STUDIES IN GERMAN LITERATURE,
LINGUISTICS, AND CULTURE
Vol. 55

Studies in German Literature, Linguistics, and Culture

Editorial Board

Frank Banta, Donald Daviau, Gerald Gillespie, Ingeborg Glier, Michael Hamburger, Gerhart Hoffmeister, Herbert Knust, Egbert Krispyn, Victor Lange, James Lyon, Erika Metzger, Michael Metzger, Hans-Gert Roloff, George C. Schoolfield, John Spalek, Eitel Timm, Frank Trommler, Heinz Wetzel

Managing Editors

James Hardin and Gunther Holst

(South Carolina)

CAMDEN HOUSE

Columbia, South Carolina

The Problem of Wealth in the Literature of Luther's Germany

John
Van Cleve

THE PROBLEM OF WEALTH IN THE LITERATURE OF LUTHER'S GERMANY

CAMDEN HOUSE

Copyright © 1991
CAMDEN HOUSE, INC.
Drawer 2025
Columbia, SC 29202 USA

Library of Congress Catalog Card Number: 90-21797
All Rights Reserved
Printed in the United States of America
First Edition

ISBN: 0-938100-86-6

Library of Congress Cataloging-in-Publication Data

Van Cleve, John Walter.
    The problem of wealth in the literature of Luther's Germany / by John Van Cleve. -- 1st ed.
        p. cm. -- (Studies in German literature, linguistics, and culture ; vol. 55)
    Includes bibliographical references and index.
    ISBN 0-938100-86-6 (hardcover : acid-free)
    1. German literature--Early modern, 1500-1700--History and criticism. 2. Wealth in literature. 3. Literature and society--Germany--History. I. Title. II. Series: Studies in German literature, linguistics, and culture ; v. 55.
PT246.V36 1990
830.9'355'09031--dc20

90-21797
CIP

Acknowledgments

MISSISSIPPI STATE UNIVERSITY GRANTED a sabbatical leave in support of this project.

H. Daniel Embree of the English Department at Mississippi State spent many hours reading the manuscript and making suggestions for improvements.

Jewel Fields typed the manuscript onto computer disk with help from Camille Mulrooney and Maria Quiñones.

Judith Arden Van Cleve always knew when to urge her husband on and when to tell him to stop.

The Problem of Wealth in the Literature of Luther's Germany contains material from two previously published articles by the author; substantial revisions have been undertaken for this monograph. The articles are:

"Two Priests for Reineke Fuchs." *Neophilologus* 65, no. 2 (1980): 239–46.

"A Genre in Crisis: The 'Volksbuch.'" *German Quarterly* 59, no. 2 (1986): 203–15.

For my parents,

Ethel Dannenmaier Van Cleve

and John Woodbridge Van Cleve

Contents

Chapter 1
Walls to Scale: The Literature of Luther's Germany
and the Modern Reader ... 1

Chapter 2
Sebastian Brant and the Treasure of the Ship of Fools ... 23

Chapter 3
Reineke Fuchs as Chancellor Not-Enough ... 63

Chapter 4
Eulenspiegel and Fortunatus: The Problem Solved ... 85

Chapter 5
Martin Luther and the Ideal of the Christian Merchant ... 111

Chapter 6
Hans Sachs asks, "Ist das gût Ewangelisch?" ... 137

Chapter 7
Historia von D. Johann Fausten: The Problem Redux ... 155

Conclusion ... 175

Bibliography ... 179

Index ... 193

Illustrations

Fig. 1. Woodcut from the *Narrenschiff* of Sebastian Brant
(from Sebastian Brant, *The Ship of Fools*, 1962) 41

Fig. 2. Woodcut from *Reynke de Vos*
(from *Reynke de Vos*, trans. Karl Langosch, 1975) 82

Fig 3. Woodcut from the "Long Sermon on Usury" of Martin Luther
(from Walther Bienert, *Martin Luther und die Juden: Ein Quellenbuch mit zeitgenössischen Illustrationen, mit Einführungen und Erläuterungen*, 1982) 119

Fig. 4. Woodcut from the "Romanusdialog" of Hans Sachs 142
(from Hans Sachs, *Die Prosadialoge*, 1970)

Fig. 5. Title page of the first edition of the *Faustbuch* 157

Chapter 1

Walls to Scale: The Literature of Luther's Germany and the Modern Reader

THOSE WHO HAVE STUDIED older literature can learn something from those who have not. What do the uninitiated see when they have our texts before them? Clumsy typefaces; impossibly long, self-righteous titles; archaic and often awkward language; primitive and occasionally vulgar woodcuts — first impressions of the literature considered here easily can be negative. Such an inexperienced reader immediately is aware of the presence of a thick wall surrounding a disjunct culture, disjunct in time. The specialist who is sensitive to the potential for confusion and retreat can help the beginner scale that wall if such assistance precedes interpretation. Understanding and appreciation are directly proportional to the extent of a latter-day reader's awareness of how the function of literature has changed in the five hundred years since Martin Luther's birth.

The tension between ethics and profits underwent a thorough reevaluation during the Protestant Reformation. What emerged was a first attempt at mediation between two powerful cultural forces by a new post-medieval, pre-middle-class German society. An historian's identification of that society with Luther emphasizes rapid change as its dominant characteristic. Ferment, radical confrontation, and paranoiac consolidation inform social, ecclesiastical, intellectual, and literary history during the tense decades before 1517, the career of Luther as a reformer, and the early years of orthodoxy-building after Luther's death in 1546.

"Luther's Germany" is modern Germany in its frenetic infancy, an infancy preoccupied with the establishment of a new social ethos. One sine qua non for broad support of a system of guiding beliefs was the ability to reconcile the traditional perception of profits as "filthy lucre" with the involvement in commerce and finance of many influential adherents of both the old faith and the new. Writers of the age approached that daunting task in a manner obscured from the modern reader's view by a wall that is half a millenium thick. The attempt to scale that wall can begin with the question, "What did such writers take to be the function of literature?"

2   The Problem of Wealth in the Literature of Luther's Germany

Recent scholarship has argued convincingly that the vernacular literature of sixteenth-century Germany should be understood as a utilitarian medium for moral instruction rather than as an autonomous vehicle for personal creative expression.[1] During the past two centuries, two developments have marked the ascendancy of the latter function of literature: the rise of "literature of experience" and the division of belletristics into one dense growth of branches labeled "literature" ("die schöne Literatur") and another labeled "popular literature" ("Trivialliteratur"). Although both developments have eighteenth-century foundations, only the emergence of experiential literature has attracted the attention of generations of Germanists.[2] If Friedrich Gottlieb Klopstock's ecstatic lyric poems threw open the gates to subjectivity, young Johann Wolfgang Goethe entered the new arena and took writers and readers of the later eighteenth century with him. For good or ill, Goethe's works, his "fragments of a great confession," have served as a standard of comparison from the 1770s to the present day. The impersonal tone and pedagogical thrust immediately apparent in the tales of Reynard the Fox, Till Eulenspiegel, and Doctor Faust constitute not just a challenge to late twentieth-century taste but a test of our ability and determination to include in the process of reception the past as it defined itself.

Because of the high visibility of popular literature, the modern reader is accustomed to evaluating fiction according to vertical categories that range upward from the lowest pornography through insipid romances, formulaic detective novels, and science fiction through stylish best-sellers and finally to the putative heirs of Dante, Shakespeare, and Goethe. In the 1960s scholarship began to assert that such evaluative categorization had been a significant factor in the mass reception of German literature since the final third of the eighteenth century.[3] There are several reasons for the relatively

---

[1] Barbara Könneker, *Die deutsche Literatur der Reformationszeit: Kommentar zu einer Epoche* (Munich: Winkler, 1975), 7-9.

[2] Of older scholarship, see for example Wilhelm Dilthey, *Das Erlebnis und die Dichtung: Lessing, Goethe, Novalis, Hölderlin* (Leipzig: Teubner, 1906), 137-200; Oskar Walzel, *Leben, Erleben und Dichten: Ein Versuch* (Leipzig: Haessel, 1912); Josef Körner, "Erlebnis — Motiv — Stoff," in *Vom Geiste neuer Literaturforschung: Festschrift für Oskar Walzel*, ed. Julius Wahle and Victor Klemperer (Potsdam: Athenaion, 1924), 80-90. Of more recent writers, see Werner Kohlschmidt, *Geschichte der deutschen Literatur vom Barock bis zur Klassik* (Stuttgart: Reclam, 1965), 503-509; Hans-Heinrich Reuter and Werner Rieck, *Geschichte der deutschen Literatur: Vom Ausgang des 17. Jahrhunderts bis 1789* (Berlin: Volk und Wissen Volkseigener Verlag, 1979), 381-89, 544-46; Erich Trunz, "Nachwort," in Johann Wolfgang von Goethe, *Gedichte und Epen I*, vol. 1 of *Goethes Werke* (Hamburg Edition), 12th ed. (Munich: Beck, 1981), 413-17.

[3] Worthy of special note is the highly influential article by Helmut Kreuzer "Trivialliteratur als Forschungsproblem: Zur Kritik des deutschen Trivialromans seit der Aufklärung," rpt. in his *Veränderung des Literaturbegriffs: Fünf Beiträge zu aktuellen Problemen der*

late advent of what is now a basic assumption of the world of book publishing: the increase in literacy, the rapid emergence of a female readership, the soaring popularity of the novel in the late eighteenth century, increasing sophistication in marketing techniques including serialized publication, and innovations in the technology of printing and binding.[4] Whatever the relative significance of individual developments may be, collectively they have led to a broad consensus concerning the hallmarks of higher and lower forms of literature. For example, inconsistent use of the elements of form or transparent dependence on sexual or scatological themes suggests lower artistic worth to a twentieth-century reader; however, these and other "faults" are common in the finest sixteenth-century literature. Within the past decade, the adverse impact of latter-day sensibilities on the scholarly response to the belletristic tradition that precedes the high-low bifurcation has attracted the attention of an increasingly self-critical Germanics.[5] Before then, the literature of Luther's Germany often failed the anachronistic, late eighteenth-century test for excellence. All self-congratulatory metacritical hindsight aside, the tone of apology evident in earlier studies of this period has become faint since the early 1970s.

Revisionist scholarship also has pointed to traditional terminology as an influence on reception. The primary texts of concern here are associated

---

Literaturwissenschaft (Göttingen: Vandenhoeck & Ruprecht, 1975).

[4] Concerning literacy, see Rolf Engelsing, *Analphabetentum und Lektüre: Zur Sozialgeschichte des Lesers in Deutschland zwischen feudaler und industrieller Gesellschaft* (Stuttgart: Metzler, 1973), 19-20, 32; Engelsing, *Der Bürger als Leser: Lesergeschichte in Deutschland 1500-1800* (Stuttgart: Metzler, 1974), 13-20; Max L. Baeumer, "Sozialkritische und revolutionäre Literatur der Reformationszeit," *Internationales Archiv für Sozialgeschichte der deutschen Literatur* 5 (1980): 187-91. Concerning the female readership, see Walter Horace Bruford, *Germany in the Eighteenth Century: The Social Background of the Literary Revival* (1935; Cambridge: Cambridge University Press, 1968), 226; Eva D. Becker, *Der deutsche Roman um 1780* (Stuttgart: Metzler, 1964), 28-29; Rolf Grimminger, "Aufklärung, Absolutismus und bürgerliche Individuen: Über den notwendigen Zusammenhang von Literatur, Gesellschaft und Staat in der Geschichte des 18. Jahrhunderts," in *Deutsche Aufklärung bis zur französischen Revolution*, ed. Grimminger, vol. 3 of *Hansers Sozialgeschichte der deutschen Literatur vom 16. Jahrhundert bis zur Gegenwart*, ed. Grimminger (Munich: Hanser, 1980), 94-95. Concerning the novel, see Becker 26-28; Michael Hadley, *Romanverzeichnis: Bibliographie der zwischen 1750-1800 erschienenen Erstausgaben* (Berne: Lang, 1977), xx; Ernst Weber and Christine Mithal, *Deutsche Originalromane zwischen 1680 und 1780: Eine Bibliographie mit Besitznachweisen* (Munich: Schmidt, 1983), 78-82. Concerning the book trade, see Peter Schmidt, "Buchmarkt, Verlagswesen und Zeitschriften," in *Zwischen Absolutismus und Aufklärung: Rationalismus, Empfindsamkeit, Sturm und Drang: 1740-1786*, ed. Ralph-Rainer Wuthenow, vol. 4 of *Deutsche Literatur: Eine Sozialgeschichte*, ed. Horst Albert Glaser (Reinbek: Rowohlt, 1980), 60-62; Wolfgang von Ungern-Sternberg, "Schriftsteller und literarischer Markt," in Grimminger, ed., 140-41.

[5] See Baeumer, 169-72. He develops and documents the observations in Könneker, 7-8.

closely with such familiar terms as "Volksbuch," "Volkspoesie," and "Volksliteratur," terms that have long confounded attempts at precise, scholarly definition.[6] The second actually diverts attention to the closing decades of the eighteenth century and the labors of Johann Gottfried Herder and the Romantics. In this context, "Volkspoesie" commonly is understood as referring to creations introduced to an unknowing literary public as examples of the oral tradition of the unsophisticated "common people," the "Volk." In fact, the formidable creative skills of Clemens Brentano, Jacob and Wilhelm Grimm, Ludwig Tieck, and others had been brought to bear to such an extent that Hermann Bausinger rejects any identification of such works as examples of a "poetry of the people."[7] He finds the widely propagated concept to be based not on historical fact but on wishful thinking, the fiction of a people ("Volk") united with its art.

In the pages that follow, "Volksliteratur" and such related genre designations as "Volksbuch" are understood as referring to that German-language literature of the fifteenth and sixteenth centuries that has been transmitted to subsequent eras in written form. While the precise identity of the "Volk" is still open to debate, a glance at the Grimms' German dictionary shows that the word has sired a host of definitions, many of which refer to the disadvantaged masses.[8] The lack of specificity concerning the occupations, social levels, and religious affiliations of those who putatively belong to the "Volk" is only magnified when the noun is linked to "Buch," a term from the world of letters. For before the second half of the nineteenth century, the great majority of the German-speaking people was both lower-class and illiterate.[9] But Max L. Baeumer has emphasized that even if a peasant could not read, exclusion from the potential audience for writers in the native tongue was not automatic.[10] The practice of reading aloud in public, on market squares, for example, saw to that. Of course, the size and composition of such audiences, the frequency of readings, and the titles of

---

[6] For a thorough presentation of this terminology, see Max L. Baeumer, "Gesellschaftliche Aspekte der 'Volks' -Literatur im 15. und 16. Jahrhundert," in *Popularität und Trivialität*, ed. Jost Hermand and Reinhold Grimm (Frankfurt am Main: Athenäum, 1974), 24-40.

[7] Hermann Bausinger, *Formen der "Volkspoesie,"* 2nd ed. (Berlin: Schmidt, 1980), 16.

[8] Jacob Grimm and Wilhelm Grimm, *Deutsches Wörterbuch* (Leipzig: Hirzel, 1951), 12.2: 453-70.

[9] Rolf Engelsing goes so far as to describe this largest segment of the population as a homogenous stratum of uneducated workers; see Engelsing, *Zur Sozialgeschichte deutscher Mittel- und Unterschichten*, 2nd ed. (Göttingen: Vandenhoeck & Ruprecht, 1978), 20-21.

[10] Baeumer, "Aspekte," 19-22.

works actually read — all await additional research into the demographics of Luther's Germany.[11]

Discussions of the late medieval society that produced German chapbooks usually employ the terms "estate" and "class." Although both designate layers within societies, only the latter has become central to modern social analysis, whether learned or lay. A common feature of societies organized by class is stratification according to personal wealth, whatever form wealth takes: liquidity, property, durable goods, or convertible holdings. In a "pure" class society, those with the greatest wealth rule, either directly or through surrogates. Those with little or no wealth enjoy only those rights accruing from interdependent relationships with the ruling nobility. While modern Western societies usually are examined with a view to relationships among constituent classes, medieval societies have been seen as illustrative of the estate system of stratification.[12] In its broadest outlines, that system traces its origins to the beginnings of feudalism, to the agreements concerning military service and peacetime security struck between lords and liege men. As time passed, the ranks of the latter group swelled, and the needs of the ruler grew and diversified. Individual vassals offered varying amounts of fealty and required varying amounts of protection. One's position in society became a function of one's utility as perceived by the local prince. In interpersonal relationships, utility was translated into status. In time status was also granted to corporate bodies such as cities or groups of cities. Such individuals and corporate bodies occupied "estates" cemented by common status or standing ("Stand") vis-à-vis temporal authority. Of course, a similar pyramidal hierarchy existed within the church. Faith and authority merged to such an extent that no credible discussion of one can ignore the other.

Even this cursory and highly simplified presentation of the two stratification systems — one based on authority, the other on wealth — suggests the difficulties inherent in their application to a time in which neither purely feudal nor purely industrial conditions existed. The fact that Luther's contemporaries thought in terms of estates suggests but does not dictate its acceptance and use by modern historians. Naive acceptance runs the risk of

---

[11] Some of that research will probably appear in the *Internationales Archiv für Sozialgeschichte der deutschen Literatur (IASL)*. For a contribution related to Baeumer, "Sozialkritische und revolutionäre Literatur," see Rudolf Schenda, "Bilder vom Lesen — Lesen von Bildern," *IASL* 12 (1987): 82-106. Research collectives at work in the German Democratic Republic are described in Irene Cannon-Geary, "Trends in Literary Research: New Developments in GDR Reception of the Sixteenth Century in Germany," *German Quarterly* 55, no. 3 (1982): 370-86.

[12] For a discussion of the estate system, see Horst Fuhrmann, *Deutsche Geschichte im hohen Mittelalter: Von der Mitte des 11. bis zum Ende des 12. Jahrhunderts* (Göttingen: Vandenhoeck & Reprecht, 1978), 196. See also Joachim Leuscher, *Deutschland im späten Mittelalter* (Göttingen: Vandenhoeck & Ruprecht, 1975), 41-45.

historicism and a resultant inattention to any ties that bind the earlier time with later, industrialized societies. Conversely, analysis by class alone can result in arrogant disregard for a legitimate goal of historiography, the documentation and discussion of self-awareness in historical groups and individuals.

It is understandable that Marx and Engels found class societies throughout history. Their openly tendentious interpretation of the origins of class conflict responds to such developments in their own nineteenth century as rapid industrialization, staggering capital formation, and gross exploitation of a rapidly growing urban proletariat. As early as *The German Ideology* (completed in 1846), Marx and Engels describe social organization in feudal Europe as an "association" directed against the interests of a subjected producing class.[13] Although the form of production featured estates and property owned by estates, the exploitive result is described as fundamentally the same two-class system that had prevailed in ancient Greece and Rome. Since the mid-1970s, this orthodox position has been altered by scholars in the German Democratic Republic, especially by members of the "Working Group for German Literature of the 15th through 17th Centuries," which has been given primary responsibility for the analysis of this portion of what socialist countries refer to as the "cultural legacy."[14] The consensus within the working group is that such terms as "class," "estate," and "bourgeoisie" should be used with careful historical qualifiers that indicate inadequate information about economic determinants before the eighteenth century.[15] This consensus is shared by Western scholarship.

The noted historian R.H. Hilton assumes a dissenting position in his book *The English Peasantry in the Later Middle Ages*. In a first chapter that addresses conditions throughout Europe, Hilton takes note of those "currently fashionable theories" that assert the primacy of what might be called "status-consciousness."[16] His fundamental premise is that the medieval peasantry was a class: "I propose to define the peasantry as a class, as determined by its place in the production of society's material needs; not as a status group determined by attributed esteem, dignity, or honour."[17] He notes that modern social historians use their own argot when discussing

---

[13] Karl Marx and Friedrich Engels, *Die deutsche Ideologie*, in *Werke*, ed. Institut für Marxismus-Leninismus beim ZK der SED (Berlin: Dietz, 1958), 3:24.

[14] See Cannon-Geary.

[15] Cannon-Geary, 376-78.

[16] R.H. Hilton, *The English Peasantry in the Late Middle Ages: The Ford Lectures for 1973 and Related Studies* (Oxford: Clarendon, 1975), 9.

[17] Hilton, 12.

the condition of the stratum in question — even when arguing for analysis by estate. The great, glaring flaw in Hilton's presentation — at least, as it relates to classical Marxist social theory — is the absence of class-consciousness within the peasantry, an absence recognized by Hilton. His attempts to relativize the significance of the characteristic only serve to accentuate the size of the ever-present gulf between two sets of perceptions of the late Middle Ages: those of the modern observer and those of the medieval observer. The most ardent practitioner of historicism, the scholar who tries to step back into time and analyze the past from within, even such a scholar must recognize the gap between twentieth-century scholarly training and medieval reportorial practices. On the other hand, modernist class-analysis tends to drag the past into the present, to emasculate itself in order to reach the topic under consideration. That the results can be highly problematic is manifest in Hilton's construct — a class with no class-consciousness.

Reportorial practices are of great importance because of the adoption of the empirical method by nineteenth-century historiography. The modern analyst either dedicates all efforts to a quest for the "objectively" true or eschews objectivity as a chimera in favor of the by now familiar introductory caveat concerning the character of authorial subjectivity. The ideology or "worldview" then employed as a touchstone may be more or less orthodox, more or less idiosyncratic, but it is at least clearly visible to the reader. If self-criticism and analysis by class have become reflexes among modern students of social history, both tend to render an understanding of medieval reporters more difficult. The absence of the former in a chronicler can lead to the unconscious presentation of what was as though it still existed or else of what could or should have been instead of what was. When detailed by a commentator from Luther's Germany, stratification by estate as adumbrated above is, at least in part, an illusion.

In broadest terms then, the noble, clerical, and municipal estates constituted society's recognized layers.[18] Distinctions within those layers, again by "estate," were legion. The peasantry, whose overwhelming numbers provided a solid base for the social structure, usually had no civil rights and either low or no "status."[19] In cities, each craft and profession, however humble, had its own guild; entry into which was carefully controlled. Occupational ranking extended to individual callings; for example, an itinerant peddler, a shopkeeper, and a wholesaler in the international market would belong to three separate guilds. That the resultant byzantine structure did not necessarily reflect the realities of everyday life is strikingly

---

[18] Compare Leuscher, 41-45.

[19] Leuscher, 42-43. See also Bernd Moeller, *Deutschland im Zeitalter der Reformation* (Göttingen: Vandenhoeck & Ruprecht, 1977), 28-29.

apparent in the case of a nobility that had survived its exuberant barbarian youth and pious Crusader middle-age only to begin its obstructionist dotage. Here, great personal status was based solely on tradition, not on social utility. Johan Huizinga has written that the fifteenth century overestimated the social importance of the nobility and underestimated that of the bourgeoisie, but he also notes that in the cultural life of the time, such false perceptions had the same significance as perceptions that modern scholarship has validated.[20] False perceptions and projections can become reality, wholly or in part. The concept of a divinely planned cosmic order with adjacent temporal and heavenly spheres was presented as an article of faith with the inertia of centuries behind it. The German nobility of the nineteenth century enjoyed privileges that had not been merited for many centuries — but the privileges were no less real for being rooted in delusion.

If evaluation of late medieval informants must mediate between reality and delusion, explication of literary texts from the period also must take into account artistic convention and tendentiousness, that is, the utilitarian role played by letters at the time. Both elements increase the difficulty of the challenge facing the modern chapbook reader, and the difficulty has methodological implications. Until the extent of tradition and myth has been clarified through further historical research into social organization and economics, the student of literature is well advised to stay close to the text. Authors and periods that are closer in time are open to documentable contrast with the real worlds that produced them. The chapters that follow attempt to incorporate recent contributions of historians, sociologists, and sociologists of literature; but as such these readings must remain tentative. The basic research that has appeared during the past two decades certainly justifies a return to the texts for new answers and, ideally, new questions.

Before those texts are considered, the designations "Volksbuch" and "chapbook" deserve close scrutiny. The German word was coined early in the nineteenth century by the writer and scholar Johann Joseph von Görres (1776-1848).[21] He and the other German Romantics had appropriated Johann Gottfried Herder's notion of a shared creative spirit ("Volksgeist") whose literary emanations supposedly had been greatest during the Middle

---

[20] Johan Huizinga, *Herbst des Mittelalters: Studien über Lebens- und Geistesformen des 14. und 15. Jahrhunderts in Frankreich und in den Niederlanden* (Stuttgart: Kröner, 1969), 74.

[21] Johann Joseph von Görres, *Die teutschen Volksbücher: Nähere Würdigung der schönen Historien-, Wetter-, und Arzneybüchlein, welche theils innerer Werth, theils Zufall, Jahrhunderte hindurch bis auf unsere Zeit erhalten hat*, vol. 3 of *Joseph Görres gesammelte Schriften*, ed. Wilhelm Schellberg (Cologne: Gilde, 1926), 169-293.

Ages.[22] Hence, the term "Volksbuch" occupies a significant place in the history of both idealistic philosophy and Romantic literature. But as a technical term for use by literary historians, the word is of dubious value; it has survived because of inertia and the power of tradition. Prudent usage has come to entail either quotation marks or the word "so-called" ("sogenannt") or else an exculpatory footnote. The reasons for such distancing are ideological.

Intensive, systematic study of the "Volksbuch" as a literary genre commenced just before the First World War with the work of Richard Benz, who edited a new collection of chapbooks for the nationalistic publishing house Eugen Diederichs.[23] The first volume had been in print for two years when Benz published a short monograph about the German chapbooks ("Volksbücher"). On the first page, the author carefully incorporates his subject into German literary tradition through use of the ambivalent term "literature" ("Dichtung"):

> "Volksbücher" are — as the term itself indicates — the share of the "Volk" in literature that has been fixed by being *written down*, rather than in *literature* in general, such as the traditional fairy tale ["Volksmärchen"] and the traditional song ["Volkslied"]....
> Only the "Volksbuch" exists in a form that is actually literary and only it has had a history — which is more than we can document in the case of either the fairy tale that is still told or the ditty that is still sung. We can say when it took shape, and we can determine how that shape changed from century to century.[24]

The significance of the first sentence is emphasized in the course of the most influential examination of the "Volksbuch" written in the past twenty years. Hans Joachim Kreutzer cites it as the beginning of what he calls the error of considering the "Volksbuch" a literary genre.[25] In defense of Benz, it should

---

[22] Görres, 174-76, 278-79.

[23] For more detailed studies of the development of the concept "Volksbuch" from Benz to the 1970s, see Hans Joachim Kreutzer, *Der Mythos vom Volksbuch: Studien zur Wirkungsgeschichte des frühen deutschen Romans seit der Romantik* (Stuttgart; Metzler, 1977). See also Georg Bollenbeck, "Das 'Volksbuch' als Projektionsformel: Zur Entstehung und Wirkung eines Konventionsbegriffes," in *Mittelalter — Rezeption: Gesammelte Vorträge des Salzburger Symposions "Die Rezeption mittelalterlicher Dichter und ihrer Werke in Literatur, bildender Kunst und Musik des 19. und 20. Jahrhunderts,"* ed. Jürgen Kühnel, Hans-Dieter Mück, and Ulrich Müller (Göppingen: Kümmerle, 1979), 141-71.

[24] Richard Benz, *Die deutschen Volksbücher: Ein Beitrag zur Geschichte der deutschen Dichtung* (Jena: Diederichs, 1913), 1. Benz' emphasis. My translation — JVC.

[25] Kreutzer, 124.

10   The Problem of Wealth in the Literature of Luther's Germany

be noted that he does place the concept in a historical framework. Görres' neologism now refers to a work that was written down at a specific time and that has undergone change since then. Nevertheless, the impetus to legitimate the "Volksbuch" as a genre of the highest order did have unmistakably nationalistic overtones. When he discusses the decline of the chapbooks and the rise of the learned poet of the seventeenth century, Benz becomes xenophobic; he charges the literary reformer Martin Opitz with having suffocated the remnants of indigenous form and national content.[26] He fumes at the "curse" of foreign governing principles for literary form finally declares:

> Our culture has been split by the Renaissance: an ideal of personal development through formal education has been put forward that is foreign to everyday life and that the "Volk" as a whole will never be able to make its own. As a result, the "Volk" holds on to its old cultural life and to poetic expressions of that life. Not only does it preserve the traditional fairy tale and the traditional song but it also preserves the "Volksbuch," which has been excluded from true literature ["Litteratur"] since the moment of the establishment of a learned literature ["Poesie"]....[27]

The inference to be drawn from this flight of cultural paranoia is clear: the "Volksbuch" is the highest and most German form of written art. Informing the dichotomy "formal education" / "everyday life" is the longing for what is perceived as an original native cultural tradition. When Benz characterizes the humanistic tradition as foreign to everyday life he is very close to asserting the superiority of German civilization.

A decade later, during the relatively stable middle years of the Weimar Republic, the young scholar Lutz Mackensen wrote a monograph that constituted a significant departure in the study of Reformation Age literature. Despite its title, *The German "Volksbücher"* evinces some discomfort with the genre designation; the author prefers to search for stylistic and structural boundaries supposedly separating what he terms the prose novel, the indigenous novel ("volkstümlicher Roman"), and the "Volk" novel. Mackensen traces a qualitatively descending series of epic genres from the verse epics of the High Middle Ages through prose translations and renditions of French chivalric epics by Elisabeth von Nassau-Saarbrücken and others to chivalric novels completely stripped of aristocratic pretensions and thrust

---

[26] Benz, 44.

[27] Benz, 45. My translation — JVC.

into indigenous costume.[28] The adjective "volkstümlich" refers to an urban bourgeoisie characterized by a rapidly developing need for literature qua entertainment. Mackensen naively equates noble authorship and noble plot with lasting high quality. When contemplating the continued "descent" of popular literature to the gothic novel and the detective story, he says that the modern phenomena lacked the characteristics that gave the "Volksbücher" life — the participation of those of the first rank in their conception.[29] While he often sounds like a latter-day toady of the medieval aristocracy, Mackensen does begin to set sociological limits on the identity of the "Volk" supposedly responsible for the "Volksbücher." But his first concern is with the place held by the "Volksbuch" in the history of the novel and in the history of popular culture.

Mackensen's preoccupation with the nobility results in a deferential attitude toward his subject that is most apparent in his repeated attribution of "spirit" and "life" to the works examined. No such reverence is to be found two years later in the first edition of the *Reallexikon der deutschen Literaturgeschichte* (Subject Lexicon of German Literary History). Wolfgang Liepe's entry for "Volksbuch" begins with these condescending words:

> The majority of the so-called "Volksbücher" are rooted in the beginnings of Early Modern German narrative prose of the fifteenth and sixteenth centuries. The "Volk" as such did not participate in the conception of the "Volksbücher." Even to a far greater extent than the "Volkslieder," the "Volksbücher" represent literary material ["Literaturgut"] that has sunk from higher levels of literary refinement down to the "Volk."[30]

The rejection of the Görres-Benz line is startlingly curt and complete. The term itself is questioned. A very late time of origin is suggested. Any thought that the "Volk" was involved in a significant way is brushed aside in a sentence that trades on the easy irony of "Volk" and "Volksbücher." Mackensen had described a tradition that passes from a higher to a lower social level. To that movement Liepe assigns a drastic fall in artistic level: "literary" can be used with reference to the aristocracy, but only "literary material" is appropriate in a reference to the "Volk." The use of "sunk down" is patronizing, even supercilious. To Liepe's way of thinking, the "Volksbücher" are something less than literature. The four-page entry offers no

---

[28] Lutz Mackensen, *Die deutschen Volksbücher* (Leipzig: Quelle und Meyer, 1927), 17.

[29] Mackensen, 41.

[30] Wolfgang Liepe, "Volksbuch," in *Reallexikon der deutschen Literaturgeschichte*, ed. Paul Merker and Wolfgang Stammler (Berlin: de Gruyter, 1928), 3:481. My translation — JVC.

stratification of the "Volk"; as he uses it, the noun refers to an undifferentiated mass with simple, coarse tastes.[31] The great bulk of the entry treats the native and foreign prose antecedents of the subject and the relationship of the "Volksbuch" to the early development of the novel.

Given its roots in irrationalism and nationalism, the concept "Volksbuch" fell easy prey to misuse during the Hitler era. In his *Geschichte der deutschen Seele* (History of the German Soul), Günther Müller speaks the unfortunate idiom of the times:

> In the strongest of these "Volksbücher," the heroes pass through the great splendor of human existence on their path toward a clear goal. Its vigorous contours lift the possibilities of human life to the vividness of graphic design. In the process, fundamental racial strengths express themselves through the types of contours, so that one may consider for example the austere, phlegmatic fearlessness and the great pleasure in accomplishment of *Duke Ernst* to be Nordic, the buoyant but noble, lustrous, and exuberant life of love and struggle in *Pontus* to be Nordic-Mediterranean; and one can demonstrate these traits in the smallest structural details.[32]

Both form and content are pressed into the service of racial "theory." With such pronouncements, tendencies present in the Görres-Benz line became extremist political dogma, and the utility of the term for postwar Germanics was permanently compromised.

It is hardly surprising that German scholarship had no great appetite for the "Volksbuch" during the late 1940s and 1950s. That lack of interest is documented indirectly in an article that appeared in a 1962 number of *Der Deutschunterricht*: much of the recent work cited is either British or American.[33] The article's title is cautious — "The 'Volksbuch' — History and Problematics" — and its author, Josef Szövérffy, is Hungarian. He affirms what he presents as a consensus position: that the "Volksbücher" constitute neither a genre nor a circumscribed literary form. The author has much more to say about "history" than he does about "problematics," and his highly factual history lesson is inferior to Mackensen's. He does cover new ground by emphasizing the international origins of his subject. But when it

---

[31] Liepe, 481.

[32] Günther Müller, *Geschichte der deutschen Seele: Vom Faustbuch zu Goethes Faust* (Freiburg: Herder, 1939), 11. My translation — JVC. "Nordic" and "Nordic-Mediterranean" were used to designate racial types.

[33] Josef Szövérffy, "Das Volksbuch: Geschichte und Problematik," *Der Deutschunterricht* 14, no. 2 (1962): 5-6.

Walls to Scale

comes to assessing the impact of chapbook heroes on the literary tradition and on their times, he is at a loss: "Are they true novel heroes or the performers of events and upheavals which step before us in a concentrated, visual form that is widely understood? Difficult to say."[34]

Helmut Prang encounters no such difficulty six years later. Questions concerning social determinants are not raised. And, in a book entitled *Formgeschichte der Dichtkunst* (A History of Literary Form), the author has little to say about works produced during an age that supposedly made no claims to literary form.[35] Prang's sole interest in the "Volksbuch" is in its position as a sagging bridge between two peaks in the history of epic literature, the Arthurian verse epic and the Baroque novel:

> That does indeed point to the fact that this form of narrative offered a kind of literary substitute for the declining heroic and knightly epic and that this literary form, which functioned as a substitute, quickly withdrew into the background when a new literary form with possibilities of its own for both expression and message came into being as the prose novel of the Baroque.[36]

At the heart of this formalist argument is a denial of inherent historical significance; the writer of a "Volksbuch" is either an epigone or a precursor. Which is to say, the chapbooks are to be understood either by looking from the sixteenth century back to the twelfth or from the seventeenth century back to the sixteenth. The approach undermines the title of Prang's book, which contains the word "history." History read backward is history read poorly. The dubious formulation "literary substitute" suggests an inferior tradition possessing little intrinsic interest in the eyes of a literary historian.

In 1977 Hans Joachim Kreutzer published his landmark study of the "Volksbuch" concept. At the conclusion of a survey of the works and their impact since Görres, Kreutzer recommends abandonment of the term as a tool for research, because it has become meaningless and therefore should be replaced by a term that relates to the book trade.[37] In fact, the term has been compromised so badly as to become a hindrance. Kreutzer urges that the concept of the novel be extended backward in time so as to begin in the fifteenth century with the prose renditions of verse epics and the translations of contemporary French novels. Most of the former "Volksbücher" will then

---

[34] Szövérffy, 19. My translation — JVC.

[35] Helmut Prang, *Formgeschichte der Dichtkunst* (Stuttgart: Kohlhammer, 1968), 93.

[36] Prang, 93. My translation — JVC.

[37] Kreutzer, 146.

be examples of the category "the early German novel." Although he follows Prang in the insistence on latter-day genre designations, Kreutzer is not burdened with the assumption of the existence of an ahistorical ideal of the eternally literary. And he consciously avoids recourse to the notion of literary forerunners. Still, he himself cites a serious problem with the use of the term "novel" before the seventeenth century.[38] Most of the works were published anonymously, whereas the common understanding of the genre includes the presence of an author whose identity or personality plays a role in reception. A novel presents the fictional reality created by an individual, and it is his attitudes and opinions that find reflection in the work. Kreutzer does not argue for the applicability of such a definition before the seventeenth century. But surely, if the meaning of the word "Volksbuch" is a product of its reception and use, so, too, is the meaning of the older word "Roman" ("novel"). Any attempt to circumvent the history of such terms will seem idiosyncratic at best and will meet with resistance. However thoughtful and self-critical his arguments may be, Kreutzer will have a hard time persuading his fellow Germanists that translations can be "novels" or that the settings of *Till Eulenspiegel* and *Reynard the Fox* are novelistic.

Written five years later, the entry "Volksbuch" in the second edition of the *Reallexikon* (Subject Lexicon) begins with a reference to Kreutzer's contention that Görres transformed the "early German novel" into a myth, the myth of the "Volksbuch." But that is all that is offered from Kreutzer. Walter Eckehart Spengler holds to the traditional concept of the novel. He does imply dissatisfaction with Görres' coinage as a technical term:

> There is ... no clearly circumscribed form "Volksbuch," neither under the aspect of verse and prose nor in the sense of the simple forms of our folk tales ["Volkserzählungen"] or folk songs ["Volkslied"]. Its literary importance lies in the spread of narrative prose, through which the development of our novel was initiated simultaneously.[39]

The second sentence manages both to establish a relationship between the chapbook and the modern novel and to emphasize the tenuous nature of that relationship. The reason behind Spengler's avoidance of Kreutzer's theory of a longer and seamless novel tradition becomes clear when Spengler equates the "Volksbücher" with "popular literature" ("Triviallitera-

---

[38] Kreutzer, 4.

[39] Walter Eckehart Spengler, "Volksbuch," in *Reallexikon der deutschen Literaturgeschichte*, 2nd ed., ed. Klaus Kanzog and Achim Masser (Berlin: de Gruyter, 1982), 4:734. My translation — JVC.

tur").[40] At least that term is clearer than "literary substitute." As is the case with Prang, Spengler's assessment of the subject at hand is rooted in the seventeenth century.

Recent studies have avoided the attribution of lesser worth that colors the analysis in both editions of the *Reallexikon*. Jan-Dirk Müller and Hans-Gert Roloff propose typologies for what the latter calls the "prose novel."[41] For Müller the word "novel" is unattractive because of the philosophical burden that its history has created.[42] Accordingly, he champions the term "prose history" in an approach that borrows from communications theory. Each scholar proposes outlines for a canon that could be reconciled easily with Kreutzer's. But both find it necessary to observe the seventeenth-century boundary. Roloff's perception of the terminological discussion is particularly revealing: "In literary scholarship one has come down either on the side of the concept 'Volksbücher,' with its ties both to Romanticism and to cultural history, or on the side of the 'prose novel.'"[43] He goes on to dismiss "Volksbuch" as unacceptable for scholarly usage. In effect, Roloff uses the old term as a straw man to demonstrate the necessity of the other term and the approach its use implies, typological genre history. And he is correct to this extent: his approach has indeed offered Germanics one avenue of escape from the miasma of mystification that surrounds the word "Volksbuch."

On those few occasions when that avenue is not taken, the discussion has quite a different look. Recently Hugo Aust has taken up the cudgels in defense of the indefensible. While his reasoning on behalf of the old concept is ultimately unconvincing, his approach to the works is unencumbered by the current preoccupation with genre. Of the "Volksbuch" he writes that understanding its relationship to its public is more important than understanding its place in genre convention.[44] Simple economics played a role in that relationship as did the utilitarian nature of the chapbooks. Writers produced and reader/listeners received responses to burning political, social, and religious issues. Whether a particular response took the

---

[40] Spengler, 737.

[41] Jan-Dirk Müller, "Gattungstransformation und Anfänge des literarischen Marktes," in *Textsorten und literarische Gattungen: Dokumentation des Germanistentages in Hamburg vom 1. bis 4. April 1979* (Berlin: Schmidt, 1983), 432-49. Hans-Gert Roloff, "Anfänge des deutschen Prosaromans," *Handbuch des deutschen Romans*, ed. Helmut Koopmann (Düsseldorf: Bagel, 1983), 54-79.

[42] Jan-Dirk Müller, 432.

[43] Roloff, 54. My translation — JVC.

[44] Hugo Aust, "Zum Stil der Volksbücher: Ein Problemaufriß," *Euphorion* 78, no. 1 (1984): 81.

form of social analysis, doctrinal suasion, or ethical guidance, popularity increased the likelihood that the response would meet with widespread acceptance. Of course before the final decades of the sixteenth century, there were few precedents by which a writer or a publisher could predict whether a work would be popular. The tradition of printed literature had just begun. In those circumstances the eclecticism that Aust notes in the chapbooks was inevitable.

A research methodology based on a fundamentally homogeneous concept, the novel, will encounter difficulty when applied to a tradition that is extraordinarily heterogeneous. A profusion of terminology has been the result; Kreutzer notes that Hans Rupprich's survey *From the Late Middle Ages to the Baroque* uses no fewer than forty terms to refer to the "Volksbücher" — including "Volksbuch."[45] Potentially more productive is a focus on the utility or social function of the chapbooks. In her seminal study, Barbara Könneker describes the era as

> ... a literary epoch whose uniqueness is determined first and foremost by the utilitarian *character* that it conferred on its literary products. But its significance rests above all on the fact that for the first time it also injected the potential utilitarian *value* of literature into the public consciousness and then made the most of that value.[46]

Those who concur with Könneker's assessment quickly find themselves in the terminological cul-de-sac to which they have been directed by Roloff — unless they are willing to follow Görres' example and use the plasticity of the German language.

The neologism of 1807 met a need of the infant discipline of Germanics as practiced by the Romantic poet/scholar. Since 1807 the discipline and its technical language have undergone tremendous change, change to which the term "Volksbuch" has proved remarkably resistant. The proposal that follows is designed to meet the needs of a maturing discipline, and it is actually less radical, less "artificial" than Görres' burst of etymological creativity. It is based on the fact that the usual English translation of "Volksbuch" is "chapbook." Usage of that second noun here has followed standard practice: no quotation marks, no "so-called." The English word is also a nineteenth-century neologism; the *Oxford English Dictionary* documents its first appearance in Thomas Frognall Dibdin's *The Library Companion, or The Young Man's Guide and the Old Man's Comfort in the*

---

[45] Kreutzer, 6.

[46] Könneker, 7-8. Könneker's emphasis. My translation — JVC.

Choice of a Library, published in 1824.[47] The definition offered was written between 1888 and 1893 by James A.H. Murray, the father of the *Oxford Engllish Dictionary*, himself:

> A modern name applied by book-collectors and others to specimens of the popular literature which was formerly circulated by itinerant dealers or chapmen, consisting chiefly of small pamphlets of popular tales, ballads, tracts, etc.[48]

The definition emphasizes physical form ("pamphlets") and the means of distribution ("chapmen"), and the action specified by the verb "circulate" is buying and selling, the retail trade. "Chapman" is the English cognate of "Kaufmann"; it was already archaic when Murray wrote. In his entry for "chapman," he cites examples for the original meaning "merchant" in Old English and Middle English. A change occurred in the sixteenth century with the appearance of the expression "petty chapman." In this sense, the noun is defined as "An itinerant dealer who travels from place to place selling or buying; one who keeps booths at markets, etc.; a hawker, pedlar."[49] Murray finds the first written use of the expression "petty chapman" in a text from 1553.

The terms "Volksbuch" and "chapbook" imply two strikingly different nineteenth-century perceptions of late medieval literature. The presence of "Buch" and "book" indicates a shared appreciation of the importance of the new printing and binding technology. The very identity of the literature in question is provided in part by technological developments. But while the word "Volk" partakes of Romantic myth-making and irrationalism, the etymological root "chap-" completes the identification of the chapbook by making it an article of trade. Both components of the English word speak to developments that signal the beginning of post-medieval "literary life." More recent institutions such as learned societies, reading societies, lending libraries, publishers who specialize in literature, literary periodicals, literary criticism, the middle-class profession "writer" — all of these institutions are based on the assumption of a continuous supply of literature made available by the retail market. In the sixteenth century, literature for sale to the public at large was something new.

German marketing conditions were similar to those sketched in Murray's definition of "chapbook." Production by printing press had reduced the

---

[47] *The Compact Edition of the Oxford English Dictionary* (Oxford: Oxford University Press, 1971), 1:379.

[48] *Oxford English Dictionary*, 379. For the dates of the definitions cited, see p. viii.

[49] *Oxford English Dictionary*, 380.

18   The Problem of Wealth in the Literature of Luther's Germany

price of the average work by 80%.[50] Low price created a growing market, which was served by a traveling merchant called a "Buchführer."[51] He would arrive in town and post announcements that he was conducting business from his room at a local inn. Customers were invited to come and inspect his wares. A list of titles was disseminated throughout the town, but the merchant was particularly careful to advertise on the doors of schools, churches, and cloisters. Even at this early date, market analysis was important to the middleman between the printer-publisher and the consumer. During the course of the sixteenth century, the "Buchführer," who represented one printer-publisher, was gradually replaced by the "Sortimenter," the shopkeeper with an "assortment" from many publishers. Josef Nadler has detailed the challenges that faced the "Buchführer" — clumsy carts, narrow and poorly maintained roads, and total dependence on sales.[52] Compensation for the effort expended depended on the popularity of the wares, and reading material that was both functional and entertaining had great potential for achieving such popularity. Literature originally published in the face of such powerful and primitive market determinants is well served by the designation "chapbook literature."

Back to Roloff and the cul-de-sac. If the term "Volksbuch" is unacceptable, and the term "novel," with whatever qualifiers, is inappropriate, then it is only logical to search for a new term. "Chapbook" would be suitable if it were a German noun, and it does have a cognate.

The word "Kaufbuch" is an old commercial term that is no longer in active use.[53] According to the Grimm dictionary, it was still current in the late eighteenth century, when it meant "ledger book."[54] It has never been either a noun used outside of commerce or a noun related in any way to Germanics. When in use, the word had only one meaning. A second meaning would provide a useful analytic tool for those who approach the literature

---

[50] Karl Ludwig, *Kurze Geschichte des Buchhandels in Deutschland*, 3rd ed. (Düsseldorf: Jung, 1964), 4.

[51] Concerning the "Buchführer," see Joachim Krause, *Der deutsche Buchhandel: Kurze Geschichte und Organisation* (Düsseldorf: Buchhändler heute, 1975), 12; Josef Nadler, *Buchhandel, Literatur und Nation in Geschichte und Gegenwart* (Berlin: Junker und Dünnhaupt, 1932), 11-12; Hans Widmann, "Geschichte des deutschen Buchhandels," in *Der deutsche Buchhandel: Wesen — Gestalt — Aufgabe*, ed. Helmut Hiller and Wolfgang Strauß (Hamburg: Verlag für Buchmarkt-Forschung, 1968), 23-24.

[52] Nadler, 11.

[53] See *Duden: Das große Wörterbuch der deutschen Sprache in sechs Bänden* (Mannheim: Bibliographisches Institut, 1978); Reinhart von Eichborn, *Der kleine Eichborn: Wirtschaft und Wirtschaftsrecht* (Hövelhof: Siebenpunkt, 1981); Dagmar von Erffa, *Wirtschaftslexikon* (Munich: Humboldt, 1976).

[54] Grimm and Grimm, 5:323.

of Luther's Germany as a utilitarian, socially engaged, nontraditional forum of communication. The following definition is offered as a provisional basis for discussion: "Kaufbuch": A work of utilitarian fictional literature printed on movable type, bound in book format, and sold on the retail market to the general reading public during the late fifteenth, sixteenth, and early seventeenth centuries.

"Kaufbücher" such as Sebastian Brant's *The Ship of Fools* (1494) and the anonymous *Reynard the Fox* (1498) began to appear in the late fifteenth century as the new printing technology was put to the service of secular literature. Their production faded during the seventeenth century because of a reemergence of aristocratic patronage and a concomitant change of target audiences. But while new literature began to cater to aristocratic tastes, humbler tastes were still served by the frequently reprinted "Kaufbücher." The definition embraces works whose authors are known as well as anonymous works — verse as well as prose. Such distinctions were not of critical importance to the writers, publishers, sellers, and readers of the chapbooks. Their innovative responses to unprecedented market conditions and to highly volatile social and ideological confrontations resulted in a new literary genre.

It is customary and prudent to supply genre designations with broad definitions. The latitude should be extended to the use of the proposed term that is present when representatives of other genres are discussed with reference to their respective genre norms. Discrepancies and deviations are to be expected. Their presence may well argue for the scrutiny of a category, and in the case of a new category, such scrutiny is appropriate. But if the truisms concerning flexibility are borne in mind, the designation "Kaufbuch" can bridge a terminological gap that has hampered research into the relationship between literature and society at the time of the Protestant Reformation. Tradition is the only legitimate reason left for continued use of the old familiar term. In this instance, Germanics would be well served by a sacrifice of tradition at the altar of clarity.

An additional argument for the term suggested concerns the dynamics of reception. At a time of overwhelming poverty and illiteracy, the chapbooks had a reliable but small consuming public. The "Buchführer" had to find a customer, that is, a member of society with disposable liquidity. Either such funds had been inherited or they had been earned through individual initiative. In either case, the purchaser belonged to the economic elite of his age. It is an inescapable conclusion that the retailer helped shape his own market by selecting works of probable interest to that elite. That is to say, he played a pivotal role in the reception of literature. The question then arises: to what extent did the chapman and his buyers influence the content of chapbooks? Demonstrable authorial response to anticipated reception and "receivers" would constitute a further argument for the use of the term "chapbook" or its German cognate.

As a merchant, the bookseller belonged to the segment of society that created an ever-increasing demand for more rapid and better developed networks for the distribution of goods and services. The balance of society followed its lead: self-aggrandizement based on merit and reified in wealth served as a guiding principle throughout the halting course of progress toward the self-aware middle class of the eighteenth century. The individual's financial condition and resultant social status entered vernacular literature as a theme at a time of intense, even martial religiosity — that is at a time when that literature had many other-worldly lessons to teach. How was personal advancement in the world of man to be reconciled with commitment to Christian faith, whether Catholic or Protestant? Of course, traditional social stratification constituted a force against such change. But as Rolf Sprandel has written, both a vehicle and an arena for overcoming that force were readily available: in urban society wealth provided admission to the highest levels of status.[55]

Social mobility was a reality in the cities of Luther's Germany, and the money that made it possible was to be made in trade and finance. The earning power of the traditional master craftsman who stayed in his workshop dwindled.[56] In sharp contrast, the master who first developed a local retail trade and then entered regional markets forged the link between production and distribution.[57] The success enjoyed by merchants and their trade centers led to what the economic historian Friedrich Lütge calls a blossoming of German urban economies in the 15th and 16th centuries.[58] The rapid rise in affluence was most noticable in the commercial hubs of southern Germany, particularly in Nuremberg and Augsburg. But during the sixteenth century, finance actually overtook trade as the most important component of most urban economies.[59] The elaborate holdings of such

---

[55] Rolf Sprandel, "Sozialgeschichte 1350-1500," in *Handbuch der deutschen Wirtschafts- und Sozialgeschichte: Von der Frühzeit bis zum Ende des 18. Jahrhunderts*, ed. Hermann Aubin and Wolfgang Zorn (Stuttgart: Klett, 1971), 376.

[56] Sprandel, 377.

[57] Friedrich Lütge, *Deutsche Sozial- und Wirtschaftsgeschichte: Ein Überblick*, 3rd ed. (Berlin: Springer, 1966), 378.

[58] Lütge, 373.

[59] See Hermann Kellenbenz, "Gewerbe und Handel," in *Handbuch der deutschen Wirtschafts- und Sozialgeschichte: Von der Frühzeit bis zum Ende des 18. Jahrhunderts*, ed. Hermann Aubin and Wolfgang Zorn (Stuttgart: Klett, 1971), 419; concerning the fall of commerce in the second half of the century, see Hans Mottek, *Wirtschaftsgeschichte Deutschlands: Ein Grundriß* (Berlin: VEB Deutscher Verlag der Wissenschaften, 1964),

families as the Fuggers and the Welsers were based on mining operations in iron, lead, copper, and the precious metals. The fortunes of such a family company often determined the financial condition of its city.[60]

Whether a product of commerce or finance, new wealth was a powerful means to rise in society, and the techniques used to generate that wealth were often relatively new. Reaction to the changing state of affairs inevitably appeared on a public forum open to the analysis of contemporary society.[61] Literature responded to the highly visible wealth of urban Germany and to a related surge of interest in material well-being.

A "utilitarian" literature produced at a time of religious strife also had to respond to the tenets of traditional Christian ethics — and the usual response was affirmation. One such tenet was the prohibition of interest on loans, an article of faith set down in a decree of the Second Lateran Synod in 1139.[62] Of course, money-based economic systems flourish or perish according to the availability of capital. That availability takes relatively few forms: to start a business, an individual may use money that has been inherited, earned, or borrowed. In the absence of interest as an incentive to the lender, that third form becomes a type of charity, in Christian terms, a demonstration of *caritas*. But the Synod's restriction on capital-formation did not become financial practice; the non-Christian, i.e., Jewish moneylender emerged as society's circumvention of the proscription.

By the fifteenth century, the same Catholic Church that had long discouraged the pursuit of wealth with moral injunctions — that same Church was filling its coffers through tithes and taxes levied against the increasing profits of Christian-owned businesses and financial institutions in Germany. It was a paradoxical state of affairs for those seeking their fortunes and for those who treated that search in their literary works. The twelfth-century tenet was contrary to contemporary thinking concerning microeconomic profitability and macroeconomic development. Doctrinal opposition to money-making as a form of temporal activity that ignores or even derogates the quest for eternal salvation confronted individual, governmental, and even ecclesiastical support for all forms of capital-formation. The clash of theory and practice over wealth and the accumulation of wealth rendered literary representation difficult at the time, but avoidance was out

---

295-97.

[60] For an overview of important trading families, see Kellenbenz, 451-55.

[61] Concerning non-literary opposition to the new forms of economic activity, particularly, to the family companies, see Hermann Kellenbenz, *Deutsche Wirtschaftsgeschichte: Von den Anfängen bis zum Ende des 18. Jahrhunderts* (Munich: Beck, 1977), 215.

[62] See Bernd Balzer, *Bürgerliche Reformationspropaganda: Die Flugschriften des Hans Sachs in den Jahren 1523-25* (Stuttgart: Metzler, 1973), 146.

of the question. The topic was too significant — and too attractive as a means of increasing sales of the "Kaufbücher."

Attention to this topic can help clarify the determinants of the stratification of the Reformation-Age Germany preserved in the chapbooks. The relationship of the print representation to historical conditions can be understood only as well as both the words and the conditions are understood. Of course, history and literature are interrelated; the intention here is not to argue for a simple-minded dialectic but to assert the hermeneutic prerogative of using social history as an aid to exegesis. Many questions are suggested by acquaintance with conditions known to have existed in the society of 1500. Still, textual explication remains the ultimate goal.

Each work studied in the following chapters considers the problem of wealth and its accumulation, whether by the "self-made man" or by the successor in a family enterprise. Of particular interest are attitudes and changes of attitude — not just in the character, but also in the chapbook narrator. How and to what extent are such attitudes conveyed to the reader — as horrifying negative examples, as lessons to be learned in a cool, rational manner, as voyeuristic glimpses of "the good life," as indirect, incomplete pleas for a thoroughly meritocratic social order, or as encouragement to labor long and well? Can any psychological or at least behavioral responses to change of status be observed in the upwardly mobile character? How does such movement come to terms with the demands of faith, Catholic or Lutheran? What are the precise dynamics of leaving one set of financial circumstances for another? And, whichever direction mobility takes, how do others respond? Who is left behind? Is the new arrival welcomed with open arms?

A survey of responses to the problem of wealth in Luther's Germany provides a terminus a quo for approaching the relationship between literature and the emergent wealth- and/or merit-based society of the eighteenth century. The literary innovations of that later society — its development of a "literature of experience" and its creation of two, parallel literary traditions — those innovations could occur only after the removal of impediments in the path into German culture that effectively excluded wealthy and potentially wealthy non-aristocrats. How did money-making come to be legitimated during an age of faith? That is the development traced from text to text in the pages that follow.

Chapter 2

Sebastian Brant and the Treasure of the Ship of Fools

SEBASTIAN BRANT'S FAMOUS *DAS Narrenschiff (The Ship of Fools*, 1494) mounts a critique of German society through presentation of a broad spectrum of aberrant personality types. Its breadth makes the company sailing on the Ship of Fools an attractive "population" to sample for attitudes determined wholly or in part by social structure and economic conditions. Factors such as intelligence, temperament, upbringing, education, and professional activity are examined as the poet separates the foolish from the wise. His observations follow no pervasive logic. The choice of topics ranges from the profound to the petty, the polemical tone from the magisterial to the mean-spirited. The lack of self-consciousness, the naiveté that characterize Brant's craftsmanship makes his critique of social mores strikingly accessible after five hundred years. The unwavering belief that the pleasures of the world are attractive, but ultimately worthless manifestations of *vanitas* — this traditional belief is the poet's sounding board as he scrutinizes one form of excessive worldliness after another. Brant finds wealth a particularly fruitful theme; he varies it throughout the work. He consistently emphasizes the effects of wealth rather than its causes. Brant's attack on money and money-making comes from a number of different directions, directions that alternate according to the nature of effects under consideration. While his underlying attitude is antagonistic, Brant must try to reconcile it with pragmatic values learned in a childhood home that was also a business. The poet's final evaluation of the pursuit of riches is not as simple as he would have the reader believe. In his life and in his one lasting work, Brant sought a measure of clarity and order that an era of change could not provide.

This examination of Sebastian Brant's *Narrenschiff* begins with a sketch of the poet's life and a description of his greatest work. Then Brant's position in the fledgling publishing trade is considered in light of his book's unprecedented success. Attention to market conditions encountered by this "Kaufbuch" leads naturally to a search of the text of the *Narrenschiff* for its responses both to the market economy of its day and to the goals of that economy, the maintenance or creation of wealth.

Sebastian Brant (1458-1521) was an energetic and prolific, if not overly inventive, writer and editor who doubled as a dedicated and revered teacher.[1] His birth must have been a particularly joyous occasion for his father, who owned and operated a Strasbourg inn. Here was a first-born son to share the hosteler's many duties. However, any hopes that Diebold Brant may have entertained concerning young Sebastian as heir to the family business evaporated at the older man's death in 1468. The widowed Barbara Picker Brant managed the family's shaky finances with such acumen that Sebastian received the necessary preparatory education and matriculated at the University of Basle in 1475. There he earned the baccalaureate in two years and in 1484 became a licentiate in law. By the time he was awarded the title *Doctor utriusque Juris* (1489), he had been teaching canon and civil law, as well as Latin literature, for several years. Brant's association with the university continued until 1501, when Basle joined the fledgling Swiss Confederation. As a staunch supporter of the Holy Roman Empire of the German Nation, he immediately returned to Strasbourg, a Free Imperial City. In the years that followed, he served his native city as a legal adviser to the city council and later as municipal secretary. Primarily because of the unprecedented success of the *Narrenschiff*, Sebastian Brant enjoyed the high esteem of his fellow citizens, esteem that grew when the Emperor called on him for advice. However, in the matter closest to Brant's heart, a proposed Crusade, Maximilian turned a deaf ear to urgent, repeated appeals from Strasbourg's famous man of letters.[2] To a man who longed for the universal rule of Empire and Church, later life brought disillusionment with Maximilian and anxiety about the sudden ascendancy of Martin Luther, whose fateful appearance before the Diet of Worms preceded Brant's death in the spring of 1521 by a few weeks.

The *Narrenschiff* is composed of 112 chapters written in "Knittelvers," a type of doggerel whose rhymed couplets are in an often ragged iambic tetrameter that was also used by Thomas Murner, Hans Sachs, and Johann Fischart.[3] The typical chapter offers a large woodcut in the middle of the

---

[1] For biographical details, see Edwin H. Zeydel, *Sebastian Brant* (New York: Twayne, 1967), 11-63. See also Klaus Manger, *Das "Narrenschiff": Entstehung, Wirkung und Deutung* (Darmstadt: Wissenschaftliche Buchgesellschaft, 1983), 11-18.

[2] Jan-Dirk Müller examines Brant's stance as a political commentator in "Poet, Prophet, Politiker: Sebastian Brant als Publizist und die Rolle der laikalen Intelligenz um 1500," *LiLi: Zeitschrift für Literaturwissenschaft und Linguistik* 10, no. 37 (1980): 102-27.

[3] Paul Habermann and Wolfgang Mohr offer a concise analysis of the "Knittelvers" in their entry "Deutsche Versmaße und Strophenformen," *Reallexikon der deutschen Literaturgeschichte*, 2nd ed. (Berlin: de Gruyter, 1958), 1:234.

first page.[4] Just above this depiction of the type of foolishness under attack stands a three-line motto; the text itself begins with four lines at the bottom of the first page. Many a chapter concludes after just thirty more lines on the second page; others add two thirty-line pages to the thirty-four line minimum. Several of the final fifty chapters break with these two patterns and expand to over two hundred lines. In a given chapter, the reader can expect to find an attack on one type of "foolish" behavior. After identifying that hapless type in the course of general comments based on the observation of his contemporaries, Brant goes through a litany of authorities intended to buttress his assertions. From the Bible, the Church Fathers, canon law, and ancient writers, he draws additional examples and sententious admonitions. Brant's fools exhibit behavior that ranges from the coarse (Chapter 9: "Of Bad Manners") to the sinful (Chapter 33: "Of Adultery"), from the harmless (Chapter 27: "Of Useless Studying") to the blasphemous (Chapter 28: "Of Speaking against God").[5] Successive chapters are completely disjunct: there are no transitions in the opening and closing couplets. In fact, the ordering of the chapters is apparently arbitrary; there is no movement, for example, from lesser foibles in the earlier chapters to cardinal sins in the later chapters.[6] Barbara Könneker has argued convincingly that what at first may appear to be randomness is in fact a logical corollary to Brant's concept of the fool.[7] In essence, the fool either cannot or will not follow the dictates of reason in his dealings with others, a characteristic rooted in a lack of self-knowledge. This leaves the fool prey to human weaknesses and, inevitably, to sin and vice. For Könneker each chapter is a variation on a single theme.

---

[4] For a study of the relationship between text and woodcut, see Konrad Hoffmann, "Wort und Bild im 'Narrenschiff,'" in *Literatur und Laienbildung im Spätmittelalter und in der Reformationszeit: Symposion Wolfenbüttel 1981*, ed. Ludger Grenzmann and Karl Stackmann (Stuttgart: Metzler, 1984), 392-422. See also Hans-Georg Kemper, *Epochen- und Gattungsprobleme: Reformationszeit*, vol. 1 of his *Deutsche Lyrik der frühen Neuzeit* (Tübingen: Niemeyer, 1987), 77-85.

[5] The critical edition of the *Narrenschiff* is still: Sebastian Brant, *[Das] Narrenschiff*, ed. Friedrich Zarncke (Leipzig: Wigand, 1854). Subsequent page references to the text will be indicated within parentheses. The Zarncke edition does not reproduce the woodcuts; they can be found in: Sebastian Brant, *The Ship of Fools*, trans. Edwin H. Zeydel (1944; New York: Dover, 1962). English translations of passages in the *Narrenschiff* have been taken from Zeydel. Page references to the translation will be indicated within parentheses.

[6] As an example of scholarship's search for internal logic in the *Narrenschiff*, see Beat Mischler, *Gliederung und Produktion des "Narrenschiffes" (1494) von Sebastian Brant* (Bonn: Bouvier, 1981), especially 322-23. The author posits three compositional concepts.

[7] Barbara Könneker, *Wesen und Wandlung der Narrenidee im Zeitalter des Humanismus: Brant — Murner — Erasmus* (Wiesbaden: Steiner, 1966), 86-89.

When viewed in this light, the mix of the heinous and the harmless is well suited to holding a reader's interest while the poet hammers home his message. And it is doubtlessly true that many a reader was interested primarily in enjoying either a good laugh at the folly of others or a wave of self-congratulation for having avoided pitfalls into which so many of his neighbors had tumbled. It is the poet's hope that such enjoyment will hold the reader's interest as chapters are encountered that occasion uneasiness and even self-criticism. The reader who regularly eats too much may repudiate such behavior if convinced that it shares a common cause with far graver offenses. Which is to say, Brant's evaluation of his audience's probable responses helped determine the structure of the *Narrenschiff*.

I have cited evidence of sensitivity to reception as an argument in favor of the use of the terms "chapbook" and "Kaufbuch." Again, authorial anonymity is characteristic of the so-called "Volksbuch," not the "Kaufbuch."

Sensitivity to the predilections of the reading public is to be expected during the infancy of book printing and bookselling. Brant's publisher Bergmann von Olpe was himself a new practitioner of the fledgling profession, and his location was a decided advantage. Basle was a Free Imperial City with a university and several monasteries.[8] Trade flourished on the Rhine, and there was even a local paper-making industry to support the printer's efforts. Basle's emergence as a center of the Northern Renaissance began with the long Church Council of 1431-48. Although the assembled clerics and academicians broke no new ground, the very presence of men such as Aeneas Sylvius (later Pope Pius II) and Nicolaus Cusanus created a relatively liberal, cosmopolitan intellectual climate. At the new University of Basle, founded first in 1440 and then successfully in 1460, Brant's philosophical faculty quickly became embroiled in the final stages of a controversy that for many years had divided scholasticism into nominalism and realism; the latter faction asserting the reality of abstract terms, the former asserting their status as names only.[9] The charismatic Johannes Heynlin, a champion of the realist camp, quickly gathered a circle of young scholars around him. Edwin Zeydel writes that, as he aged, Heynlin came to view the world as morally bankrupt and that the great teacher passed on this

---

[8] For more about economic and social conditions in Basle at this time, see Traugott Geering, *Handel und Industrie der Stadt Basel: Zunftwesen und Wirtschaftsgeschichte bis zum Ende des 17. Jahrhunderts* (Basle: Schneider, 1886), 296-354.

[9] Concerning the final stages of the controversy, see Gerhard Ritter, *Studien zur Spätscholastik: Via antiqua und via moderna auf den deutschen Universitäten des 15. Jahrhunderts* (Heidelberg: Winter, 1921-27), 65-68, 127-28.

perception to students like young Brant.[10] Individuals had to be weaned away from a worldly society that was leading them to perdition.

Whether because of this urgent message or the means used to convey it, the *Narrenschiff* was a great and lasting success. In fact, the work's high profile in literary history may be due to its reception as much as to its content. Zeydel's study of Brant devotes one fifteen-page chapter to a "History and Characterization of the *Narrenschiff*" and one fifteen-page chapter to a reception survey.[11] In part, this organization reflects the commendable sensitivity of an American Germanist to the interests of his Anglo-American audience. It also indicates that popularity, as manifest in numbers of editions, translations, and adaptations, was particularly vital to the nascent publishing trade — which Brant knew as he was writing the *Narrenschiff*. After all, he had already worked for the Strasbourg presses as an editor. It is hardly surprising that he wrote a book that sold well; in fact, it is tempting to suspect that he wrote a book to sell well. Whatever the intent, the publication history is extraordinary for an incunabulum: six authorized editions during the poet's lifetime; thirteen more during the balance of the sixteenth century.[12] Pirated editions also appeared, some in local dialects. In the century between Brant's death and the beginning of the Thirty Years' War, twenty-nine authorized reprints and editions were published. Translations into most of the other major European languages soon made the work an international phenomenon.[13] A few examples of *Narrenschiff* reception are particularly famous. In 1498 the renowned preacher Geiler von Kaysersberg gave a series of sermons in the Strasbourg cathedral, a series drawn from chapters in the *Narrenschiff*; each Sunday one of Brant's fools met with eloquent excoriation. And soon a whole new literary tradition, the "literature of fools," was in full bloom with such works as Erasmus's *Moriae Encomium* (*The Praise of Folly*, 1509), Thomas Murner's *Narrenbeschwörung* (*Conjuration of Fools*, 1512), and the *Epistolae obscurorum virorum* (*Letters of Obscure Men*, 1515 and 1517) of the embattled humanists Crotus Rubeanus and Ulrich von Hutten.[14] While the nature and extent of Brant's influence has been debated for decades, it

---

[10] Zeydel, *Sebastian Brant*, 32.

[11] Zeydel, *Sebastian Brant*, 74-89, 90-105.

[12] See Manger, 66-69, 78-81 and Zeydel, *Sebastian Brant*, 90-91.

[13] Manger, 70-74, 85-92.

[14] For a detailed study of the origin and development of the "Literature of Fools," see Könneker, *Narrenidee*. For a recent comparison of the *Narrenschiff* with the *Narrenbeschwörung* (1512) of Thomas Murner, see H.-G. Kemper, 85-90.

is clear that, as a prototype, the *Narrenschiff* held out the promise of audience interest in similar works.

Its great success made Brant's work a significant factor in the book trade of Luther's Germany. It was a reliable commodity in a growing, increasingly competitive market. From a bookseller's point of view, the response to the *Narrenschiff* constituted an assurance of the viability of the book trade and underscored the connection between popularity and profitability. From a reader's point of view, a book like the *Narrenschiff* came to be seen as an appropriate purchase. With increasing sales, printed matter was becoming a familiar consumer item. To be sure, a technological breakthrough, the invention of movable type, had made possible the production of many copies at low cost. And Humanism's mission of general enlightenment legitimated the replacement of Latin by the vernacular on the printed page. Pan-German patriotism during the reign of Maximilian supported the new acceptance accorded the German language. However, any broadly based support for literary production — support from beyond the academy — had to be founded on a canon of works that would retain their appeal through the decades as their numbers swelled to respectable proportions. Books that would be purchased by successive generations — "Kaufbücher" — were the works that made literature a part of general economic growth. As a domestic industry that was not dependent on transcontinental transportation systems, the book-trade was well positioned to survive the economic doldrums of the last decades of the sixteenth century and the social chaos of the Thirty Years' War. As it grew, it created a steady demand for the products of the domestic timber and paper industries. Such commercial interdependency increased the stability of a book-trade that could then diversify and specialize. With the rise of literacy and the advent of literary publishers, the middle-class professional writer could become possible. Of course, over two centuries were required for these developments, a span of time that included the retrenchment of the seventeenth century. However, it was the chapbooks that established the set of relationships among writers, manufacturers, merchants, and readers that still exists today.

It would be reasonable to assume that, because of their involvement in the book-trade and therefore in early capital formation, the chapbook texts assume a positive or at least neutral stance vis-à-vis the problem of wealth. After all, a man like Brant knew the printer-publishers of his city; they moved in the same social circles. The financial status of a Bergmann von Olpe was both readily apparent and critically important. Brant in particular had understood the role of business in human affairs since his childhood at the family inn. Later, personal impoverishment might have suggested the indispensability of financial assets. And yet, the response to wealth recorded in the *Narrenschiff* is largely negative; or, more precisely, most of the responses to wealth are negative.

From the early chapters on, Brant draws a distinction between two large groups of fools. One appears in clear profile as the subject of the third chapter, "Of Greed"; the other group is introduced by the seventeenth chapter, "Of Useless Riches." Because the two chapters are paradigmatic for the analyses that follow, they are reproduced here in their entirety; the three-line motto precedes each chapter title:

>Wer setzt sin lust vff zyttlich gůt
>Vnd dar jnn sůcht sin freyd vnd můt
>Der ist eyn narr jnn lib vnd blůt
>[3.] Von gytikeit
>Der ist eyn narr der samlet gůt
>Vnd hat dar by keyn fryd noch můt
>Vnd weysz nit wem er solches spart
>So er zům finstren keller fart
>Vyl narrechter ist der verdůt
>Mit üppykeit vnd lichtem můt
>Das so jm got hat geben heyn
>Dar jnn er schaffner ist allein
>Vnd dar vmb rechnung geben můsz
>Die me gilt dan ein hand vnd fůsz
>Ein narr verläszt sin fründen vil
>Sin sel er nit versorgen wil
>Vnd vörcht jm brest hie zitlich gůt
>Nit sorgend, wasz dasz ewig důt,
>O armer narr wie bist so blindt
>Du vörchst die rud, vnd findst den grindt
>Mancher mit sunden gůt gewynt
>Dar vmb er jn der hellen brynt
>Syn erben achten das gar klein
>Sie hülffen jm nit mit eym stein
>Sie löszten jnn kum mit eym pfundt
>So er dieff ligt in hellen grundt,
>Gib wil du lebst durch gottes ere
>Noch dym dot wirt ein ander here,
>Esz hat keyn wyser nye begerdt
>Das er möcht rich syn hie vff erdt
>Sunder das er lert kennen sych
>Wer wys ist, der ist me dann rich,
>Crassus das golt zů letzst vsztrangk

Noch dem jnn hat gedürstet langk,
Crates syn gelt warff jn das mer
Das es nyt hyndert jnn zůr ler,
Wer samlet das zergenglich ist
Der grabt sin sel jn kott vnd mist

(6)

Who sets his heart on earthly ware
And seeks his joy and comfort there,
Inveterate foolishness his share.
3. OF GREED
A fool who gathers earthly ware
And finds no joy or comfort there
And hardly knows for whom to save
When once he finds his dark, cool grave;
More foolish still is he who spends
To frivolous and wasteful ends
What God once gave for him to own,
What he should husband all alone.
Some day accounting he must make,
Where more than limb will be at stake.
A fool gives liberally to friends,
His own salvation never tends
And dreads the lack of earthly wares,
But ne'er for things eternal cares.
O silly fool, how blind you are,
You fear the mange, invite a scar.
The man who wrongful riches wins
Will burn in hell for all his sins;
To that his heirs pay little heed,
They'd not assist in time of need,
They'd not redeem him for a sou
When once in hell he needs must stew.
For God's sake, give the while you may,
When you've died other men hold sway;
No wise man ever deemed it worth
His while to garner wealth on earth,
He'd rather learn to know himself.
Who's wise has more than trifling pelf;
Crassus did drink the gold, they say,
For which he craved and thirsted ay;
Crates his gold tossed out to sea,

So that for studies he'd be free.
Who piles up goods that evanesce
Inters his soul in filthiness.

(66-67)

Wer gůt hat, vnd ergetzt sich mit
Vnd nit dem armen do von gytt
Dem wurt verseit, so er ouch bitt
[17.] Von vnnutzem richtum
Die grösszt torheit jn aller welt
Ist, das man eret für wiszheit gelt,
Vnd zücht harfür eyn richen man
Der oren hat, vnd schellen dran
Der můsz alleyn ouch jn den rat
Das er vil zů verlieren hat,
Eym yeden gloubt soviel die welt
Als er hat jnn sinr täschen gelt
Her pfenning der můsz vornen dran
Wer noch jn leben Salomon
Man liesz jn, jnn den rat nit gon
Wann er eyn armer weber wer
Oder jm stünd sin seckel ler,
Die richen ladt man zů dem tisch
Vnd bringt jnn wiltpret, vogel, visch,
Vnd důt on end mit jnn hofiern
Die wile der arm stat vor der türen
Vnd switzet, das er möcht erfrieren,
Zům richen spricht man, essen herr,
O pfening, man düt dir die ere
Du schaffst, dasz vil dir günstig sint
Wer pfening hat, der hat vil fründ
Den grüszt vnd swagert yederman,
Wolt eyner gern eyn ee frow han,
Die erst frag ist, was hat er doch,
Man fragt der erberkeyt, nym noch
Oder der wiszheit, ler, vernunfft
Man sůcht eyn vsz der narren zunfft
Der jnn die mylch zů brocken hab
Ob er joch sy eyn köppels knab
All kunst, ere, wiszheit, ist vmb sunst
Wo an dem pfening ist gebrust
Wer syn or, vor dem armen stopfft

Den hört got nit, so er ouch klopft

(19-20)

> The wealthy man of foolish creed
> Who nevermore would beggars heed
> Will be denied when he's in need.
> 17. OF USELESS RICHES
> The greatest folly ever told
> Is honoring wisdom less than gold,
> With such beliefs one only rears
> Rich men with bells on asses' ears.
> Such councilmen one fain would choose
> As have the greatest wealth to lose;
> The world believes a man as much
> As he has funds inside his pouch.
> Lord Lucre leads the greedy on:
> If still alive were Solomon,
> The council he would have to shun
> If but a simple weaver he,
> Or if his purse of gold were free.
> To rich men dinners we will proffer,
> And game, fowl, fish to them we offer,
> The scraping host cajoles and flatters
> The while the beggar waits in tatters
> And from the cold his jawbone chatters.
> The wealthy guest is greeted: "Sir,
> Please eat!" Yes, riches cause a stir;
> You force all men to scrape and bend.
> Who has the coin has many a friend,
> He's called a chum on every side,
> And if a man would take a bride,
> The first thing is: How rich is he?
> No one inspects his honesty
> Or asks if wisdom in him rules;
> He's chosen from the guild of fools,
> Who can afford some bread with milk,
> Though he be rowdyish of ilk.
> Nor wisdom, honor have much backing
> Wherever shining gold is lacking.
> Who from the poor his treasure locks
> Will find God deaf whene'er he knocks.

(100-101)

The first lines of Chapter 3 confirm expectations created by the title that the pursuit of new or additional wealth is to be the subject. Brant selects the simplest strategy for his attack when he uses the first line to establish his target as the man who is consumed with greed. Brant juxtaposes that sin with an image of death in order to underscore the significance of time and its uses. The time one has been granted on earth should be spent on one's inner being; "earthly ware" is a reification of time wasted. Completely irrelevant is the possibility that altruism will be attributed to those who labor for the comfort of future generations. Brant's fool is unable to assign correct values to the various human activities and, as a result, strives after that which is valueless. The first lines of Chapter 17 establish a tension between title and text. The title suggests a highly judgmental analysis of wealth; however, the text takes up not wealth, but the response to wealth. Here, the greedy striving of Chapter 3 either has already occurred or will occur in the generation to come. Between this past and future is a present that understands personal treasure to be a permanent commodity, like wisdom. Chapter 3 considers wealth sought; Chapter 17 considers wealth possessed. Through the change of focus, Brant can expand his appeal to include those who have a high regard for wealth and who are willing to spend time seeking or "honoring" it. Those who only revere gold from a distance are still guilty of valuing the valueless. They, too, must share the blame for raising the avaricious fool of Chapter 3.

The fact that one man's greed may bring unexpected gain to his friends cannot mitigate the sin. That message in lines 11-12 and 17-22 of Chapter 3 reinforces the earlier reference to legacies: the individual is responsible for his own path to salvation. Brant's emphasis on the miser's friends and family indicates a decision by the poet not to restrict his denunciation to the personal decision to live for the things of this transitory sphere. Of course, that latter, more traditional accusation is leveled (lines 13-14), but the type of fool and the nature of the foolishness are so well known that the poet is able to go beyond exposition and anticipate the response from defensive wealthy readers. Brant will not accept as expiation the security and comfort of dependents. While some may be able to pursue wealth without committing ethical transgressions, many will "win wrongful riches." Which is to say, while material success in itself is not sinful, it constitutes a condition that is tantamount to sin. Lines 17 through 27 carry the defensive position of wealthy readers to its logical, immoral extreme, sinning for the sake of others, and then notes the irony that possessions bought at the price of eternal hellfire cannot be inherited with commensurate gratitude. The strong implication that acquisitiveness leads to sin gives way in the final couplet to the next logical position. The verb "samlet" ("gathers") echoes from the first line of the chapter. There it partakes of a laughably irrational approach to life; here it is an act of self-damnation. The image of chilly, dark death in the fourth line is replaced by that of filth and putrefaction in lines 33-34. The poet has moved from a presentation of greed as a serious failing ("no joy or comfort") to a description of self-loathing and spiritual suicide.

The wealthy fool of Chapter 17 also faces an unhappy fate in the final couplet; however, the image of God turning a deaf ear is not calculated to sicken or horrify. The remonstrance itself could apply to those who have only a little more than they need as well as to those who are truly wealthy. However, it is used to reinforce the motto with its sharp focus on the rich man and the poor man. Hence the chapter begins and ends in a manner that is consistent with its title. But the balance of the presentation concerns not that small portion of the population composed of those who have possessions and liquidity, but rather that group of townsmen who hover about the wealthy to flatter, to pander, and to feather their own nests. Others may not have the opportunity to bow and scrape, but their veneration of wealth knows no bounds. It dominates their attitude toward life to such an extent that it eclipses the esteem accorded such characteristics as intelligence, honesty, and wisdom. Of course, it was the author's intention that the reader would agree that this perception of wealth was in fact widespread and that it constituted a deplorable perversion of Christian ethics. The mere proximity of a wealthy burgher endangers the moral rectitude of his financially strapped neighbor. In the two chapters, that neighbor is Brant's chief concern.

To recapitulate, Sebastian Brant's attack on wealth in these early chapters of the *Narrenschiff* is mounted against two personality types: the fool who actively pursues money and property and the fool who can only honor those who have achieved worldly success. In neither chapter does the poet evince great concern for the rich man himself, whether or not the latter parades his status through conspicuous consumption. The man of wealth *is* subjected to thoroughgoing criticism in the later chapters, but the treatment of wealth begins, logically enough, with those groups within the population that are "saved" most easily from the blandishments of the world. And in fact, when the rich are considered, it is frequently with a view to the deleterious influence exerted on those who belong to Brant's economic stratum — whether or not they are trying to escape it.

Brant moves to avoid a potential charge of harboring hostility born of envy by presenting the moneyed townsman as a victim of his own worldliness. After all, the wastrel fool is in his midst, and possibly under his roof. This familiar type, whose very existence still triggers resentment, is the subject of one of the earlier long chapters, "Of Gluttony and Feasting." As the motto of this sixteenth chapter makes clear, the behavior in question is associated with affluence:

> Billich jn kunfftig armůt feltt
> Wer stäts noch schleck vnd füllen stelt
> Vnd sich den brassern zů geselt
>
> (18)

> He merits future poverty
> Who always lives in luxury
> And joins the spendthrift's revelry.
>
> (96)

The inference to be drawn is that poverty would be a particularly fitting punishment for the behavior described because it would represent a reversal of financial circumstances. The underlying assumption is that the reveler is rich.

Before the breadth of his transgression is measured, it should be noted that poverty is presented here neither as a cure nor as a state of innocence, but as a punishment. Deprivation of the things of this world is undesirable. While this position is later reversed, other passages will be cited as support for the contention that Brant's attitude toward wealth is riddled with ambiguity.

Nevertheless, the dominant message of Chapter 16 is that excessive eating and especially excessive drinking lead to degradation of all forms. Such a fool will suffer the shakes, lose the ability to think, and ultimately stray from the path of chastity. The poet echoes the New Testament (Luke 16, 19) in hammering home his warning to the wealthy: "Der richman tranck als eyn gesell/Vnd asz des morndes jnn der hell ..." (19) ("The rich man reveled once so well/That on the morn he ate in hell," 98). Still, Brant shows an awareness of two potential weaknesses in his presentation of the victim of over-indulgence. On one hand, the maladies from which the victim is sure to suffer summon forth the image of the drunken beggar sprawled in the street. Even alcoholics only partially capable of "normal" professional and personal contacts will not identify themselves with so wretched a figure. Hence, the emphasis on wealth, which effectively raises the drunkard's status to heights commonly deemed unattainable by abstemious townsmen. The message is not simply that wealth is dangerous, but that wealth is dangerous because it leads to a condition, alcoholism, that erodes social stratification. On the other hand, Brant must come to grips with society's traditional, paradoxical tendency to "enable" a drinker to continue his self-destructive behavior. For centuries that tendency has led to the attitudes that overindulgence is enjoyable and companionable, that drunks are not deceptive, but to the contrary, refreshingly candid, that a person should not be held responsible for unacceptable acts committed while inebriated. Of course, the above characterization of the moneyed fool as a reveler suggests that his wealth and its associated malady guarantee that he will not dine alone in hell. His drinking companions are also at hazard. Against the general society's tendency to excuse, support, and even esteem drunkenness and the drunk, Brant ranges the time-worn argument that the world honors what it should loathe. He cites Seneca as asserting, "Das man würd ettwann geben mer / Eym druncknen, dann eim nühtern ere" (19) ("... one pays a drunken man / More heed than many a sober man ..." 99). Accordingly, the right-thinking reader must avoid this "worldly" perception and hold the drunk responsible for his actions, including the endangerment of others and the act of drinking itself.

Of course, healthy behavior characterizes the one who avoids both the ways of the world and those fellow creatures who are devoted to such ways. His wealthy counterpart, whether drunk or sober, always has a retinue around him:

> Eyn armer bhalt wol heymlicheyt
> Eyns richen sach, würt wyt gespreyt
> Vnd würt durch vntruw huszgesynd
> Geöffnet vnd vszbrocht geschwynd ...
>
> (42)

> A poor man lives in privacy,
> Rich men are watched quite eagerly,
> By all their faithless retinue
> All their affairs are aired anew.
>
> (153)

Wealth brings a special form of paranoia based on the inability to speak in confidence. No one is to be trusted; any plans made are immediately known to the public — hence the title of the chapter from which the citation is drawn, "Of Open Plans." Here the poet's animosity has clouded his reason: without effective, successful planning, many of the wealthy could not remain wealthy. And the concept of family confidentiality clearly is not restricted to those of modest incomes. The very existence of wealthy merchant families refutes Brant's argument.

Because he is not in a position to trust others, the man of substance is denied true friendship. Each relationship will have a financial basis:

> Wer vil gůt hat, der hat vil fründ
> Dem hilfft man redlich ouch zů sünd
> Eyn yeder lügt wie er jn schynd

> So lang das wärt, bisz er würt arm
> So spricht er, heu das gott erbarm
> Wie hat ich vor, nochlouff so vil
> Keyn fründ ist der mich trösten wil ...
>
> (67)

> The rich man gathers hosts of friends
> Who walk the sinful way he wends
> And swindle him for sinful ends.
> They persevere until he's poor
> And he exclaims: "My friends grow fewer,
> O Godamercy, how they wane,
> No friend consoles me, stills my pain!"
>
> (227)

Both sinning and sinned against, the wealthy fool is admonished once again that his path leads to penury. His pursuit of temporal goals means that in a crisis he cannot turn to faith for solace, but only to others whose materialism matches his own. In fact, the ironic use of "friend" calls into question the concept of friendship as a worthy focus of human energy. Interpersonal relationships are of this world and are therefore as transitory as riches. The sharing of thoughts and plans with one's fellow man is one of the many ways of wasting time, all of which divert the mind from its proper study, the self. Barbara Könneker has asserted that Brant views his contemporaries as lacking a focus for their existence; in urging them to turn to their own lives for such a focus, he foresees and accepts the resultant diminution in their capacity to have impact on their society.[15] Self-reliance emerges as a virtue, but, as Könneker points out, at considerable cost — particularly to a townsman. His opportunity for having an impact on the society around him comprised intangibles such as setting an optimistic, forward-looking example for his neighbors and applying indirect but steady pressure on secular authority to improve the social and economic prospects of the small middle stratum of society — such intangibles in addition to his palpable contributions in providing goods and services. In the passage above, Brant rules out any argument that wealth can improve the human condition if it is only used properly. His position here is simple: wealth can only harm. Still, it should be borne in mind that this is the same writer who presents the absence of money as a punishment. Brant's advice to his contemporaries cannot be reduced to a simple, satisfying formulation such as the one Könneker suggests.

---

[15] Könneker, *Narrenidee*, 98.

Particularly revealing in this context is the poet's approach to poverty; he devotes a chapter to a denunciation of those who hold the poor in contempt. The polemic uses the example of Christ as ballast:

> Wer gůt vff erden rich hye syn
> Christus wer nit der ärmst gsyn,
> Wer spricht das jm sunst nüt gebrest
> Dann das on pfenning sy sin täsch
> Der selb ist aller wiszheit on
> Im gbrüst me dann er sagen kan
> Vnd vor vsz das er nit erkennt
> Das er sy ärmer dann er wänt
>
> (81)

> If riches were a blessing sure
> Would Christ have been so bare and poor?
> Who says: "For me the only curse
> Is this: I've nothing in my purse,"
> He's ignorant of wisdom's way,
> He lacks far more than he can say.
> Precisely this he never knows:
> He's needier than he'd suppose.
>
> (275)

Here, at the conclusion of Chapter 83: "Contempt of Poverty," Brant has already countered the traditional condescension of those accustomed to material comfort with the divine model. However, he finds just as culpable the behavior of those who lament their own poverty. They too have forgotten that the life of Christ is the cornerstone of Christian ethics. Nevertheless, the playful use of "needier" in the last line relativizes that message by implying that a continuum exists between poverty that is purely spiritual and poverty that is purely material. Of course, the naive suggestion that wisdom should be the first concern of the one whose purse is empty is in line with the poet's fundamental conservatism in matters of socioeconomic inequity. A far more pragmatic response to the relative attractiveness of wisdom and wealth is evident in the chapbook *Fortunatus* (1507). In fairness to Brant, his conservative stance is self-critical rather than reactionary; the punning with "needier" bespeaks a sardonic posture vis-à-vis his own argument.

The same glorification of poverty extends to historical and sociohistorical analysis. In the chapter just cited, the rise and fall of Rome is explained as a consequence of the absence and then presence of wealth.

Brant delights in the irony that fame and glory were preceded by rustic poverty:

> Dann wer merckt, vnd gedenckt do by
> Das Rom von hyrten gbuwen sy
> Von armen buren lang regiert
> Dar noch durch richtům gantz verfürt,
> Der mag wol mercken das armůt
> Rom basz hat gthon, dann grosses gůt ...
>
> (81)

> For who will note what's much expounded
> That Rome by shepherds once was founded
> And long by peasants poor was ruled
> And then by riches was befooled,
> He'll realize that poverty
> Did Rome more good than property.
>
> (274)

The irony of the second line becomes the oxymoron of the third as the bucolic vision of Rome's early days becomes utopian in the reference to peasants who ruled. The fabled classless society faltered with the advent of materialism and, by extension, stratification based on personal wealth. The poet does not miss the opportunity presented by the notorious example of imperial Rome to contrast poor, honest builders with wealthy, dissolute destroyers.

Brant's championing of poverty in Chapter 83 is paradigmatic for his analysis of wealth: he is careful to demonstrate two sets of effects, those on the individual and those on the society. Wealth renders impossible the private "imitation of Christ" and the public pursuit of the "common weal." Its impact on the individual extends not only to final salvation, but also to satisfaction with daily activities, intellectual development, and self-esteem. The results of the pursuit of money are presented in such a way as to shock any reader who might be tempted to conclude that business affairs can be left outside of the front door of one's home:

> Gar kum vff erd yetz kumen vsz
> Die tugend hant, sunst nüt jm husz
> Man důt wiszheit keyn ere me an
> Erberkeyt můsz verr hynden stan
> ...
> Vnd wer vff richtům flysset sich

> Der lůgt ouch, das er bald werd rich
> Vnd acht keyn sünd, mort, wůcher, schād
> Des glich verretery der land
> Das yetz gemeyn ist jnn der welt
> All boszheit, fyndt man yetz vmb gelt
>
> (80)

> Men cannot live on earth alone
> With virtue, if that's all they own,
> For wisdom now is spurned and scored,
> Respectability ignored ...
> ...
> And who for riches has an itch
> Will hatch a plan for getting rich
> And heeds no sin at any season
> Nor murder, usury, nor treason,
> Which now is common here on earth,
> All evil's done for money's worth.
>
> (271-72)

There is one source for all of these forms of self-betrayal. Money is also a destructive influence on interpersonal relationships. Brant has concluded that the modern world necessarily frustrates attempts to set and pursue goals in a virtuous fashion. The second couplet suggests that the societal response itself constitutes a barrier in the path to intellectual and moral self-improvement. The inference to be drawn is that wealth has replaced wisdom and respectability with the result that all who walk the earth only await the opportunity to transgress against their neighbor, their country, and their God. The lines that immediately follow those above emphasize the extent of social decay by imputing it to precisely that institution charged with safeguarding public mores, the judiciary. Brant's irony becomes particularly bitter as he adumbrates the fatal consequences of the rampant subversion of justice.

The passages cited demonstrate that Brant's survey of the effects of wealth takes stands on a myriad of issues metaphysical, interpersonal, and institutional. He who has financial means is ipso facto susceptible to situational temptations that will lead him to betray himself and others. One clear implication has anyone with substantial assets teetering on the brink of perdition at each encounter with a fellow creature.

Just in case any doubt might remain as to precisely what would push a modern Croesus over the brink, a heavy money-bag is shown in the full-page woodcut that accompanies Chapter 103: "Of the Antichrist" (Fig. 1). High

Fig. 1. Woodcut from the *Narrenschiff* of Sebastian Brant

atop the foundering hulk of the Ship of Fools sits the Antichrist as though on a throne. His crown is the snake-like body of a demon; instead of a scepter, the emblem of a king's power on earth, he holds a flail in his left hand. The money-bag is in his right, where rulers of the Holy Roman Empire traditionally held an orb, the bejeweled sphere surmounted by a crucifix. Since the coronation of Heinrich II in 1014, the "imperial apple" had symbolized the Emperor's claim to universal sovereignty under the authority of the cross. Of course, as a ceremonial weapon, the scepter represents the monarch's ability to defend his subjects by force of arms. Antichrist's "scepter" is designed not to provide protection for, but to mete out punishment to his subjects. The ersatz orb constitutes a still greater perversion since the faith is involved. It is not just that the worship of Christ has been replaced by the worship of gold, but that the entire medieval cosmology has been lost. Accordingly, the Antichrist is a ruler without a realm; the flotsam throne bobs about aimlessly on the open sea. Just as directionless are his drowning subjects, some of whom can be spotted only by the tips of their dunce caps. Meanwhile, Saint Peter uses his key to pull a boatload of pious men to shore. The apostle holds out the promise of the solid ground of institutional Christianity to the few readers who bear in mind the order of the cosmos represented by the true orb.

Brant reinforces the message of the woodcut by according wealth extensive consideration in passages concerning the Antichrist. In one sustained treatment, the poet describes those souls who have fallen away from virtue in their quest for riches. "Der" ("His") refers to the Antichrist:

> Der würt er han vil jnn der weltt
> Wann er vsz teylen würt syn gelt
> Vnd all syn schätz würt fürhar bringen
> Darff er nit vil mit streichen zwyngen
> Das merteyl, würt selbs zů jnn louffen
> Durch geltt würt er vil zů jm kouffen
> Die helfen jm, das er dann mag
> Die gůten bringen alle tag,
> Doch werden sie die leng nit faren
> Inn würt bald brechen schiff, vnd karren
> Wie wol sie faren vmb vnd vmb
> Vnd würt die worheyt machen krumb
> So würt zů letst doch worheyt bliben
> Vnd würt jr falscheyt gantz vertriben
> Die yetz vmbfert jnn allem standt
> Ich vörcht das schiff kum nym zů landt

(99)

> His retinue will be untold,
> And when he pays his shining gold
> And shows that he's not treasureless
> He will not have to use duress,
> They'll come and join of their accord,
> And money coaxes more aboard.
> They'll help him wherewith well he may
> Enlist good people every day,
> But brief and sad will be their trip,
> They will be wrecked with skiff and ship,
> Though traveling everywhere for ay,
> Distorting truth in every way,
> Yet truth will live and ever be,
> Expelling all their falsity
> Which now from no estate is banned,
> I fear the ship will never land.
>
> (333)

The money-bag is presented as the most effective of Antichrist's means of enticing humanity — most effective because victims do not avoid it as a deadly trap, but instead eagerly seek it. Recourse to the flail is seldom necessary. The perception that such sinners trade salvation for the coin of the realm is expressed starkly in the image of the Antichrist "buying himself" most of his shipmates. Of course, their reward is comfort and luxury until the final shipwreck; however, even their brief happiness serves the purposes of Satan's agent. It is put on display as a trap set for still others, here identified as "good people." Some of the passengers on the ship have always had or sought wealth. Others have made the decision to forsake the faith and forfeit their standing among "good people." Use of that designation indicates the existence of a clear distinction in Brant's mind between those who view affluence uncritically and positively and those who have surveyed the various paths through life only to choose badly. Members of the first group are already on board, whereas many members of the second are still swimming toward the doomed ship. Use of "good people" with reference to those in the water indicates that their fall is not yet complete and could be reversed. In light of this perception, it is logical that the poet devotes particular attention to those in search of new wealth; in his eyes, their tie to the Antichrist can be broken.

Given this straightforward analysis and given the biographies of Diebold and Sebastian Brant, it comes as no surprise that the *Narrenschiff* speaks most frequently, most fervently, and in greatest detail to those who actively seek economic advancement. At the family inn and later in Basle, Brant was in a position to observe closely those busily engaged in making money. By chance of birth and then by choice of occupation, he lived in the midst of commercial activity without experiencing the responsibilities and rewards of full participation. The inevitable distancing that ensued did not lead him to underestimate the attractiveness of money-making, however. The first structurally anomalous chapter, the twenty-second, takes as its theme the self-discipline necessary to reject the acquisition of assets when the techniques of acquisition are as clearly understood as are the benefits of the assets. In "The Teaching of Wisdom," Brant breaks with his pattern of one type of foolishness per chapter to offer a hortatory address by an allegorical figure. In a speech to all of mankind, Wisdom divides the various channels for human energy into two categories:

> Vff bschydikeyt hant acht jr kyndt
> Mercken all, die jn dorheyt synt,
> Sůchen die ler vnd nit das gelt
> Wiszheyt ist besser dann all welt
> Vnd alles das man wünschen mag
> Stellen noch wiszheyt nacht vnd tag
> Nüt ist, das ir glich vff der erd
> In rätten ist wiszheyt gar werdt
>
> (24)

> You must be prudent, wise, and shrewd,
> Hear me in all your folly crude,
> Seek teachings ever, never gold,
> Wisdom holds preciousness untold,
> 'Tis better than mundane delight,
> Pursue it ever, day and night.
> There's nothing like it here on earth,
> In councils it's of sterling worth.
>
> (112-13)

The third and fourth lines establish an equality between teachings and wisdom, an equality given special prominence through the wordplay with the chapter title.[16] The woodcut features a crowned angel at a podium; from the upper right, the hand of God blesses her labors. The inference to be drawn from the lines cited is that learning leads to wisdom and a concomitant state of grace. What at first reads as a heavy-handed attempt to

---

[16] Raimund Kemper emphasizes the significance of Brant's concept of wisdom and its relationship to education in "Zur Beurteilung des Sebastian Brant," *Leuvense Bijdragen* 73, no. 1 (1984): 4-6. See also Könneker, *Narrenidee*, 91, 125-32.

deify education should be understood in the context of the tension within humanism between traditional religiosity and the rising secularism of the intellectual elite. The passage invites anagogical interpretation even as it supplies potential opponents of the new learning with a substitute foeman. "Seek teachings ever, never gold." Those who have chosen the latter pursuit are "in folly"; it is they who desire that which is of this world ("mundane delight"). Brant's penchant for presenting ethical problems as questions with yes-or-no answers is particularly apparent in Wisdom's parting couplet: "Wer mich findt, der fyndt heil vnd glück / Der mich hasszt, der verdyrbt gar dick" (25) ("'Who finds me, also finds salvation, / Who hates me, suffers harsh damnation,'" 113). The only alternatives offered are love of wisdom and salvation or else hatred of wisdom and ruin. The implicit denial of any middle ground suggests the necessity of unremitting self-discipline as a response to the presence of continual temptation. The accompanying woodcut emphasizes the power of temptation by sprinkling Wisdom's audience with listeners in foolscaps; one is directly beneath the podium.

The pursuit of wealth leads such fools to engage in several kinds of aberrant behavior on a number of forums: within the family, within each social stratum, within the church, within government. In private life, the foolish preoccupation with money-making leads to disaster in the raising of children:

> Des ist zů wundern nit dar an
> Das narrē narrecht kynder han
> Crates der allt sprach, wān es jm
> Zů stůnd, wolt er mit heller stym
> Schryē, jer narrē vnbedacht
> Ir hant vff gůtsamlē grosz acht
> Vnd achtē nit vff vwer kind
> Den jr sölich richtum samlen sindt
>
> (9)

> It's little wonder that a fool
> Has foolish children as a rule.
> Old Crates said, if 'twere allowed
> And proper he would loudly shout:
> You fools, who think of getting rich
> And have this constant burning itch
> And ne'er to children pay much heed
> Since riches are your only need!
>
> (74)

There is no equivocation about the future that awaits such children:

> Ettlich důnt sich in bůben rott
> Die lästern vnd gesmächen gott
> Die andren hencken an sich säck
> Dise verspielen rosz vnd röck
> Die vierden prassen tag vnd nacht
> Das würt vsz solchen kynden gmacht
>
> (9)

> Some join a brutal ruffian's horde,
> Blaspheming they malign our Lord,
> Some go about with slattern whores,
> Some gamble, losing shirt and horse,
> Others carouse by day and night,
> That, mark you, that's our children's plight
> ...
>
> (74-75)

The poet's condemnation of the pursuit of wealth is seldom as sweeping as it is here, where he presents the trait as a legacy transmitted from one generation to the next. Accordingly, it is not enough to condemn the wanton man; if a careful observer studies not only the son, but also the father, he usually will find two worshippers of the Golden Calf. The rites of such worship take place in public and therefore are readily observable as a shockingly demeaning pattern of behavior. The depth of Brant's dislike emerges from a passage that intimates the existence of a secular order of flagellants:

> Mancher der liesz sich halber schynden
> Vnd jm alle viere mit seylen bynden
> Das jm alleyn ging gelt dar vsz
> Vnd er vil golds hett jnn sym husz
> Der lytt ouch das er läg zů bett
> Vnd er der richen siechtag hett
> Vnd man jn wie eyn bůben schiltt
> Echt er dar von hett zyns vnd gültt
>
> (68)

> Some men would let themselves be flayed
> And tied with ropes from foot to head
> If only that would net them gold

> And bring them affluence untold,
> And some in bed would gladly be
> And have the rich man's malady,
> Or take a scolding like a knave,
> If only riches were their slave.
>
> (228-29)

A total surrender of self-determination is adumbrated here. In order to worship money, the fool will submit himself to demeaning treatment despite any resultant humiliation or disease. Such passive admiration brings about dehumanization. At the same time, Brant believes that a person can be debased through an equally focused, but ruthlessly active search for wealth, a search that can involve immoral acts committed against life and property.

Brant takes care to present the consequences of the acquisitive urge for the society as well as for the individual. One such consequence supposedly has been the growth of Germany's pariah caste:

> Man lyhet eym yetz müntz vmb goltt,
> Für zehen schribt man eylff jnns bůch
> Gar lydlich wer der juden gesůch
> Aber sie mögen nit me bliben
> Die krysten juden, sie vertriben
> Mit juden spiesz die selben rennen
> Ich kenn vil die ich nit will nennen
> Die triben doch wild kouffmanschatz
> Vnd schwygt dar zů all reht, vnd gsatz ...
>
> (89-90)

> [Some] lend in silver, ask for gold,
> You borrow ten, eleven's due,
> They're more usurious than the Jew.
> Their business now the Jews may lose,
> For it is done by Christian Jews.
> With Jewish spears they run about,
> I could name many such a lout,
> Unsavory are their transactions
> Yet are not stopped by legal actions.
>
> (303)

As the traditional, Christian proscription of the charging of interest was undermined gradually, the unsavory reputation of the traditionally Jewish occupation moneylender lay in wait for rising Christian financiers. Brant implies that the amount of interest now received would be filling Jewish coffers were it not for the existence of Christian moneylenders. The inference to be drawn is that the Christians now bleed their debtors more rapidly than have their Jewish colleagues. Of course, the phrase "Christian Jews" has the force of an epithet. Their act of driving the Jews out of the lending business has lowered such Christians to a social position that can be described only by recourse to a paradox. It is in effect a "non-position" since the Jews had at best a clearly defined relationship to, albeit outside of, society at large. The metaphor "juden spiesz" ("Jewish spears") created problems for Friedrich Zarncke, the nineteenth-century scholar who produced what is still *the* critical edition.[17] While the usage in Chapter 76: "Of Great Boasting" (line 11) is unclear, the passage cited above from Chapter 93: "Usury and Profiteering" contains a strong clue. Brant first ascribes actions to "Christian Jews" ("Some lend ..."), then offers a commentary ("They're more usurious ..."), and finally describes the action of running about with "Jewish spears." The first actions, indicated by "lyhet" ("lend") and "schribt" (literally "write"), are to be understood in the *sensus litteralis*, the second action in the *sensus allegoricus* suggested by the first. The Jew's "spear" is his pen; he wields it in his account books. In the hands of "Christian Jews," these weapons have rendered their bearers insuperable on the financial battlefield. The moral conventions and legal regulations and institutions that have limited the commercial activities of the Jews will not apply to rapacious Christian merchants and financiers. The use of "wild" ("wild") in the original suggests an author recoiling in horror before his two oxymora, Christians who are "Jews" and Jews with and without quotation marks who approach those with whom they have business dealings from a position of ("armed") strength. Those who should be powerless are instead powerful. In Brant's view, society is newly bereft of its traditional veneration for morality and law as guarantors of order within society. One result has been an ironic perversion of the faith, the "armed" Christian "Jew." Another result has been damage to the secular community of man. The poet closes Chapter 93 as follows: "Wer rich will syn, mit schad der gmeyn / Der ist eyn narr, doch nit allein," (90) ("Harm common weal and help your own, / And you're a fool, but not alone," 303). The second half of the first line is not intended solely as a qualifier; the comma introduces enough ambiguity to allow a causal reading. The fools referred to in the second line break the natural cohesion among members of the same social level. Elsewhere in the text, Brant points to the effects of the resultant chaos, the sundry types of

---

[17] Brant, *Narrenschiff*, 420, 437. Compare Zarncke's clarifications of the phrase as offered on these pages of the editor's "Commentar."

disintegration triggered by the search for wealth by members of the nobility, the urban middle strata, and the peasantry.

The ruling nobility has a berth for passage to Narragonia. The woodcut adorning Chapter 46: "Of the Power of Fools" features Queen Folly and her courtiers, advisers young and old who are bound together with chains that she holds. The text is particularly rich in biblical allusion.[18] The critique of temporal power begins with such allusions as a sign to the reader that prudence and sensitivity will be employed throughout the chapter. At the same time, the familiar point of attack is cited:

> Myet, früntschafft, all worheyt vmb kert
> Als moysen syn schwäher lert
> Pfēnīg, nyd, früntschafft, gwalt vñ gūst
> Zerbrechen yetz, recht, brieff, vnd kunst
> ...
>
> (48)

> All money, favors help us naught,
> So Moses learned, by Jethro taught.
> Greed, money, friendship, favor, power
> Break laws and charters every hour.
>
> (168)

The lesson taught to Moses has not been learned by those presently in a position to curry favor and give rewards. The implication that money and power unite to subvert law is protected from censure both by the circumlocution of the passage and by the express reference to Old Testament authority.

After establishing precedent for his critique, Brant moves on to words of praise for "the good old days" when princes had wise advisers and when justice and peace were enjoyed by all. He then reintroduces Queen Folly, whom he charges with having led the princes away from wisdom and toward selfish gain. Of course, both the reminiscence of past glory and the imputation of princely passivity in the face of an allegorical Folly are gentle rebukes; but the author does pass on to more trenchant language:

> Grosz narrheyt ist by grossem gwalt
> Gott liesz, das mancher fürst regiert
> Langzyt, wann er nit würd verfürt
> Vnd vnmylt wurd, vnd vngerecht

---

[18] Brant, *Narrenschiff*: "Commentar," 382.

> Durch anreytz valscher rätt vnd knecht
> Die nämen gaben, schenck, vnd myet
> Vor den eyn furst sich billich hůt
> Wer gaben nymbt, der ist nit fry
> Schenck nemen, macht verretery
>
> (48-49)

> Great folly goes with copious power.
> Our Lord would let the princeling rule
> A long time, were he not a fool,
> Becoming bitter and unjust
> Through councilors whom none can trust.
> No prince should trust that vicious tribe
> That takes of money, gift, or bribe:
> The man who takes a bribe's not free,
> Accepting gifts breeds treachery ...
>
> (169)

The first line links power and foolishness, but no equation is drawn. The conditional statement that follows is cast in the subjunctive mood in order to avoid the appearance of opposition to the rule of the aristocracy. God would grant a long and popular reign if the prince would only hold at bay the folly that is inevitably attracted to the source of power. The use of the passive voice is also crucial to Brant's strategy for criticism: the prince does not become bitter and unjust if left to his own devices. The danger is that he will be suborned by advisers whose only true allegiance is to personal financial advancement. The pursuit of wealth leads to treason. The poet takes care to avoid the attribution of venal motives to the prince who is harsh and unjust. Still, in the midst of all of his circumspection, Brant does attribute inappropriate, harmful behavior to some unspecified crowned heads.

The *Narrenschiff* presents the lower nobility as an estate whose claim to favored status within society has been badly compromised. Its very identity as a homogenous group is called into question because of the easy availability of letters of patent:

> Vil hant des brieff vnd sygel gůt
> Wie das sie sint von edelm blůt
> Sie went die ersten sin von recht
> Die edel sint jn jrm gschlecht,
> Wie wol ichs nit gantz straff noch acht
> Vsz tugent ist all adel gemacht

> Wer noch gût sytt, ere, tugent kan
> Den haltt ich für eyn edel man
> Aber wer hett keyn tugent nitt
> Keyn zûcht, scham, ere, noch gûte sytt
> Den haltt ich alles adels lär
> Ob joch eyn fürst syn vatter wer
> Adel alleyn by tugent stat
> Vsz tugend aller adel gat ...
>
> (75)

> Some own a seal and patent good,
> They prove they are of noble blood.
> They're first, they claim quite rightfully,
> To be dubbed in that family,
> And I nor blame nor disagree.
> 'Tis virtue makes nobility,
> For breeding, honor, virtue can
> Alone proclaim the nobleman,
> But if unvirtuous you be —
> No breeding, honor, modesty —
> Of nobleness for me you're bare,
> E'en though a prince your father were;
> Nobility with virtue goes,
> Nobility from virtue flows ...
>
> (253)

While Brant does not question directly the process of elevation to the nobility, he does offer an additional definition of "edel" ("noble") and "adel" ("nobility") that would make nobility a function of virtue. It has been noted that this argument would be voiced with increasing fervor by the middle class during the centuries to come.[19] However, it should be apparent that Brant does not use the argument either to undermine the stratification system or to imply that those of lower status be admitted into the aristocracy in recognition of their ethical purity. This is after all the chapter that begins "Die gäckken, narrren, ich ouch bring / Die sich berümen hoher ding / Vnd wellent syn, das sie nit sint" (74) ("Of louts and fools I also sing / Who boast of many a lofty thing / And want to be what they are not ..." 251). It is not possible to be both socially ambitious and spotlessly virtuous. Those who "want to be what they are not," who wish to purchase high status, do not fall under the additional definition of nobility. The passage concerning the

---

[19] Brant, *Ship of Fools*: "Commentary" by Zeydel, 381.

prince's son demonstrates that Brant is aware that some members of old ruling families have behaved disgracefully. Still, the cautious subjunctive implies that such occurrences are infrequent, even unusual. Brant sees the true source of the problem as the substitution of money for virtue as a condition for elevation.

Those whose occupation put them in the best position to purchase entry were the merchants, and it is to them that Brant addresses Chapter 102: "Of Falsity and Deception." In it he rails against common forms of market-square deception: selling cure-alls that actually damage the health, representing old horses as young, using inaccurate scales and dim lighting, or offering worthless articles that have been made to appear valuable. Such practices supposedly have become the rule:

>Keyn kouffmanschatz stat jnn sym werdt
>Jeder mit falsch vertriben bgert
>Das er syns kroms mög kumē ab
>Ob es Gall, vberbeyn, joch hab
>
>(98)

>No trade is what it's claimed to be,
>Men sell their wares with falsity,
>Dispose of them with zealous skill
>Although their quality be nil.
>
>(330)

The withering evaluation equates commerce in all forms with deception: through mendacious practices, merchants unload goods of uneven quality. Because medieval cities flourished or faded according to the degree of their participation in trade, a rejection of that field of endeavor was tantamount to an attack on city life.

However, the *Narrenschiff* does not offer the alternative of a rustic idyll. Fair Justice no longer resides with the peasantry:

>Gerechtikeyt was by den buren
>Do sie floch vsz den stett vnd muren
>Woltt sie jnn ströwen hüttlin syn
>Ee dann die buren druncken wyn
>Den sie ouch yetz wol mögen tulden
>Sie stecken sich jnn grosse schulden
>Wie wol jn korn, vnd wyn gilt vil
>Nämen sie doch vff borg vnd zyl

> Vnd went bezahlen nit by ziten
>
> (79)

> To [the peasant folk] was justice never dead.
> When Justice from the cities fled
> She went to live in huts of straw
> And peasants bare of wine she saw,
> While now on drinking wine they're set.
> They plunge themselves in heavy debt,
> And though their corn and wine sell well
> They borrow more than I can tell
> And payments are alway belated.
>
> (268-69)

Under the influence of drink, the once virtuous country folk have abandoned their simple ways in an ill-starred attempt to live beyond their means. Chapter 82: "Of Peasants' Squandering" goes on to list attitudes and patterns of behavior that are similarly inappropriate for those of low estate. Peasants have begun to emulate the manners and dress of the nobility, a development that the poet milks for all of its easy humor. The outlandish figure of a peasant in silk is used to introduce the argument that the esteem universally accorded wealth has blurred the boundary lines that properly separate the estates. Having described the horrible fall that awaits avaricious peasants, Brant continues as follows:

> Des glich by vnsern zytten ouch
> Ist vff gestanden mancher gouch
> Der vor eyn burger, kouffman was,
> Will edel syn, vnd ritter gnasz
> Der edelman gert syn eyn fry
> Der Groff, das er gefürstet sy
> Der fürst die kron des künigs gert
>
> (79)

> And now for such a reason too
> We've hatched full many a cuckoo
> Who burgher, peasant used to be,
> Now he'd profess nobility.
> A noble would be a baronet,
> A count a prince's title get,
> At royal crowns the princes aim ...
>
> (269)

The breakdown of social stratification is particularly apparent in the cities — and not just in the rise of an amoral stratum of merchants.

> Man findt eyns hantwercks mannes wib
> Die bessers wert dreit an dem lib
> Von röck, ryng, mäntel, borten schmal
> Dan sie jm husz hat überall
> Do mit verdyrbt manch byderman
> Der mit sym wib mûsz bättlen gan
> Im wynter drincken vsz eym krûg
> Das er sym wib mög thûn genûg
> Wann sy hüt hatt alls das sy gelangt
> Gar bald es vor dem koüffler hangt
>
> (79-80)

> A tradesman's wife one often finds
> Who wears more gauds of various kinds,
> Skirts, rings, cloaks, broid'ries scant and rare,
> Than in her home is anywhere.
> It's ruined many a good man's life,
> He must go begging with his wife,
> From jugs in winter time drinks he
> To keep his wife in finery,
> And if today she has her fill
> She sells it soon to junkman Will.
>
> (270)

Urban artisans also have left the path of virtue in order to indulge a penchant for ostentation. Here, the addiction to the things that money can buy has perverted the traditional familial hierarchy by installing the craftsman's wife as the effective head of the house. The contemporary reader would have cringed at a scenario of progressive degeneration that begins beside a comfortable hearth and ends at a beggar's post on the street. Brant is holding up the specter of familial and social instability to that portion of the urban middle stratum that enjoyed the greatest stability during the poet's lifetime.[20] While commerce has always entailed risk, the position of master craftsman was entrenched, respected, and modestly prosperous in the

---

[20] See Könneker, *Narrenidee*, 95. Könneker finds in Brant a belief that the search for wealth, power, and prestige leads to a reliance on uncontrollable forces, a loss of self-control, and a susceptibility to the whims of fate.

decades before and after 1500.[21] The warning issued here points to the insidious nature of avarice: it will seek out weaker members of a family as stepping stones to the strongest. Brant uses the traditional, sexist analysis: the surest way to seduce Adam is to first seduce Eve.

The condition of the church was a topic of great concern to Brant because service rendered to Rome often yielded upward mobility. The attainment of higher social status meant entry into a world of wealth and power; a young churchman born into the peasantry and educated at the behest of Rome must have experienced intellectual and ethical vertigo upon assuming his duties. The poet is not sympathetic. Chapter 73: "Of Becoming a Priest" charges that many cynically abuse their opportunities for spiritual development in order to pursue a comfortable life-style unburdened by responsibility. Peasant families urge their sons along this path in order to enjoy the benefits of the steady income guaranteed for life by the wealth of the church. An additional chapter, "On Too Many Benefices," castigates the complex system of tithes and offices that keeps church coffers full. Not only has the prince, and with him temporal authority, succumbed to the blandishments of wealth, but the integrity of ecclesiastical authority also has been compromised.

Whatever area of human activity is under consideration, Brant's attitude toward wealth, the treasure of the Ship of Fools, is largely consistent: a preoccupation with money and property makes happiness in this world possible, but not inevitable and salvation in the world to come impossible. However, that dominant message is undercut repeatedly. Even the angelic Wisdom of Chapter 22: "The Teaching of Wisdom" has an ambivalent attitude toward wealth:

>   Wer mich lieb hat, den lieb ouch ich
>   Wer mich frü sucht, der fyndt mich
>   By mir ist richtům, gůt, vnd ere
>   Mich hat besessen gott der herre
>   Von anbegynn jn ewikeyt
>   Durch mich hatt got all ding bereit
>   (25)

>   "Who loves me dearly's loved by me,
>   Who seeks me early him I see.
>   Through me are wealth and honor stored,
>   I am possessed by God, the Lord,
>   Forever, in eternity,

---

[21] Moeller, 33.

And God created all through me."

(113)

At first reading it is only natural to attempt to reconcile this expression with the earlier admonition "Sůchen die ler vnd nit das gelt" (24) ("Seek teachings ever, never gold ..." 112). One such attempt might understand wealth as a happy by-product of a prudent life: as long as wisdom is the goal, the trappings of virtue do not constitute a danger. However, an underlying assumption of that position is that it is acquisitiveness, not possession, that is dangerous. Of course, elsewhere in the text, wealth and property — not just positive responses to wealth and property — are attacked. The "byproduct" reading cannot be reconciled with such repeated, categorical rejection. Furthermore, in the middle of the brief, hortatory address, such an enticing digression would distract the audience gathered at Wisdom's feet.

A more satisfying interpretation of the lines above identifies as their purpose the inclusion of wisdom among the greatest gifts that existence — on earth or in heaven — can bestow, whether upon those listening to the angel or upon those reading the *Narrenschiff*. As he reaches for those things that his readers will recognize immediately as the greatest things that man can attain, Brant momentarily forsakes his campaign against wealth and its pursuit. The rhetorical crescendo leads to a statement that cannot be reconciled with what might be called his standard position on wealth. Several questions arise. Does the text contain passages that resonate with this striking departure from the standard position? Do such passages share common features? And finally, what grounds can be postulated for authorial ambivalence?

Before leaving Wisdom and her audience, it is worth noting that both the admonition, "Seek teachings ever, never gold" and the passage cited above hinge on the verb "suchen" ("seek"). The person who actively seeks wisdom will find wealth. From her pulpit, the angel recommends kinesis rather than stasis, the pursuit of goals rather than the cultivation of the status quo. Self-improvement is the theme of the sermon; but there is tension between the abstract distillation of that theme ("Seek teachings ...") and its practical interpretation for a congregation that measures self-improvement in monetary terms ("Through me are wealth ...").

Brant's standard position on money-making activity shifts when he considers the world of work; in that world honor and financial reward are attendant upon determination and diligence. The esteem in which Brant holds those qualities is apparent in Chapter 97: "Of Indolence and Sloth."

Die müssig gänden, strofft der her
Vnd gibt der arbeyt lon, vnd ere,

> Der bösz vyndt, nymbt der tragkeyt war
> Vnd sägt gar bald syn somen dar,
> Tragkeit eyn vrsach aller sünd
> Macht murmelen Israhel die kynd
>
> (93)

> An idle man can try the Lord,
> Good work God always will reward.
> The devil notes all idleness
> And sows his seeds in wickedness.
> One cause of sinfulness is sloth,
> The Israelites it rendered wroth.
>
> (312)

Here again divine favor is guaranteed to those who attempt to better their condition; the completely passive are threatened with hellfire. In spite of all of his fulminations against the power of wealth, Brant goes so far as to assert the presence of God as a force in the money economy of 1500. Not a subtile thinker, the poet is unable to establish for the reader that point beyond which the reward for services rendered is excessive. In fact, the *Narrenschiff* offers what only can be called business advice — to employers and to employees. One of the passengers to Narragonia is the businessman who overextends his line of credit. The woodcut to Chapter 25: "Of Borrowing Too Much" portrays a debtor tormented by three fools and kicked by a donkey whose tail the debtor holds. In the background a wolf lowers near a tombstone. That the poet is particularly incensed at this variety of foolishness is evident in the first lines:

> Der ist me dann eyn ander narr
> Wer stäts vff nymbt vff borg vnd harr
> Vnd jn jm nit betrahten wil
> Das man spricht, wölff essen keyn zyl
>
> (27)

> A prominent, outstanding fool
> Who must make borrowing a rule
> And credits not the man who quotes:
> "Wolves eat no promissory notes".
>
> (118)

A logical explanation for the use of the vehement comparative degree is close familiarity with the inept businessman as a type; here Brant's family background should be called to mind. Imprudent money-management leads to pain and mockery, then to bankruptcy, and eventually to a tombstone. The saying that wolves do not eat (paper) IOUs (but flesh-and-blood debtors) trades on the superstition that wolves devour people; the IOU is an instrument of financial suicide even as the wolf can be an instrument of physical suicide. Inviting the presence of IOUs is analogous to inviting the presence of wolves. The passage suggests a belief that financial and physical existence are closely related and that, at the final judgment, the soul will be held accountable for financial incompetence. Brant compares this fool with those who receive divine forgiveness from sin only to sin again. It is a comparison that suggests little sympathy for arguments that failure at business might result from inexperience, from a series of understandable mistakes, from bad luck. Brant believes that bankruptcy results from the obdurate refusal to learn from one's mistakes.

Brant begins his apologia in the penultimate chapter "Apology of the Poet" with the assurance that his critique of society would not have been softened if his publishers had paid him in advance. In fact, such an action would have constituted a poor business practice:

>   Der ist eyn narr, vnd grosser dor
>   Wer eym werckmā dē lon gibt vor
>   Der macht nit werschafft vff dem merckt
>   Wer nit vff kunfftig blonung werckt,
>   Gar seltten würt verdient der lon
>   Der vor verzert ist, vnd verthon
>   Das werck gar langsam naher got
>   Das man macht vff vorgessen brott ...
>
>   (113)

>   A fool is he, a silly loon,
>   Who pays a workman far too soon,
>   He never plies an honest trade
>   Who ere he's finished would be paid.
>   The pay for work that's scarce begun
>   Is seldom earned by anyone.
>   All work will slowly go ahead
>   Rewarded with devoured bread.
>
>   (359-60)

Brant's concern here is for the employer rather than the employee; in fact, it is easy to infer a jaundiced, even cynical attitude about the working man. Honesty and pride in craftsmanship cannot be assumed. The consumer of such services is best advised to expect the worst. In this same vein, Chapter 97 "Of Indolence and Sloth" specifies the servant stratum as a major offender. The woodcut depicts a house maid who has fallen asleep at the spinning wheel and a male servant who is daydreaming as he sews seed. The motto bristles with animosity:

> Tragkeit fyndt man jn allen gschlechten
> Vor vsz jnn dienst mägten, vnd knechten
> Den kan man nit genůgsam lonen
> Sie künnen doch jr selbst wol schonen

(92)

> There's laziness in all the classes
> And most among the servant classes;
> Pay any wage, it will not please,
> Still they will spare their energies.

(311)

On one hand, employees will always be dissatisfied with their wages; on the other hand, they will never devote their full energy to the task at hand. Brant considers this a fatal state of affairs for the slothful because work brings happiness:

> Sellig der werckt mit synem karst
> Wer müssig gat, der ist der narrst

(93)

> He's happy who with pickax works,
> The idle man's the one who irks ...

(312)

Reference to the "Karst" or "pickax" indicates that one of the levels of society, one of the "gschlechten" about which he is troubled is the peasantry. Here again the poet associates laziness with low social status and thus indirectly justifies the payment of low wages and the maintenance of close oversight at the workplace.

Brant's empathy with the businessman and with the challenges inherent in a career in commerce is evident in his warning that the pleasures of the flesh, specifically drink, can render financial advancement impossible:

> Der mensch wer fry, keyn knecht gesin
> Wann drunckenheit nit wer, vnd wyn,

> Wer wyns vnd feiszt dings flysset sich
> Der wurt nit selig oder rich,
> Dem we vnd synem vatter we
> Dem wurt krieg, vnd vil vnglucks me
>
> (19)

> Man would not be a slave, in fine,
> If he disowned the demon wine:
> Are wine and sumptuous food your itch?
> You'll not be happy, not get rich.
> Woe's him and woe's his father too,
> He'll have misfortunes not a few ...
>
> (98)

Once again, the underlying assumption is that the pursuit of wealth and happiness is natural and commendable. The first lines go so far as to suggest that alcoholism can lead to a fall in social standing, which in turn is described as both a personal and familial tragedy. Of course, the immoderate feasting and revelry excoriated in this chapter "Of Gluttony and Feasting" was far beyond the means of the lower social levels; the poet is attacking a vice that he sees among his social peers. The use of "wurt" (literally "will become") in these lines is of crucial importance. When Brant focuses on those social groups for which change, "becoming," is possible, his attitude toward wealth is at odds with the traditional concept of *turpe lucrum*. In such passages, the poet places some value on what would come to be called upward mobility.

The occasional ambivalence toward wealth that appears in the *Narrenschiff* results from the expansion of the social level within which Sebastian Brant grew to adulthood. Its participation in the relatively new and increasingly complex money economy brought it into conflict with the static estate system rooted in medieval Catholicism. Brant still embraces the old polarized cosmology of the church fathers; he does not champion the world view of European humanism. Nor is he sufficiently self-critical to recognize the contradictions in his own thinking and respond to them. Indeed, had he been capable of greater self-reflection, he probably would have eliminated his tips for would-be entrepreneurs. Instead, Brant's naiveté led him to reflect rather than shape perceived reality. From the presence of wealth, members of his social level could draw the traditional inference of sinful temporality; but the presence of new wealth could be interpreted just as easily as the reification of exemplary self-improvement.

This apparent logical inconsistency entered the literary tradition as Germany underwent a period of convulsive social change. Because the

Narrenschiff stands at the beginning of a canon of widely distributed works in the vernacular, it is only natural to ask whether Brant's work is paradigmatic for the chapbooks of the early sixteenth century. Do writers apply a separate set of standards to new wealth and to the social level that was creating it? How is upward mobility evaluated? Do writers suggest norms for the disposition of new wealth? Are metaphysical implications of money-making activity presented in any detail? Or, is there any evidence of the kind of self-censorship that a more self-critical Sebastian Brant would have practiced?

Among Brant's literate contemporaries, the huge success of the *Narrenschiff* argued for its author's use of a Horatian blend of *prodesse et delectare*, and specifically, for the pedagogical thrust of his social analysis. His preoccupation with money and property resulted from the increasing prominence of wealth as a means of stratifying his society. His highly visible treatment stood as a precedent to which writers and printer/publishers would respond. The nature of that response before the emergence of Luther is the subject of the two chapters that follow.

Chapter 3

Reineke Fuchs as Chancellor Not-Enough

CHANCELLOR. MENTION OF THIS position of high public trust calls to mind personality traits of the model citizen: earnestness, probity, selflessness. In a medieval monarchy, the chief minister of state also functioned as confidential adviser and private secretary to the ruler; hence, the chancellor owed final allegiance to both a system of governance and a person. Both the status of second-in-command and a professional future that excluded advancement tended to promote circumspection, even deference.

Since his earliest appearances in the Flemish *Ysengrimus* (ca. 1150) by Nivardus and in the better-known *Roman de Renart* (ca. 1200) by an anonymous French troubadour, Reynard the Fox has never personified any lofty qualities of morality and will. High intelligence does afford him access to the king; however, it also enables him to distinguish between the welfare of the community and the welfare of Reynard. Given a choice, the fox pursues his own agenda. In the Middle Low German *Reynke de Vos*, that agenda countenances mendacity, theft, betrayal, rape, and murder. This most popular version of the fable presents a "villainous hero" who flourishes in court society precisely by going after his own advantage — at the expense of equally ruthless and more powerful enemies. Reineke's advantage is defined consistently by his own materialism and that of others, including the king. Here, as elsewhere in the fable, fiction intentionally mirrors life.

The famous animal epic appeared in its best-known German form in 1498 — the collaboration of an anonymous poet and a Lübeck printer. The northern poet had translated and adapted a Dutch work by Hinrek van Alckmer.[1] The precise nature of Hinrek's contribution to Reineke's long march through the literature of northern Europe has occasioned debate among philologists, a debate that is particularly intense because the text

---

[1] For a thorough study of textual history, see William Foerste, "Von Reinaerts Historie zum Reinke de vos," *Niederdeutsche Studien (Münstersche Beiträge zur niederdeutschen Philologie)* 6 (1960): 105-46. See also Niclas Witton, "Die Vorlage des Reinke de Vos," in *Reynaert Reynard Reynke: Studien zu einem mittelalterlichen Tierepos*, ed. Jan Goossens and Timothy Sedmann (Cologne and Vienna: Böhlau, 1980), 1-159.

itself is incomplete.[2] However, it is generally agreed that he divided the tale passed down to him into books and chapters, supplied the latter with superscriptions, and interjected moralizing prose interpretations of the action. He is also credited with having written either much or all of two prefaces retained in the Lübeck version. The second and longer of the two provides a key to the epic: the types of animals that appear in the text are assigned counterparts from the several levels of human society. Beasts of burden represent "de stad van den arbeyders," from which three other estates supposedly have developed: the merchants, the clergy, and the nobility.[3]

Of the four books composing *Reynke de Vos*, the first is fully as long as the others combined. It presents a complete adventure that begins at a public audience held by King Nobel. There an absent Reineke is accused of criminal acts by a procession of wounded parties led by the wolf. Impressed by the gravity of the charges, the lion decides to summon the fox to his court so that Reineke will have to face his accusers and respond to all complaints. First the powerful bear and then the clever tomcat are dispatched to fetch Reineke; both are lured into traps by the miscreant and then badly mauled by human peasants. The enraged lion is pacified only when Reineke's nephew, Grimbart the Badger, volunteers to bring his kinsman before king and court. Grimbart is able to persuade Reineke that such an appearance is not to be avoided. Along the way, the fox has his young relative act as priest-confessor so that Reineke can enter a hostile arena with a clear conscience.[4] Soon after his arrival, the fox is found guilty and led off to the gallows. There he is granted permission to make a final confession, during the course of which Reineke invents a fabulous buried treasure whose location is known to him alone. Soon the gullible and greedy Nobel has pardoned the fox and subjected Reineke's principal accusers to abuse and imprisonment. In order to avoid the futile treasure hunt, Reineke announces that he must undertake

---

[2] See Klaas Heeroma, "Henric van Alckmaer: Versuch einer neuen Würdigung," *Niederdeutsches Jahrbuch: Jahrbuch des Vereins für niederdeutsche Sprachforschung* 93 (1970): 16-18. Heeroma takes issue with Foerste on several points. For a discussion of Reineke's first appearances in English, see Kenneth Varty, "The Earliest illustrated English Editions of 'Reynard the Fox'; and Their Links with the Earliest Illustrated Continental Editions," in Goossens and Sedmann, 160-95.

[3] *Reinke de Vos*, ed. Friedrich Prien and Albert Leitzmann, 3rd ed. (Halle/Saale: Niemeyer, 1960), 4-5. Subsequent references to the text will be indicated within parentheses; references will be by line(s) of verse unless otherwise indicated. For an excellent translation into modern German, see *Reineke Fuchs: Das niederdeutsche Epos "Reynke de Vos" von 1498 mit 40 Holzschnitten des Originals*, trans. and with an afterword by Karl Langosch (Stuttgart: Reclam, 1975).

[4] Concerning Grimbart's role as priest-confessor, see John Van Cleve, "Two Priests for Reineke Fuchs," *Neophilologus* 65, no. 2 (1980): 239-46.

a pilgrimage to the Pope immediately. He celebrates his arrival home by devouring the hare, who has joined him on the "pilgrimage."

The remaining three books constitute a second adventure, which recycles the major plot elements of the first. At a second public audience, additional charges are leveled at Reineke, and the incensed lion decides to bring the fox to justice. Grimbart undertakes the role of emissary once again and persuades his wily uncle that a return to court is preferable to the siege of the fox's castle planned by Nobel. During the journey to court, the badger hears an even longer confession, a confession that includes an extensive critique of both church and state. The travelers then cross paths with their relative Martin the Ape, who promises to champion Reineke's cause with Martin's many friends at the Vatican. Once at Nobel's court, the fox uses lies and tall tales to win his way back into the king's good graces. But the wolf Isegrim, whose wife Reineke has raped, demands satisfaction. Thanks to his use of some particularly vicious tactics suggested by the ape's wife, Reineke wins his fight with the wolf. In the midst of a boisterous celebration, the fox assures Nobel of his obedience, and Nobel responds by naming Reineke the new chancellor of the realm.

King Nobel occupies his position at the top of the social ladder by virtue of birthright. While he is less strong than some of his subjects and less intelligent than others, only he can appear to lead. The extent to which he follows the advice of others has no effect on his incumbency. Such security is completely unknown to the individual subject, whose status changes as the lion's perception of him changes. At the beginning of the first book, the wolf and the bear are Nobel's closest advisers, but the precarious nature of that status becomes apparent as one physically inferior enemy engineers their complete fall. Reineke actually rises beyond the highest position attainable at the beginning of the chapbook, that of unofficial adviser. Nobel's creation of the office of chancellor indicates his willingness to extend his own security to a uniquely deserving second person. In taking the step, the king effectively changes the structure of his government: power-sharing is open to the subject who can demonstrate extraordinary merit. How has Reineke taken this first step toward meritocracy? His every action is predicated on his outsider's analysis of society and of interaction among particular members of society.

Reineke belongs to the landed aristocracy. His residence is described as a castle; his assets include the local peasantry (2954-59). Such high rank makes his absence from the first audience significant. The text makes clear that long-standing tension has led to a break in relations:

> [Nobel] hadde vorbodet dar to houe
> Alle de dere, groet vnde kleyne

> Sunder Reynken den vos alleyne;
> He hadde in den hoff so vele myßdan,
> Dat he dar nicht endorste komen noch gan.
> De quad deyt, de schuwet gern dat lycht;
> Alzo dede ok Reynke, de bözewycht:
> He schuwede sere des konnynges hoff,
> Dar in he hadde seer krancken loff.
>
> (20-28)

> For Noble to this sumptuous feast
> Had summon'd every bird and beast,
> Save crafty Reynard, who alone,
> For vilest mischief he had done,
> Was holden in such ill report,
> He durst not show his face at Court.
> As deeds of darkness shun the light,
> So Rankey did; that treach'rous wight,
> Convinc'd he would not be commended
> By those he had so oft offended.[5]

Both the king and his errant subject perceive that Reineke stands outside of the court community. The needs of the community transcend the individual needs of its members, and it is up to the lion to articulate those common needs. Although it becomes clear that in reality certain nobles and the king himself follow secret, selfish agendas, all public utterances are in line with the policy that the common good is of paramount importance. Reineke's ostracism has resulted from his open rejection of that policy and from his notorious pursuit of goals determined by self-interest.

In his two extended confessions to the badger, the fox gives candid expression to his analysis of the very feudal society that seems bent on his destruction. Reineke minces few words in his deflation of Nobel:

> Wente de lauwe is yo vnse here
> Vnde holt yd al vor grote ere,
> Wat he to syk rapen kan.
> He sprickt, wy syn alle syne man.

---

[5] *Reynard the Fox: Pictured by J.J. Mora* (Boston: Estes, 1901), 2. The *National Union Catalogue: Pre-1956 Imprints* assigns the translation to Dietrich Wilhelm Soltau. Subsequent page references to this translation are given in parentheses. Where the exigencies of versification have lead the translator to change or omit words or phrases critical to the analysis, I have supplied my own plain prose translations. They are marked "JVC."

> Dat is noch neyne grote eddelycheyt,
> Dat he den vndersaten schaden deyt.
> Seet, oem, wan ick yd seggen dorste,
> De konnynck is eyn eddel vorste,
> Men he heft leeff den, de eme vele brynget
> Vnde de so dantzet, alze he vore synget.
>
> (3885-94)

> Nay, even our liege Lord, the King,
> Doth not refrain from pilfering,
> And though not openly himself
> He comes, to take away our pelf,
> Yet Wolves and Bears with loaves and fishes
> Know mighty well to meet his wishes.
> But still he thinks, this all is fair;
> For none to him the truth declare.
> Confessors, Chaplains and their crew
> Make him believe, 'tis all his due ...
>
> (109)

A clash between appearance and reality is readily apparent to Reineke when he considers his ruler. A king who should devote his every thought to the welfare of his subjects is instead ready to use and abuse those subjects in order to snatch up as much wealth and material comfort as he can. The ironic references to "grote eddelycheyt" ("great nobility") and to the king as "eyn eddle vorste" ("a noble prince") reveal an underlying hostility to those who have betrayed the ideals of governance to which they pay lip service. It is an attitude of disillusionment that leads either to resignation or to revolution. After all, the lion is entrenched; he has powerful supporters:

> Yd en is noch nicht al so klare,
> Dat nu de wulff vnde ok de bare
> Myt dem konnynge wedder ghan to raden;
> Dat wyl noch mannygem sere schaden.
> He seth vppe se groten louen,
> Se konnen vele stelen vnde rouen,
> Eyn yslyk denne mede stylle swycht.
> Yd is alleyns, wo men dat kricht.
>
> (3895-3902)

> And basely they ["Confessor, Chaplains and their crew"] neglect their duty,

> Because they all share the booty,
> Though 'twere but for a hood, or gown.
> Poor Commoners are thus kept down,
> Unheard, unjudg'd, they must refrain,
> Of their oppressors to complain.
> For since the Lion hath the sway,
> And Bears and Wolves have won the day,
> 'Tis honour thought by them to steal
> And prey upon the Common-weal.
>
> (109)

Reineke sees before him a ruling establishment with a base in the concept of the king as God's agent in temporal affairs, with a single-minded focus on material self-interest, and with a completely amoral modus operandi.

Reineke's response to authority is ambiguous in that it partakes of both rejection and affirmation. On one hand, the fox chooses not to "play by the rules of the game" and join the inner counsel of thieves composed of lion, wolf, and bear. He stands apart, follows his own rules, and faces first ostracism and then execution as a result. The creation of the position of chancellor can be interpreted not only as a personal victory, but as a victory for a force for institutional change. Because the chapbook concludes with Reineke's appointment, the direction that the new regime will take cannot be specified. Read in this light, the tale presents only the advent of change and, in the defeat of the wolf, the "revolutionary" act — not the course of government and the ethics of society after the upheaval.

On the other hand, Reineke's instincts are those of a predator; as such they tend to affirm the status quo. After Reineke notes the privileged position of the lion's rapacious courtiers, he turns in the confession to his own contrasting situation:

> Arm man Reynke, nympt de men eyn hoen,
> Dar wylt se alle denne vele vmme doen,
> Den wylt se denne soeken vnde vangen,
> Ja, se ropen alle, men schal ene hangen.
> De kleynen deue henget men wech,
> De groten hebben nu starck vorhech,
> De mothen vorstaen borghe vnde lant.
> Seet, oem, so ick dyt hebbe bekant
> Vnde wan my dyt kumpt to synne,
> So spele ick ok na myneme ghewynne.
> Ik dencke vaken, yd is so recht.

Wente men nu des vele plecht.

(3907-18)

But if poor Reynard lifts a Goose,
The hounds of Justice are let loose,
And "Hang the thief," and "Crucify,"
Becomes the universal cry.
For small thieves are hang'd out of hand,
Whilst wholesale robbers rule the land.
Such bad examples have seduc'd me,
And to foul play they have induc'd me,
Because I thought, what others did
Was not to me alone forbid ...

(109-10)

In no sense of the word is Reineke "poor." While some members of the nobility were impoverished by the end of the fifteenth century, Reineke's domestic life is presented as comfortable, his property holdings as extensive. The fox certainly deserves no pity, either before or after he commits an act that flaunts the authority of the court. Even in life-threatening situations, his self-confidence knows no bounds. The assertion that thieves fall into two categories contains an implicit admission of guilt, but even here Reineke finds a way to play for sympathy. Either the wolf and bear should be hanged, too, or the fox should be left in peace to pursue his self-interest even as "de groten deue" ("the great thieves") are given free rein. Of course, both the amount of mayhem that the fox creates and his resultant standing as one of the major problems facing the kingdom render absurd Reineke's inclusion among "de kleynen deue" ("the petty thieves"). Still, he displays a measure of honesty in admitting that he has made a conscious decision to live as a thief, to adhere to idiosyncratic standards of personal behavior despite any attendant opprobrium. The final couplet in the citation above is the ultimate justification offered: the only way to survive in a society of thieves is to become a thief. Because that couplet blatantly contravenes the teachings of the church, Reineke goes on to acknowledge that his version of a thieves' ethic is in conflict with his conscience and with the word of God. But first by noting the presence of worldliness within the clergy and then by passing on to a full-blown critique of the second estate, Reineke tries to shift onto the shoulders of others the burden of responsibility he should bear for the ethical choices he has made. He does observe that the best course of action would be to follow the example set by virtuous members of the clergy (3929-30). But, above all, the fox wants to survive, and he has already observed: "De nu dorch de werlt schal varen, / De en kan syck nicht so hyllych bewaren, / Alze de in eyn kloster höret" (3843-45) ("Whoever wants to get by in this world cannot remain as pure as he who belongs in a cloister." JVC). It is his perception that the pious churchman does not live in the world of the wolf and bear. Hence, the suggestion that such a person might serve as a model is disingenuous. Instead of confronting his own history of conscious acquiescence to society's immorality, Reineke obfuscates.

The thoroughgoing critique of the priesthood introduced by this defensive self-analysis can be taken at face value or understood with reference to an observer who is anything but dispassionate and uninvolved. The reader who always bears in mind the presence of a wily reporter with several axes to grind must also determine whether Reineke's bias necessarily mitigates the accuracy of his perceptions of others. His constant pursuit of his own self-interest provides a frame of reference for statements about himself that are contradictory upon first inspection. Reineke's every action, his every utterance is consistent and logical within that framework. With his single focus, the fox affirms the unspoken principle of social organization to which governing authority adheres. In hypocritical fashion, the lion and his advisers make a show of beneficent, paternalistic rule even as they covertly seek their own enrichment at the expense of their subjects. The fox is perfectly willing to engage in that same hypocrisy and, when possible, to turn the hypocrisy of others to his own advantage. But such self-awareness carries with it the germ of rejection: Reineke understands that an ethical system has evolved that cannot coexist with Christian morality. And he expresses that perception to another, if in a tentative, evasive fashion. Having outlined the ethical conflict to the badger, Reineke is not prepared to take a stand. At the same time, it is noteworthy that, when his silence would serve to affirm hypocritical governance, Reineke chooses to reveal the true state of affairs. In so doing, he undermines authority. Within the context of the chapbook, that act is rendered less significant by its inclusion in a confession, where the tradition of strict confidentiality obtains. Nevertheless, soon after the second confession, it becomes apparent that Reineke's analysis of society is shared by other members of his large family. And of course, a third party is present for the confession: the reader of an animal fable expects to draw comparisons with human society at each significant point in the tale. That reader must decide whether to contemplate the step from critical analysis to revolution.

As the centerpiece of an alternative system of ethics in *Reynke de Vos*, self-interest is defined in terms of personal wealth and material comfort. The most dramatic demonstration of the power of wealth begins toward the end of the first book when Reineke faces the gallows. To buy himself time, the condemned fox fabricates a plot against the throne conceived by his enemies the wolf and bear. To lend credence to the outrageous lie, he implicates his own dead father and his one prominent ally at court, the badger Grimbart. Upon first hearing of a plot and a treasure, the king and queen have Reineke brought down from the ladder, and they take him aside (2064-75). In view of the alleged plot, their desire for privacy is understandable enough. But the conspiracy that the fox invents is presented as ancient history. Reineke is careful to increase the size of the cache even as he decreases the amount of present danger to the king. When he concludes his tale of intrigue, the embattled fox has painted himself as a subject whose loyalty transcends family ties and personal safety. But any sense of gratitude that the king may feel is lessened by the fact that the events he has heard related are set in the past and by the fact that he has a right to expect such loyalty from all subjects, including Reineke. If the king determines that certain courtiers have conspired against him, he can deal with them at his leisure. Nobel must still respond immediately to the numerous charges against the fox, many of which have been brought by subjects not implicated by Reineke.

As Reineke finishes his story of a conspiracy, the royal couple has one consuming interest. Reineke's private audience has taken place just out of earshot of the assembled court, but now that distance is no longer adequate. The three leave the scene. At this point (2359-63), Reineke's survival depends upon the fictitious treasure. The king's decision to keep information about the treasure secret suggests that it does not occur to him to use the windfall to improve the lives of his subjects; he means to spend it on himself. Nobel's greed becomes apparent when the fox tells him where the cache is located: the remote site is unknown to the lion.

> De konninck sprack: "horet my, Reynart,
> Sy möten myt my vp de vart;
> Ik kan de stede allene nicht raken
> Ik hebbe wol horen nomen Aken,
> Lupke, Kollen vnde Parys,
> Men wor Husterloh efte Krekelput is,
> Dar en hebbe ick ne er van ghehort.
> Ik vruchte, yd is men eyn dichtet wort."
> (2481-88)

> "Come with us then, and show the way,"
> Said Nobel, "and full well you may,
> Unless this story, with intent
> To trick and cheat us, you invent.
> We've read in our Geography
> Of Brentford, Staines and Coventry;
> But Quarrelpit and Hufferslow

> Are names of which we nothing know."
>
> (69)

If the lion knew where to find Husterloh and Krekelput, he would go alone — despite the size of the hoard and the problem of transport. Nobel's only other concern is his lingering suspicion that Reineke is lying, a suspicion laid to rest when the slow-witted hare Lampe is summoned to confirm the existence of Husterloh and Krekelput. When Lampe does so, Nobel is convinced and proceeds to ignore his kingdom's need for justice. He frees Reineke in exchange for the mere promise of wealth.

Reineke cannot be a fully integrated member of the court as it is presented in the early chapters of the first book because such membership requires uncritical acceptance of its materialistic goals and its hypocritical system of ethics. His perspicacity sets the fox apart. It enables him to manipulate court machinations, but it also excludes him from membership in the high counsels of state. In order for Reineke to be integrated, the system of leadership must be changed so as to include high office for the most sagacious subject. Nobel makes the decision to allow that change when he decides that the fox and the wolf may do battle. The wolf is a vassal in the traditional sense: he serves his feudal lord through his ability to coerce others. The fable represents the armed forces of such a vassal with the daunting power and boundless voracity of Isegrim. The wolf serves his monarch with tireless strength that stands ready to obey without reflection. The lion's decision to allow the battle constitutes a recognition that he who lives by his wits serves the throne as well as does he who lives by physical prowess. To a contemporary reader of the chapbook, "he who lives by his wits" would have been readily identifiable as the townsman. Accordingly, the text is suggesting that the most successful townsman has a place at the right hand of hereditary authority. The weakened position of the nobility by the late fifteenth century makes such a suggestion possible.

The chapbook reader had been prepared for the king's decision and its implications through the use of a precedent. When he meets Reineke and Grimbart during their journey to court, Martin the Ape speaks about Rome and about the sort of help he can arrange for the fox through his many contacts at the Vatican.[6]

> Wente ick to Rome den loep wol weet,

---

[6] Reineke later recounts his meeting with Martin when the fox appears before King Nobel. Jan Goossens uses that recounting to establish relationships between the Low German text and its Dutch predecessor. Goossens, "Reynaerts und Reynkes Begegnung mit dem Affen Martin," *Niederdeutsches Wort* 20 (1980): 73-84. The article concerns itself with textual comparison rather than with content analysis.

> Wat ik schal laten efte doen.
> Dar is ock myn oem Symon,
> De mechtich is vnde seer vorheuen;
> He helpet deme gherne, de wat mach gheuen.
> Her Schalkevunt is dar ock eyn here,
> Ock doctor Grypto vnde der noch mere,
> Her Wendehoyke myt her Lozevunde,
> Dyt synt alle dar vnse vrunde.
> Ik hebbe gelt vor henghesant,
> Hir mede werde ick best bekant.
>
> (4150-60)

> My worthy friend and uncle Simon,
> Who is a pow'rful and a sly man,
> Hath everything at his command,
> And will help those who fill his hand.
> Nay, he is not the only friend,
> On whom at Rome I can depend;
> There's Doctor Wrest, and bach'lor Civil,
> Who'll gain a supper from the devil,
> And both will follow, while we've money,
> As busily, as flies do honey.
> The proverb says, and all men know:
> 'Tis money makes the Mare to go.
>
> (116)

The same pursuit of self-interest that guides activity behind the scenes at Nobel's court has been institutionalized at the court of the Pope. There, the practice of simony makes possible both the short-term profit of those who sell offices and the potential long-term gains available to those who buy and then use offices to their best advantage. Nobel's interest in Reineke's treasure constitutes the first step for a society down a path that leads to the sophisticated materialism of Rome — to all appearances a locus of authority, but in reality also a nexus for investment interests. The ongoing stability of that "market" is guaranteed by a system of power-sharing that has grown up around a member of the College of Cardinals who limits access to and controls decisions made by the Pope.

> De pawes is eyn old kranck man,
> He nympt syck nenes dynges meer an,
> Alze datmen syner nicht vele acht.
> Men alto male des houes macht

> Heft de cardinal van Vnghenöghe,
> Eyn man yunck, mechtich, van behendem töge.
> Ick kenne eyne vrouwen, de heft he leeff,
> De schal eme bryngen eynen breff;
> Myt der byn ick seer wol bekant,
> Ja, wat se wyl, dat blyft neen tant.
>
> (4193-4202)

> The Pope is old and sick, and cares
> But little about all affairs;
> But there's a jolly Cardinal,
> Hight Bonnyblade, who governs all.
> I know a pretty, buxom Lass,
> With whom his evenings he doth pass:
> To all requests, which she presents,
> He always readily consents.
>
> (117)

Martin goes on to describe the lieutenants of Vnghenöghe (literally "Not-Enough"), men who control the flow of wealth through manipulation of canon law — lawyers, judges, and courtiers. All derive their power from Cardinal Not-Enough. As the head of this shadow court, he refutes the traditional morality embodied in the figurehead Pope by keeping a concubine. An appeal to her on behalf of Reineke will put the influence of the church at the disposal of the fox. Through such individuals and channels of communication, the throne of St. Peter offers forgiveness from sin and determines punishment for the sinner. The chapbook goes so far as to suggest that an entire people can be released from a papal ban at the whim of a concubine (4219). The power of acquisitiveness has become that entrenched; he for whom there is "not enough" embodies the curia's aspirations. His name is its motto.

At the conclusion of the chapbook, Reineke occupies a similar position in secular government.[7] Unlike the Pope, the lion is neither old nor sickly. He *is* stupid and therefore, from Reineke's point of view, malleable. The fox ascends to a position that is even more secure structurally because it has no equal. Vnghenöghe is one of many cardinals. Potentially, Reineke will wield relatively more power because he will not be limited to behind-the-scenes activity. And he will wield it longer because he and the lion are still young.

---

[7] The significance of Vnghenöghe escapes the notice of even Hartmut Kokott in his detailed analysis of the plot. Martin is cited as a "weiterer Repräsentant füchsischer Art," but no mention is made of the character who is the most successful representative of that "kind." Kokott, *"Reynke de Vos"* (Munich: Fink, 1981), 57-58.

The description of the curia by Martin the Ape provides a basis for predicting the composition and operating philosophy of a government led by the fox as "Chancellor Not-Enough." A coterie of close associates will divide up administrative functions and advise the chancellor. The rationalization of government will proceed with dispatch because a system of patronage will be used. As the new chancellor leaves the court in triumph, he contemplates the future:

> He dachte: "hir schal neen schade aff komen,
> Weme ik nu wyl, deme mach ik vromen,
> Vnde mach mynen vrunden alle tyd syn holt.
> Noch pryse ik wyßheyt bouen dat golt."
>
> (6787-90)

> He thought, "No harm will come of this. It will go well for whomever I favor, and I always shall be partial to friends. I value wisdom even more highly than gold." JVC

Reineke's friends are primarily members of his own large family. His first plans for the kingdom concern their welfare, not his own enrichment. The reference to gold indicates that he is well aware of the many lucrative opportunities that will come to his office and that his first concern should be the meritocratic system itself, not the system's rewards. Of course, what he has in mind is government by the few and for the few. No thought is given to the improvement of conditions for all subjects. The altruistic commitment to the use of wisdom as *the* tool of decision-making cannot obscure the materialistic ends that the new administration will pursue. Martin has learned how to approach such an administration for help: he sends money to Rome in advance of a visit at the Vatican (4159-60). In Martin, the chapbook offers a prototype of the administrators with which the fox will man a bureaucracy that will guide an evolution from true monarchy to de facto plutocracy. In *Reynke de Vos* the pursuit of wealth becomes government's reason for being.

In the real world of 1500, such a government would have been of considerable appeal to merchants, their suppliers, and those in allied or support professions. Wealth created by entrepreneurs eventually flows through the treasury of their state. They have a natural affinity for a ruler whose sole concern is material prosperity. What is good for a Chancellor Not-Enough is good for business. Allied professionals such as bankers, moneylenders, and lawyers stand to gain right along with wholesalers and retailers — itinerant traders as well as shopkeepers. One striking demographic change associated with the development of an economy based on the availability of large amounts of liquidity was the growth of cities as arenas for the exchange of cash and credit. Not only craftsmen but also physicians, builders, and academicians were dependent upon the fiscal stability of their communities. The response of such townsmen to the ethical message of *Reynke de Vos* will be considered below; here it should be noted that their response to the change in governmental structure suggested by the chapbook would have been positive. But to view the fox as a representative of the interests of an urban proto-bourgeoisie is to ignore his status as a noble and his narrow motives in becoming chancellor: he will advance the self-interest of each member of his administration. The dedication to one's subjects implicit in the medieval king's role as the divinely instituted "father of his country" is nowhere to be found. A townsman reading the chapbook would have had to balance the loss of such altruistic paternalism against the gain of a primitive form of laissez-faire economic policy. The deliberation would have been brief. However, then such a reader would have had to consider the work as a moral satire: does the chapbook mean to condemn all that the fox does and all that he represents?

A literal interpretation of the text offers much to support an affirmative answer to that question. The very names of the characters invite disapproval; after all, Martin's contacts in the curia include not only Simon, Not-Enough, and Dr. Grab-It ("doctor Grypto" 4156) but also Judge Donar and Judge Moneta (4212). The ecclesiastical model for the future administration of Chancellor Reineke is a veritable rogue's gallery. The likelihood of immorality in the new bureaucracy is all the more apparent when Reineke's mendacious and murderous conduct before and during the action of the chapbook is taken into consideration. Thus, as the historical context of *Reynke de Vos* has become remote, it has become easy to evaluate the fox as a negative exemplum with few redeeming features.[8]

Such a reading finds apparent confirmation in the narrator's commentary at the conclusion of the chapbook. Chancellor Reineke requests permission to return to his estate so that he can be reunited with his worried family. After the fox leaves the court "Myt schonen worden vnde groter gunst" (6755) ("with fair words and in high favor" JVC), the narrator offers his own extended interpretation of the text:

Ja, de sus noch kan Reynkens kunst,

---

[8] For instance, Hans Rupprich's surprisingly brief treatment of *Reynke de Vos* characterizes the fox as "der schlaue Übeltäter." The fable uses the evil in one figure to expose the greater evil in court society. Rupprich, *Die deutsche Literatur vom späten Mittelalter bis zum Barock: Erster Teil: Das ausgehende Mittelalter, Humanismus und Renaissance 1370-1520*, vol. 4, part 1 of Helmut de Boor and Richard Newald, *Geschichte der deutschen Literatur von den Anfängen bis zur Gegenwart* (Munich: Beck, 1970), 308-09.

Syn wol ghehoret vnde leffghetal
By den heren ouer al.
Isset gheystlyk efte werltlyk stad,
An Reynken slut nu meyst de rad.
Reynkens slechte is grod by macht
Vnde wasset alle tyd, ya, dach vnde nacht.
De Reynkens kunst nicht heft ghelerd,
De is tor werlde nicht vele werd,
Syn word wert nicht draden ghehord;
Men myt Reynkens kunst kumpt mannich vord
Dar synt vele Reynken nu in der warde
(Wol hebben se nicht al rode barde)
Isset in des pawes efte keysers hoff.
Se makent eyn deel nu yo to groff.
Symon vnde Gheuerd holden dat velt,
Men kent to houe nicht beth dan ghelt.
Dat ghelt vlüth alder wegen bouen,
De gelt heft, de krycht ok wol eyne pröuen.
De Reynkens lyst nu bruken kan,
De wert ok draden eyn vpperman.

(6756-76)

Whoever practices Reineke's art today is admitted readily to the court of any lord, clerical or secular. In fact the council usually acts as Reineke would. The fox's family is powerful and growing day and night. Whoever has not been taught the fox's art is of little value to the world. His words usually fall on deaf ears; however, he who practices Reineke's art will prosper. There are now many of Reineke's kind at the side of emperor and pope, although not all of them wear the red beard. Of course some of the things they do are simply too bad. Simon and Grant command the field; those at court know only money. And money rises to the top in the world, so that the man who has money receives the prebends. Whoever knows how to use Reineke's cunning soon will become a man of high station. JVC

Stripped away is the thin veneer of genre that separates the world of talking animals with its harsh rules for survival from the world of men with its harsh rules for survival. Reineke's kind is strong and growing stronger in the real world of 1500. He who follows Reineke's example and joins his kind will surely rise in the esteem of the world. The direct condemnation of that kind is both brief and qualified. As the example of Brant makes clear, literary sensibilities of the late fifteenth century sustained extended diatribes —

replete with biblical allusions — against sin, both mortal and petty. But at this point in *Reynke de Vos*, the appropriate point for a flailing of the foxes who are rapidly taking over secular and ecclesiastical government — at this point stands only the tentative "Se makent eyn deel nu yo to groff." The "yo" that reaches to the reader for confirmation is a sign of insecurity; the "eyn deel" mitigates the seriousness of any improper dealings. If some of the activities of the "human foxes" are improper, it follows that others are not. Finally, the single pejorative word has no bite; the Grimm dictionary equates "groff" as used in *Reynke de Vos* with modern German "schlimm" ("bad").[9] In sum, this a mild rebuke.

The narrator is far from suggesting that Reineke's kind should be banned from court, let alone from society. Rather, he is urging that one behavioral characteristic be eliminated, a characteristic specified in the two couplets that follow "groff." Acquiescence to or participation in simony and bribery are unacceptable. The narrator censures the fox when Reineke's materialistic, even Darwinian approach to governance leads to extremes. But the point must be emphasized that such excessive, reprehensible behavior constitutes only a portion ("eyn deel") of Reineke's leadership activity. And if the nascent rule of the fox is flawed, so has been that of the lion. The plot does not detail a fall into corruption from a pristine state of Eden-like harmony. To the contrary, by the conclusion of the chapbook, governance through physical intimidation is giving way to governance through political manipulation. As a result, while royal policy will still revolve around material self-interest, fewer subjects will be brutalized and greater prosperity will be divided among far more subjects — the rapidly expanding ranks of government functionaries. Reineke Fuchs will inaugurate a new era of relations between the king and his subjects, an era that will be relatively benign.

Traditional interpretations of *Reynke de Vos* have led to the conclusion that the machinations of the animal court and the ultimate triumph of the scheming fox merge to form a sweeping indictment of contemporary secular government.[10] The royal courts have fallen to such a low state that an animal fable featuring an amoral king will find resonance. The reader is entertained by a reductio ad absurdum that is intended to be both comic and monitory: in this arena the worst scoundrel will attain the loftiest position. Such interpretations suggest an authorial posture of resignation: circumstances in this mortal realm can only proceed from bad to worse. Reineke will leave the scene only to be replaced by a still more objectionable figure as society spirals ever downward. Of course, resignation in the face of an

---

[9] Grimm and Grimm, 4.1.6: 391.

[10] *Reineke Fuchs*, Langosch, "Nachwort," 278-79.

objectionable status quo can be perceived as acceptance or even affirmation of the social order. By extension, if the literature of this era has what Könneker calls pedagogical function, it would be logical to understand the work as a call for the adoption of a cynical stance vis-à-vis an immutably corrupt society.

Such a reading of the text accounts neither for the attitude of the narrator as expressed in the long passage above nor for the putative shape of a Reineke chancellorship. Strong, vehement condemnation of avaricious behavior, condemnation in the manner of Sebastian Brant is totally absent. And if outrage is in short supply, so too is bitterness. Instead, the narrator prattles along in bouncy couplets about the success enjoyed by the fox and his kind. Of course, if the narrator attaches no significance to affairs of this world, such comments can only be understood as ironic. However, as the presence of a "key" in the longer preface to the tale demonstrates, the contemporary reader was supposed to learn a lesson about governance. *Reynke de Vos* is pedagogical and any attribution of an attitude of resignation is problematic.

In that preface, the author is described both as a "lerer" ("teacher") and as a "poete" (5). In his role as teacher, he has demonstrated that those who think only of their greedy goals cannot flourish at court:

> He bewyset ok, dat den vorsten vnde heren dat vele nutter is, to hebben den wysen in ereme rade, dan den ghyrygen; wente neynes vorsten hoff efte stad sunder wyßheyt vnde klockheyt stande mach blyuen lange in eren. (5-6)

> He also proves that it is much more advantageous to lords and princes to have the wise man rather than the greedy man as their councillor. For no princely court or estate can long remain honored that neglects intelligence and wisdom. JVC

The poet has an optimistic faith in his ability to convince readers that wisdom and intelligence, not avarice, should and can have the king's ear. Reineke's unspoken thoughts upon leaving the court as chancellor echo that optimism:

> Weme ik nu wyl, deme mach ik vromen,
> Vnde mach mynen vrunden alle tyd syn holt.
> Noch pryse ik wyßheyt bouen dat golt.
> (6788-90)

It will go well for whomever I favor, and I always shall be partial to friends. I value wisdom even more highly than gold. JVC

Both the narrator and his central character evince a determination to make the world better.

The chancellorship of Reineke Fuchs will represent an improvement in government. To be sure, simony and graft will flourish, and a system of cronyism will be installed. However, physical coercion as practiced by the wolf Isegrim will no longer be the sole means of exercising authority. Economic self-interest will guarantee a measure of order, and those who can create wealth will have access to those who forge state policy. What obtains in the Rome of Martin the Ape will obtain at Nobel's court.

If the means of delivering that message are ambiguous, it is therefore safe from any charge of revolutionary intent. Apes and foxes do not populate utopias. Aristocratic readers of the chapbook easily could find in it mocking caricatures of those who are consumed with venality — stereotypically, merchant townsmen. At the same time, they could find an affirmation of their own intelligence and superiority in the aristocratic Reineke. The ruling nobility could find a concern for the honor of the court, as in the passage above, and a wish that wisdom might have the highest seat at the council of the king. For their part, townsmen could take heart in the rise of intelligence and meritocratic rule and in the weakening of feudalism with the erosion in influence of physical force. An interpretation of the chapbook as a transparent demolition of contemporary society is insensitive to its layers of interrelated — here complementary, there off-setting — appeals to disparate and fundamentally antagonistic levels of a society in change.

Brant's *Narrenschiff* offers one traditional negative assessment of the accumulation of wealth as the reason-for-being of mankind and a second, positive assessment when the poet considers the aspirations of representatives of his own social level. Of the two, the first is clearly dominant; Brant passionately yearns for the simpler, more devout age that he believes existed in the recent past. When he considers the general condition of man, Brant uses as his yardstick a clear, ever-present image of a golden age. It is adherence to that image that supports a protracted litany of the evils of modernity. The poet holds a naive belief that the image can become reality, if only each fool will recognize his own departures from the dictates of reason and from revealed truth. "Naive" because Brant exempts his own social stratum from a confrontation with his projection of a halcyon past.

The pursuit of material gain also separates mythic past from mundane present in *Reynke de Vos*. However, all leading members of the court of the lion *and* the court of the Pope view the past as irretrievably lost. In their public actions, they carefully maintain a facade of beliefs and values that they privately regard as superseded. The ruling elite uses the widespread longing for a return to older, better ways to manipulate the ethical reflexes of the masses. Nobel uses his subjects' expectations of a selfless, just, patriarchal king as a blind behind which he pursues a selfish agenda. However, Reineke is the master of this artifice. For example, when the fox is charged with outrages by a procession of animals at the first public audience, the badger at first is able to make excuses for the absent Reineke. However, when Henning the Rooster tells his tale of murder, no rebuttal is possible, and the decision is made that the fox must appear at court. Henning recounts how the fox appeared before the rooster's family in the guise of a hermit monk and convinced the family of his new-found religiosity. Once he had lured the family outside of their protective enclosure, Reineke blocked the path back and devoured most of the rooster's brood. For the reader, the gravity of the offense is largely balanced by the disguise of the fox (Fig. 2) and by the gullibility of the fatally stupid rooster. This comic portrayal of hypocrisy and its startling consequences (decapitation!) suggest an authorial posture that is at odds with that of Brant. Whereas Brant is horrified at the growth of what he perceives as an un-Christian basis for social interaction, the author of *Reynke de Vos* is amused. The transparent delight in the excesses of the aristocracy, including the ruling aristocracy, smacks of cultural voyeurism. It also suggests empathy for the exploiters' attitudes and contempt for those of the exploited. While the anonymous writer certainly does not commend the new, materialistic world-view to his readers, neither can he bring himself to sing the praises of earlier times. The poet is reconciled to the replacement of feudal allegiance based on force by material self-advancement based on intelligence. It is a cautiously open attitude toward change.[11]

The type of change depicted in the chapbook would have been of appeal to the urban intelligentsia of 1500 because it did not appear to be change. After all, Nobel is still king and the ordering of social levels remains the same. Nevertheless, the chapbook sends the message to those who are ruled that intelligence will inevitably replace force. As the reality behind an unchanging facade, the pursuit of wealth by a large group with similar goals will eclipse the satisfaction of greed by predatory individuals. At the same time, a member of the governing stratum could read *Reynke de Vos* without trepidation, indeed, with gratification at seeing the animal king's ability to bring order out of chaos. Reineke's elevation could be seen as the disarming of an antagonist of the tiny ruling clique through absorption into the clique. For his part, a townsman could find in the same text an assurance of supportive rather than exploitive governance in the near future. Reineke's

---

[11] For an interpretation of the chapbook as an attack on all aspects of a degenerate society, see Kokott, 86-88.

Fig. 2. Woodcut from *Reynke de Vos*
(from *Reynke de Vos*, trans. Karl Langosch, 1975)

elevation could be seen as the unofficial emergence as state policy of the progressive economic agenda of the merchants, professionals, and craftsmen.

This two-track approach to the small audience for literature in 1500 constitutes a recognition of the increasing polarization within society, polarization triggered by the decline of feudalism. The author has foreseen that the reception of his work will take two different paths. The calculated, carefully counterbalanced response to anticipated reception points to a level of artistic sophistication considerably above that of the impassioned Sebastian Brant. That sophistication leads to a representation of acquisitiveness that includes advantages as well as dangers both for the society and for the individual. The status of the individual in an increasingly materialistic society is a primary concern of the chapbooks *Dil Ulenspiegel* and *Fortunatus*. They detail the careers of a poor man and a rich man — each trying to make his way in the realm of Chancellor Not-Enough.

Chapter 4

Eulenspiegel and Fortunatus: The Problem Solved

THE ADVENTURES OF TILL Eulenspiegel and Fortunatus are set against a common background, a society that is unabashedly and relentlessly devoted to material gain. Gone is Sebastian Brant's fading vision of a return to the virtue and simplicity of a fabled past. Gone are King Nobel's attention to appearances and his reliance on force to maintain the integrity of the social hierarchy. Here, the ideals of Christian feudalism have all but disappeared from a world preoccupied with money and what it can buy — not just comfort but power. The two chapbooks under consideration entertained the sixteenth-century reader/auditor in part because they presented unusual, extreme perspectives on that materialistic society. While Till is barely able to keep body and soul together as an itinerant member of a low social level, Fortunatus experiences wealth as well as want, fabulous wealth and concomitant political power. Taken together, the tales can support an analysis of mores in German-speaking Europe on the eve of the great religious revival.

Ein kurtzweilig Lesen von Dil Ulenspiegel, geboren uß dem Land zu Brunßwick. Wie er sein Leben volbracht hatt. 96 seiner Geschichten (*A Pleasant Vintage of Till Eulenspiegel, Born in the Country of Brunswick. How He Spent His Life. 96 of His Tales*) was first published in 1510-11 by the Strasbourg printer Johannes Grieninger.[1] The foreword identifies the title character as a native of Braunschweig, and recent scholarship has assigned authorship of the anonymous chapbook to a native of that same Low German speaking area, Hermen Bote.[2] But, since the earliest editions are in

---

[1] Concerning the history of the text, see Wolfgang Lindow, "Nachwort," in *Ein kurtzweilig Lesen von Dil Ulenspiegel*, ed. Lindow (Stuttgart: Reclam, 1968), 269-71, 275-77. See also Werner Wunderlich, "Till Eulenspiegel: Zur Karriere eines Schalksnarren in Geschichte und Gegenwart," *Monatshefte* 78, no. 1 (1986): 41-44. The English title is from Paul Eugene Oppenheimer, trans., *A Pleasant Vintage of Till Eulenspiegel, Born in the Country of Brunswick. How He Spent His Life. 96 of His Tales*, diss., Columbia University, 1970 (Ann Arbor: UMI, 1971), 7106235. Subsequent references to this translation are given in parentheses.

[2] Peter Honegger, *Ulenspiegel: Ein Beitrag zur Druckgeschichte und zur Verfasserfrage* (Neumünster: Wachholtz, 1973), 92-94.

High German, in the absence of texts, long-held assumptions concerning one or more missing Low German originals remain speculative. Well documented, on the other hand, is the popularity of the work as measured in number of editions: Werner Wunderlich lists twenty-five in the sixteenth century alone, editions published in both southern and northern cities.[3] The chapbook has been widely available in Low German, English, and French translations since the sixteenth century; it also has appeared in Latin, Yiddish, Swedish, Danish, Czech, Polish, Russian, and Finnish.[4]

There is evidence of the existence of an historical model for the character Till Eulenspiegel, although, as Gerhard Steiner points out, the debate concerning such a flesh-and-blood Till has little impact on a reading of the chapbook.[5] The historical hypothesis posits a wandering journeyman or laborer who lived in the first half of the fourteenth century. Born in or near Braunschweig, he became known as a prankster. He supposedly fell victim to the Black Death and was buried in the town of Mölln. While no contemporary records the existence of what would have been an "attention-getting" personality, circumstantial evidence does exist. In 1592 a visitor to Mölln reported seeing Till's gravestone, and the name "Ulenspiegel" *is* documented as early as 1335 in the environs of Braunschweig.

Unlike *Reynke de Vos* and *Fortunatus*, *Dil Ulenspiegel* offered the contemporary reader a collection of independent stories about the central character. There is no architectonic plot, no character development. The first chapter or "Histori" recounts how the newborn Till was "baptized" three times in one day: first at the font, then in some dirty puddles along the path home by drunken godfathers, and finally in a tub of soapy water. A propensity to lewd behavior surfaces as early as the second chapter, in which the young rogue bares his behind at some peasants who have complained about his outrageous antics. At the conclusion of the ninth chapter, Till begins to wander from town to town and from prank to prank. At the beginning of the eighty-ninth chapter, those wanderings are coming to an end: Till is old and weary. The tricks he plays while dying constitute a structural counterpoint to the boyhood adventures, and, just as the newly baptized infant is accidentally dropped into the mud, Till's coffin is accidentally dropped into the grave in an upright position. Those present persuade the pallbearers not to reposition the coffin: "Da sprachen sie alle, die dabeistunden: 'Lassen ihn ston, wan er ist wunderlich gewesen in seinem

---

[3] Wunderlich, 46.

[4] Willy Krogmann, "Ulenspegel," in *Die deutsche Literatur des Mittelalters: Verfasserlexikon*, ed. Karl Langosch (Berlin: de Gruyter, 1953), 4:567-70.

[5] Gerhard Steiner, "Zur Exegese des Volksbuchs von Till Eulenspiegel," *Acta Litteraria Academiae Scientiarum Hungaricae* 2 (1959): 251.

Leben, wunderlich wil er auch sein in seinem Tod'"[6] ("Everybody who was standing there now said, 'Let him stand. As he was strange while he lived, he wants to be strange in death too,'" 316). An unconventional interment is appropriate at the end of an unconventional life. Unlike Reineke Fuchs, Till Eulenspiegel remains an outsider to the end. Like a chemical catalyst, his presence creates instability and change while he himself remains unaffected. In the midst of that instability, those with established positions in society give unreflected, even naive expression to their always pragmatic and often acquisitive world-views. Till's own attitudes toward money constitute a basis for his ability to generate chaos.

Eulenspiegel is a two-dimensional character. He undergoes no psychological development; large gaps in his personality render impossible any empathy with him. He does not demonstrate so much as a modicum of concern for his fellow man. He has no love life; there is no hint of sexuality. Even in the face of death, he offers no analysis of his life and beliefs. His adventures result from a limited number of constant, clearly and repeatedly expressed motivations.

The chapbook text takes pains to establish the dominant trait of its central character at an early point; the second chapter begins as follows:

> Alsbald nun Ulenspiegel so alt ward, daz er gon und ston kunt, da macht er vil Spils mit den jungen Kindern, wann er waz nötlich. Wie ein Aff domlet er sich uff den Küsn und im Graß, so lang, biß er 3 Jar alt ward. Da fliß er sich aller Schalckheit also, daz alle Nachburen gemeinlich uber Ulenspiegel clagten, daz sein Sun Dil Ulenspiegel wär ein Schalck. (12-13)

> As soon as Eulenspiegel was old enough to walk and stand, he played lots of games with the young children. Like a monkey, he tumbled about and lay around on pillows and in the grass until he was three years old. Then he began to apply himself to all sorts of mischief, so all the neighbors complained together to Eulenspiegel that his son Till Eulenspiegel was a rogue. (7-8)

The text offers no explanation for such unusual behavior, behavior that begins before most children are capable of coherent speech. The boy's parents are not described as singular in any way; in fact, as the second chapter makes clear, Father Eulenspiegel is blithely unaware of his son's singular demeanor. Till shows his backside to others only when his father is

---

[6] *Ein kurtzweilig Lesen von Dil Ulenspiegel*, ed. Wolfgang Lindow (Stuttgart: Reclam, 1968) 266. Subsequent references to the text will be indicated within parentheses.

looking the other way, so adept at trickery is the child. Each subsequent chapter is to be understood as an expression of this innate roguishness. Till's first victims respond by identifying him as a rogue. A procession of new acquaintances uses the epithet as one outrageous prank follows another, and the reader is given to understand that during his career, Till achieves notoriety throughout German-speaking Europe. A striking feature of that reputation is that Till is not perceived to be a unique, bizarre aberration, as something not completely human, but rather as a familiar type — the rogue.[7] That perception, shared by those who are duped and those who only watch, is significant because it constitutes a textual basis for an assessment of Till as a representative of a segment of his society.

As Till enters manhood, the question of his occupation arises. It is then that a second character trait becomes apparent. The fifth chapter relates a short conversation that takes place just after Till has played a trick on a number of peasants and their sons. Fearing to set foot outside his parents' house, the young rascal has busied himself quietly indoors. The chapter begins with these words:

Und Ulenspiegels Muter, die waz fro, daz ihr Son so stil waß, und strafft ihn, daz er kein Hantwerck wolt lernen. Da schweig er stil. Da ließ die Muter nit nach, ihn zu straffen. Da sprach Ulenspiegel: "Liebe Muter, wozu sich einer begibt, daz würt ihm sein Lebtag gnug." (19)

Well, Eulenspiegel's mother was happy that her son was so quiet. But she reproved him for not wishing to learn any trade. He kept silent, though, so his mother continued to admonish him.

Eulenspiegel then said, "Dear Mother, anything a man takes up will provide for him all his life." (15)

Till's use of the saying is ironical since he has yet to devote himself to any occupation. Irony aside, the response anticipates a lifelong commitment to idleness. But Till must reconcile his aversion to work with his prime motivation of expressing roguishness, since the latter requires effort on his part. That reconciliation occurs when Till has achieved so much notoriety that he must begin to use disguises. That is to say, he must alter his modus operandi. The narrator uses the occasion of the change to comment that, while the means have changed, the ends remain the same:

Also gieng es an demselben End mit ihm zu, das er sich mit Müsiggon nit mer trüwt zu ernären und waz doch guter Ding von Jugent uff

---

[7] Wunderlich, 39-40.

gwesen und Gelts gnug uberkumen mit allerlei Gükelspil. Da aber sein Schalckeit in allen Landen bekant ward und ihm sein Narung hinder sich gieng, da gedacht er, waz er treiben solt, daz er gut uberkäm mit Müssiggon, und nam ihm für ein Statzinierer ußzuthun und mit dem Heiltumb im Land umherzureiten. (92-93)

Nonetheless, it finally became clear to him that he could no longer trust himself to make his living by idleness — despite his having been a cheery fellow from his youth up and having gotten money enough through all sorts of clever games. And now that his roguery was becoming known through all countries, and his profits were declining, he reflected on what he might undertake — to support himself in idleness anyhow — and had the idea of doing himself up as a wandering monk and riding, with relics, throughout the surrounding country. (99-100)

In order to satisfy his need for idleness, Till has decided not to work for a living; he will accept the hand-to-mouth existence that such a decision enjoins. But the need for sustenance and the need to express roguishness are specified here as stimuli for the one form of activity that is acceptable — the playing of pranks. In the passage above, Till hits upon an activity that is both an ongoing prank and a form of idleness. That congenial pursuit is the peddling of religious relics, a practice that would have been rendered laughable in the eyes of the contemporary reader.

The third consistent motivation in Eulenspiegel's life is then the need for food and shelter and therefore for money.[8] Shelter is frequently on Till's mind. The editor of the German text, Wolfgang Lindow comments that, when a chapter specifies the time of year, the season is usually winter (152). In such passages, the text makes clear that harsh economic conditions prevail. The first sentence of the fifty-second chapter is typical: "Einsmals kam Ulenspiegel gen Ascherleue und waz Wintersnot und dürre Zeit und gedacht er: 'Waz wilt du nun anfahen, daz du uß dem Winter kumest?'" (152) ("Eulenspiegel once arrived in Aschersleben. Now, it was deep winter and a bitter time, and he thought, 'What'll you take up now, to bring you through the winter?'" 175). In an earlier passage, high unemployment among servants and unskilled workers is specified as a symptom of such hard

---

[8] See Wolfgang Fritz Haug, "Die Einübung bürgerlicher Verkehrsformen bei Eulenspiegel," *Argument-Sonderbände* 3 (1976): 12-13.

times (120, 135). The resultant competition for positions would lend a sense of great urgency to the search for work.[9]

The observation about increasing joblessness appears at the beginning of the fortieth chapter. In the adventure related there, Till finds a haven with a blacksmith. Hunger forces him to tell himself: "'Leid, was du leiden kanst. Solang der Finger wider in die lück Erd gat, du, waz der Schmid wil'" (120-21) ("'Bear what you can bear, and do what the smith wants — till you can stick your finger into spongy earth again,'" 135-36). Until he can poke his finger into the soft soil of springtime, he will curb his usual motivations and serve the new master. Of course, the smith soon proves to be a slave driver. On Till's first day of work, the smith plays a trick that deprives his new helper of a much needed mid-day meal. The smith then leaves Till to his thoughts:

> Ulenspiegel swig stil und gedacht: "Du hast dich verrent und hast daz vil ander Lüten gethon. Mit dem Maß würt dir wider gemessen. Wa wilt du nun das ihm bezalen? Das muß bezalt werden, und wär der Winter noch so hart." (121)

> Eulenspiegel kept quiet, but he thought, "You've run the wrong way here, and done such things yourself to many people — to the extent to which it's now being measured out to you. How do you plan to pay him back for this? For it's got to be paid back, though the winter were twice as harsh." (136)

The immediate response is neither anger nor sorrow at the prospect of an afternoon of hunger. Instead, the prankster recalls his prime motivation and is conscious of the irony that his recollection has been prompted by one who has turned the tables on Till Eulenspiegel. Till's priorities emerge in sharp relief from the last sentence: he will be true to himself even if that idealism endangers his life.

---

[9] Georg Bollenbeck points to overpopulation in the second half of the fifteenth century and the resultant difficulties facing those looking for menial and semi-skilled work. He sees Till as to a certain extent representative of this "excess population." Bollenbeck, *Till Eulenspiegel: Der dauerhafte Schwankheld: Zum Verhältnis von Produktions- und Rezeptionsgeschichte* (Stuttgart: Metzler, 1985), 76-79. Because Hans Hagen Hildebrandt interprets the text as reflective of the century in which Till supposedly lived (the fourteenth), he must attempt to reconcile such passages with reduced population figures caused by the plague. The attempt is not convincing. Hildebrandt, "Sozialkritik in der List Till Eulenspiegels: Sozialgeschichtliches zum Verständnis der Historien von Till Eulenspiegel (1971)," in *Eulenspiegel-Interpretationen: Der Schalk im Spiegel der Forschung 1807-1977*, ed. Werner Wunderlich (Munich: Fink, 1979), 188-89.

Money is a constant concern for Till as a means to immediate physical comfort, not as an end in itself. This attitude becomes clear when Till enjoys such success as a preacher that the text describes him as wealthy (94, 102). The device used to commit fraud in Chapter 31 is a skull that Till represents as that of St. Brandon. He is supposedly taking contributions for the construction of a church; those who kiss the head and make a contribution will receive remission of sin. Till enriches himself by using a disguise and by disciplining himself to practice only one type of trickery. The strictures thereby imposed on his inclination to give varied and creative expression to his roguishness soon prove to be too tight. Chapter 32 begins:

> Ulenspiegel was künstlich in der Schalckeit. Als er nun mit dem Hopt weit umbgezogen waz und die Lüt vast betrogen het, da kam er geen Nürnberg und wolt sein Gelt da verzeren, daz er mit dem Heilthom gewunnen. Und da er nun ein Zeitlang da gelegen was unnd alle Umbständ gesehen het, da kunt er von Natur nit lassen, er müst da auch ein Schalckheit thun. (95)

> Eulenspiegel was inventive in his roguishness. After he had traveled widely with the head, greatly deceiving people, he arrived in Nürnberg, intending to spend the money he had won with his relic. But when he had lived there for a while, and had seen all aspects of the city, he was unable to abandon his nature and had to perpetrate a clever trick there too. (103)

The first sentence is more than a formulaic introduction; it abruptly reminds the reader of both Till's prime motivation and his creativity. The career as a confidence man must come to an end because the character is "by profession" not a swindler but a rogue. The second sentence contains his attitude toward wealth: it is not a desirable state of being, but rather a means to the end of physical comfort. The third sentence then reinforces the first by reminding the reader who Eulenspiegel is by nature, that is, by reminding the reader of the prime motivation. The prank that Till is about to play will bring about the end of his career as a preacher.

This is not to derogate the significance that Till attaches to money. Many of his pranks bring him monetary benefit. His focus on the rewards that money can bring enables him to endure temporary unpleasantness. That much is shockingly clear at the end of an adventure that features coprophagy. In Chapter 24 Till competes with the court jester of the King of Poland for new clothing and twenty guilders. The king has declared that the winner will be the contestant who plays a prank so outrageous that his competitor will not imitate it. After the two have countered one another with one form of foolishness after another, Till walks to the center of the hall, defecates, uses a spoon to make two portions, eats one, and offers the spoon to the jester. The king immediately ends the contest and declares Eulenspiegel the victor. Till's thoughts just before the repulsive act are reported as follows: "'20 Guldin und ein nüw Cleid, das wär fast gut. Ich wil darumb thun, das ich sunst ungern thät'..." (72) ("'Twenty guilders and a new wardrobe — that would be rather nice. I shall therefore do something I would otherwise find unpleasant,'" 75). Money is this important to Till.

It is more often the case that Till is able to express his roguishness and secure the money he needs for survival without experiencing unpleasantness. In Chapter 78 he plays a trick on an innkeeper who has mocked three traveling merchants. The merchants agree to pay Till if he can make a fool of their host. When the prank is successful, they pay Till's bill at the inn. The reconciliation of Till's prime motivation with his need for funds is usually so complete that he is in a position to offer the resultant ability as a service. In this instance he is a prankster for hire.

But when circumstance forces Till to choose between food and shelter on the one hand and a prank on the other, the choice is made without reflection. The setting for Chapters 52 and 53 is again a hard winter during which the need for workers has dropped sharply. When Till does find a job, it is with a furrier who does not subject Till to abuse. Nevertheless, the rascal plays one trick after another, and at the conclusion Till must run out the door. He has not been goaded into action; his behavior is not a response to humiliation. His behavior contravenes his economic self-interest: he literally runs away from certain compensation.

The attitudes toward the pursuit of wealth held by the chapbook's other characters are considered below. The point of interest here is that the central character has a prime motivation capable of eclipsing all other motivations. But that character is a rogue, that is, a social type. He therefore represents a segment of his society that attaches only secondary importance to money and the things it can buy.

Till Eulenspiegel finds jobs in a broad spectrum of callings.[10] In stark contrast to those with whom he comes into contact, he is rootless. His interlocutors are consistently portrayed as occupying established positions in society. Both Till and the narrator often describe the victims of his pranks in stereotypical terms. Peasants are simple-minded (251-52, 294-95) and deserving of contempt (130, 149). Jews are treacherous businessmen who deserve to be tricked (104-6, 113-16). Village priests are arrogant and irreligious (37-38, 35-36); they ignore the rule of celibacy (113, 105).

---

[10] For a recent discussion of the chapbook as a "Ständespiegel," see Werner Wunderlich, *"Till Eulenspiegel"* (Munich: Fink, 1984), 65-74.

University professors and their students waste their time contemplating useless subjects (82-85, 88-92). Pious Christians are narrow-minded (221, 259-60). Members of the nobility are fickle in matters of life and death (73-74, 77-79). The church hierarchy fosters absurd practices such as the veneration of relics (92-94, 99-102), and the Pope himself is easily duped (101-3, 109-12). In sum, the chapbook does not pit unique individuals against Till Eulenspiegel; instead, the reader witnesses the responses of one type after another to the archetypical rogue. It is reasonable to conclude that the author saw or wanted the reader to see society as a forum for interactions among types. Any common denominator shared by those interactions demands attention as a force for cohesion among the estates. The quest for money and property is the most obvious common denominator.

The approach of death clarifies Till's priorities. Beginning with Chapter 89, Till is aware that his time is short. The woodcut for that chapter shows a rogue with thinning hair, sagging jaw, and a prominent age line on the one visible cheek. In the last chapters, Till continues to find new ways to express his prime motivation. His final act is to bequeath a chest containing his valuables to three groups for fair division (262-63, 311-12). After his death, representatives of the groups convene, open the chest, and find that it contains only stones. Each group suspects the other of having made a substitution. Till has managed to play a prank after his own death. The stones are a metaphor for Till's attitude toward wealth, an attitude that remains consistent even at a time of traditionally great concern about worldly goods. The three groups that care only about Till's financial legacy are the local church, the town council of Mölln, and the dying man's friends. No one offers the rogue any solace — which is to say, none of the characters present at Till's death evince a priority more significant in their eyes than financial gain. Ecclesiastical authority, secular authority, and personal relationships are revealed as sharing a common underlying venality.

The bitter satire on the deathbed audiences gives sweeping expression to a theme to which the chapbook returns in one variation after another: the pursuit of wealth and property as the prime motivation of Till's contemporaries. Whether it is an innkeeper who is consumed with greed (206, 240-41) or a wallet-maker who ignores common sense in his zeal to amass an extraordinary profit (169-70, 196-97), providers of goods and services are portrayed as balance-sheets incarnate. Till's tricks are highly successful because it is a simple matter to dupe characters who always wear blinders, and the very possibility of financial loss makes them quake to their foundations. Whether he is a baker (Chapters 19 and 20), a smith (Chapters 39 and 40), a cobbler (Chapters 43 and 46), or a tailor (Chapter 48), Till's master inevitably suffers losses of cash or inventory. The only portion of his humanity presented in one or two short chapters is his status as a participant in the rapidly developing urban, money-based economy of the late fifteenth and early sixteenth centuries. That status is his identity. A contemporary reader naturally would compare the comic reduction with its real-world counterpart. The gap between the two is narrowed by a cumulative effect that the chapbook achieves by injecting Till into one business establishment after another. The reader is to perceive that the life of a proprietor is synonymous with the life of his business.

When Till tricks members of the ruling nobility, he affords them the opportunity to demonstrate their financial strength by making light of substantial losses. The King of Denmark laughs upon learning that he has been duped into giving Till four golden horseshoes (69-70, 71-73). He sees that Till has only followed instructions literally and so keeps the outlandish courtier until he himself dies. When the Landgrave of Hessia finds himself in a similar position, he banishes the trickster, who has already fled the scene. But he too speaks of a sizable loss as though it were of little consequence (81, 87). Disdain for that which others value most, the accumulation of wealth and property, is a form of representation reserved for princes. When such figures are acquisitive, the material goal must be whimsical rather than practical. The Duke of Braunschweig has Eulenspiegel trick a pastor out of a horse that the Duke wants (113-16, 125-30). The reader is to understand that the Duke is accustomed to acquiring whatever he desires, whether he needs it or not. The expression of a cavalier attitude toward property is a means of representing exalted status.

Although a prince affects disdain for wealth and property before his courtiers, when he sits as judge, his sole concern is the size of the next bribe. Till levels that charge against the judicial system in a conversation with the Bishop of Trier (178-80, 205-8). The vagabond has introduced himself as a maker of eyeglasses whose profession supposedly has fallen on hard times. The demand for glasses has declined because ecclesiastical and secular judges no longer read books of law. Eulenspiegel tells the bishop:

> ... Ihr und andere groß Herren, Babst, Cardinal, Bischoff, Keiser, Künig, Fürsten, Radt, Regierer, Richter der Stat und Land (Got erbarmß) nun zur Zeit durch die Finger sehen, waz Recht ist, daz zu Zeite von Geltgaben sich ursacht. (180)

> ... You and other great Lords, Popes, Cardinals, Bishops, Kaisers, Kings, Princes, Councilors, Governors, Judges of the cities and countries (God save us!) presently just wink at what is right — and this, presently, because of gifts of money. (207)

The occasional loss that serves as representation can be borne easily if such bribes amount to a regular and sizable source of income. In the final analysis then, the ruling nobility is as concerned about making a profit as are townsmen.

While Till's accusation of acquisitiveness in high places in the church remains largely unsubstantiated, the behavior of the priest who is to hear Till's last confession reveals the presence of greed in the lower levels of the hierarchy. Remission of sin and a place in heaven have become commodities to be bought and sold (260, 308-9). Of course, the contemporary reader might not have reacted to what was by 1510 a commonplace criticism of churchmen. But that reader must have been struck by the venality of Till's friends and, particularly, by Till's mother. At her son's deathbed, the old woman weeps and expresses concern about his illness. She then asks that he leave her with a sweet thought or sentiment, and Till responds with quips and jokes. Their last exchange is as follows:

> Die Muter sprach: "Lieber Sun, gib mir doch etwas von deinem Gut." Ulenspiegel sagt: "Liebe Muter, wer dat nüt hat, dem sol man geben, und der etwas hat, dem sol man etwas nemen. Mein Gut ist verborgen, das niemans weiß. Findest du etwas, das mein ist, das magchst du angreiffen, doch ich gib dir von meinem Gut alles, das krumb ist und recht ist." (257)

> His mother said, "Dear son, give me some of your belongings."
> Eulenspiegel said, "Dear Mother, one should give to him who has nothing and take from him who has something. My goods are hidden — where, nobody knows. If you find something that's mine, you may take it, for of my goods I leave you all that's crooked and straight." (303)

While each of her earlier pleas has been answered by a single witty rejoinder, her final request elicits several. By positioning it at the end of a series of exchanges and by having Till respond in an exaggerated fashion, the chapbook author suggests that his mother's final request has been her all too transparent purpose in visiting her child. If a mother's feeling for her son has an economic basis, it is only logical that other, less intimate relationships will have profitability as their common goal. In his response Till is still in character: each of his jokes depends for its humor upon the supreme importance that society attaches to personal financial holdings. By repeatedly making light of the putative legacy, Till firmly resists the pressure generated by society's expectation that a dying man will put his financial house in order. Till refuses to act in deference to the prime motivation of his fellow creatures. As he lies dying, the rogue has no further use for money and therefore refuses even to consider it.

In the chapbook *Dil Ulenspiegel*, materialism pervades every level of society. Individuals — whether noble or peasant, rural or urban — are therefore unable to establish normal relationships with the one human type that rejects materialism. Communication breaks down continually because society's language serves common-sensical, practical, materialistic goals, while Till's language serves roguish goals.[11] Till is an effective tool for social analysis because he creates an instability that frequently involves money and property. The text constantly holds up venality to the reader's laughter, scorn, and rejection. At the same time, Till plays the clown so often and in such extreme fashions that any reader identification with him as an idealistic free spirit is all but impossible. The type that he represents does not oppose society; it neither seeks nor causes attitudinal change. On the contrary, it is an integral component of a society in stasis. That society has a time-tested method of dealing with the type, as is clear at the conclusion of Chapter Forty-Five. Till has broken the shop windows of a bootmaker, and the craftsman expresses his anger — but that anger is not directed at Till:

> Ich hon allweg gehört, wer mit Schalckßlüten beladen ist, der sol den Schlupff abschneiden und sie lassen gon. Hät ich das auch gethon, so wären mein Fenster wol gantz bliben. (133)

> I've always heard whoever's bothered by knaves should cut the traces and let them go. If I'd done so, my windows would still be in one piece. (152)

According to folk wisdom, the best response to a rogue is to let him have his way and not have much to do with him. As folk wisdom the piece of advice is nothing new; it has proven itself over time. Hence, knaves have been recognizable as a group within society for some time. Till has spiritual ancestors — and brothers. Their type is to be looked upon as are destructive acts of nature. Nothing can be done; a victim can only wait until the destructive force passes. The advice recalled by the master contains the assurance that rogues eventually will leave.

It cannot be the intention of the chapbook to warn readers against contact with the rogue type since Till's movements are under no more

---

[11] Till's language is studied in Dieter Arendt, "Eulenspiegel: Sprachwitz und Widerstand," *Kürbiskern* 2 (1977): 108-16.

control than are those of a thunderstorm.[12] In view of Till's prime motivation, it is ill-advised to characterize him as in any way representative of economic strata such as urban servants and laborers or peasants.[13] In no sense is Till a revolutionary because, wherever he creates chaos, the local population is certain that he soon will leave. Finally, because of the repugnant nature of many of Till's pranks, the reader is not tempted to model attitudes and patterns of behavior after him.

Instead, the reader is to note what the rogue reveals about German society. That society is presented as unchanging; it is in a static balance that subsumes even the personality type that rejects its prime motivation, the pursuit of wealth. Viewed through the eyes of a rogue, the stasis is humorous, entertaining. Entertainment is the reason cited in the narrator's foreword for writing down the adventures: "Nun allein umb ein frölich Gemüt zu machen in schweren Zeiten, und die Lesenden und Zuhörenden mögen gute kurtzweilige Fröden und Schwänck daruß fabulleren" (7) ("My only ambition is to create a happy feeling in hard times, so my readers and listeners may experience good, pleasant entertainment and fun," 2). Fluctuating economic conditions constitute one cause of the hard times; as indicated above, the chapbook refers to times of high unemployment. As a response to such conditions, *Dil Ulenspiegel* offers neither a program for change nor a revolutionary to emulate, but only the palliative of laughter. The harsh, materialistic world is to be endured, if possible, with a smile.

Fortunatus and his son Andolosia also live in that world. But the chapbook *Fortunatus* (1509) offers a cohesive narrative rather than a series of independent pranks. It is the tale of the young son of a fallen family who attains fabulous wealth and success but whose own sons meet tragic ends. The plot pivots on Fortunatus's conscious decision to secure wealth for himself because it is the most significant determinant of the quality of human existence. The circumstances of the character's moment of decision, his motivations in placing wealth before other traditionally prized determi-

---

[12] Compare Hans Wiswe, "Sozialgeschichtliches um Till Eulenspiegel (1971)," in *Eulenspiegel-Interpretationen*, 179.

[13] For such an identification, see Ingeborg Spriewald, *Vom "Eulenspiegel" zum "Simplicissimus": Zur Genesis des Realismus in den Anfängen der deutschen Prosaerzählung* (Berlin: Akademie-Verlag, 1978), 82. Dieter Arendt refers to Till as a "plebejischer Tribun": Dieter Arendt, *Eulenspiegel — ein Narrenspiegel der Gesellschaft* (Stuttgart: Klett-Cotta, 1978), 82. Gerhard Steiner had already voiced this orthodox Marxist perception in 1959, albeit in less colorful language: Steiner, 260. Bollenbeck is still arguing the line in 1985 — but with qualifiers. Till supposedly numbers among the "entstehendes Vorproletariat" — a statement that is itself immediately qualified. Bollenbeck, *Till Eulenspiegel*, 80.

nants, and the consequences of the decision are the primary concerns of the analysis that follows.

The earliest extant edition of *Fortunatus* was published in Augsburg by Johann Otmar. Scholarship has yet to establish the identity of the anonymous author; but descriptions of non-German landforms and customs in terms that Germans could have understood suggest German origins.[14] The importance of international commerce to the plot and the text's attention to merchandise, trade routes, and business practices have drawn the attention of researchers to major commercial centers as likely candidates for provenance. Of such centers, Augsburg is the most likely because of the presence there of Otmar. The chronicler Burkhardt Zink has been proposed as a possible author.[15]

Reader response to the chapbook was both enthusiastic and lasting.[16] Approximately twenty editions appeared in the sixteenth century alone an additional twenty during the following two centuries. Use of the Fortunatus subject matter in other literary genres has been relatively infrequent. But in translation, the work became known throughout Europe before the end of the sixteenth century. If *Fortunatus* is less familiar outside of German-speaking Europe than are *Dil Ulenspiegel* and the *Faustbuch*, it may be in part because of the chapbook's inability to satisfy latter-day expectations about the novel. As the chronicle of the rise and fall of a family, *Fortunatus* does invite comparison with, for instance, Thomas Mann's *Buddenbrooks*. Of course, such comparisons, while tempting and even unavoidable, are anachronistic. *Fortunatus* makes no attempt to lay bare the psyches of unique individuals. It is relatively short — 191 pages in the latest student edition.[17] Those pages offer journeys throughout the known world, nonstop adventures, a large cast of characters, magic devices, and a metaphysical vision. While all of this is still eminently readable, the work's observations and message are impersonal. As the "Preface" indicates, the chapbook was

---

[14] Marjatta Wis, "Zum deutschen 'Fortunatus': Die mittelalterlichen Pilger als Erweiterer des Weltbildes," *Neuphilologische Mitteilungen* 63, no. 1 (1962): 16-18.

[15] Walter Raitz, *"Fortunatus"* (Munich: Fink, 1984), 7. Marjatta Wis has suggested possible German sources used by the author: Wis, "Nochmals zum 'Fortunatus'-Volksbuch: Quellen- und Datierungsprobleme," *Neuphilologische Mitteilungen* 66, no. 2 (1965): 199-209.

[16] For details concerning reception, see Wis, "Zum deutschen 'Fortunatus,'" 6-9.

[17] *Fortunatus: Studienausgabe nach der editio princeps von 1509*, ed. and with an appendix by Hans-Gert Roloff (Stuttgart: Reclam, 1981). Subsequent references to the text will be indicated in parentheses. The only complete English translation of *Fortunatus* was prepared by Thomas Churchyard, who died in 1604. Because copies of the Churchyard translation are difficult to procure and because its English is archaic, I offer my own translations here with the thought that a new English translation of *Fortunatus* would be a significant contribution to research in the literature of Luther's Germany.

conceived as a source of entertainment and instruction, instruction concerning the relative merits of wealth and wisdom (5).

The story of Fortunatus and his sons begins in the city of Famagusta on Cyprus. Theodorus, the son of a wealthy old patrician family, squanders his inheritance trying to live in the style of the nobility. He is particularly enamored of tournaments and the hunt. When financial ruin looms, he marries the daughter of a wealthy family, and within a year Fortunatus is born. Theodorus soon returns to his favorite diversions and quickly impoverishes his small family.

When Fortunatus leaves his destitute parents at age eighteen, his only education has been in the ways of the hunt. He immediately enters the service of a homeward-bound Flemish count. In Flanders, Fortunatus's skills on the hunt and at the tournament earn him the favor of the count and the enmity of the other servants. Duped by several of the latter into believing that his manhood will soon be forfeited, the young man steals away to London, where he throws away his savings on riotous living and loose women. After six months of debauchery, he enters the service of an upright, wealthy Florentine merchant named Roberti, who soon comes to place great trust in Fortunatus. While the Cypriot is away from London on an errand for his master, a nobleman is murdered in Roberti's large house without the merchant's knowledge. The Florentine and his servants are found guilty of the crime and are summarily executed, a fate that the returning Fortunatus barely avoids.

It is a penniless Fortunatus who flees England for northern France, where he is unable to find work. Soon he is wandering about the forests of Brittany, hopelessly lost, in rags, starving. The hero is envisioning his imminent demise when "die junckfraw des glücks" ("the Maiden of Fortune" appears before him, 46). She offers the pitiful wretch a choice from six possible gifts: wisdom, wealth, strength, health, beauty, and long life. After he chooses wealth, she gives him a purse that will contain money as long as he or one of his children is alive — and she gives him directions out of the woods.

In the course of a suspenseful episode with a rural count, Fortunatus learns to use his magic purse with great discretion, to avoid immediate "conspicuous consumption." Only when he arrives in a large city does he set aside his beggar's rags and acquire some of the trappings of a rich traveller. It is there in Nantes that he meets old Lüpoldus, whom he engages as a travel guide and adviser. Together they criss-cross Europe from Ireland to Constantinople, from Poland to the Iberian peninsula. Finally, after a fifteen-year absence, Fortunatus returns home to his native land amid great pomp.

In Famagusta he learns that his parents have died. Soon he builds a splendid residence and a church to which he makes extraordinary bequests.

100   The Problem of Wealth in the Literature of Luther's Germany

He also marries Cassandra, the thirteen-year-old daughter of a count. Within a year of the wedding, Lüpoldus dies. Cassandra later bears two sons, Ampedo and Andolosia. After twelve years in Famagusta, Fortunatus travels off to see the rest of the world. His travels take him from Egypt to Persia and beyond to China and India. Returning through Alexandria, he steals a magic hat from the Sultan. The hat enables its wearer to wish himself from one place to another. After a two-year absence, he returns to Cyprus where he lives happily for many years. Finally, Cassandra falls ill and dies. The aged Fortunatus's mourning becomes mortal illness. Just before death, he reveals the nature of the two magical possessions to his sons, warns them to keep the nature of the purse and hat secret, and dies — sixty years after meeting the Maiden of Fortune.

After a year of mourning, Andolosia sets forth with the magic purse to travel through Europe in the manner of his father. The sober Ampedo remains at home with the magic hat. With the aid of his wealth and chivalric skills, Andolosia soon wins renown at the royal court in Paris. But an infatuation with a married noblewoman leads to victimization and a hasty departure. After some years in Spain and Portugal, he travels to England, where he falls in love with the scheming Agripina, the daughter of the King. She tricks him into revealing the secret of the purse and steals the source of his wealth. After a series of adventures, Andolosia recovers the purse and marries Agripina to the son of the King of Cyprus.

At a tournament celebrating the marriage, Andolosia surpasses all others in knightly prowess, but the prize is given to Count Theodorus of England in order to honor Agripina's escort. When Theodorus hears all of the spectators saying that Andolosia deserves the prize, the count conceives a hatred for him. Together with the Cypriot Count Lymosy, who despises Andolosia for affecting an aristocratic life-style that does not befit a commoner, Theodorus kidnaps Andolosia, steals the purse, and finally murders Andolosia. Ampedo succumbs to despair, destroys the magic hat, and dies of grief. When the King of Cyprus learns the truth, he has the two miscreants executed.

The "Preface" to the chapbook concludes by specifying the lesson that is to be learned from the example of Fortunatus and his sons: "[wie] in alweg vernufft und weißhait für all schätz diser welt / zu begeren und zu erwölen ist" (5) ("that in all matters reason and wisdom are to be sought or chosen rather than all of the treasures of this world"). Thus, from the onset a reader knows to expect that the text will present its hero with a choice, and that Fortunatus and his children will have to face the consequences of making the wrong choice. But when the Maiden of Fortune appears before a starving Fortunatus, she offers six highly desirable gifts, not just two. Of the five choices rejected, only two are logical alternatives to wealth from the young man's perspective. His chivalric talents, already demonstrated in Flanders, would have comprehended mastery of the social graces as well as prowess at arms. Which is to say, strength, health, and beauty are qualities that he already possesses.[18] Longevity and wisdom fall into a different category because the youth does not possess them; but at his age, it is reasonable to assume both many more years of life and some degree of resultant wisdom. By the same token, as the poor son of poor parents, Fortunatus has no basis for assuming that he will attain to wealth. Of the six choices, it is the only one that may well elude him for the rest of his life. Such are Fortunatus's prospects as he faces the momentous decision. But he must also consult his past experiences with wisdom and wealth in order to determine their relative worth. The improbability of possessing great wealth would be counterbalanced by a reverence for wisdom, a reverence either taught by his parents or learned during his first experiences as an independent adult. No such counterbalancing has occurred.

In fact, the course of the hero's life up to his moment of decision dictates his choice. Scholarship has already demonstrated the supreme importance of money and what it represents as presented from the beginning of the chapbook; the choice has been viewed as logical.[19] While his childhood gave him a close familiarity with poverty, time spent in the service of two wealthy men, the Flemish count and the Florentine merchant, has acquainted Fortunatus with the other end of the economic spectrum. Most recently he has learned that the inability to earn wages can lead not just to poverty but to starvation. The immediate prospect of a lingering death argues powerfully for wealth as a guarantor of life. On the other hand, the young man has seen little evidence of the value of wisdom. His formal education is described as woefully deficient: at eighteen he can read and write his name only (7). While his father Theodorus has imparted enthusiasm for and knowledge of huntsmanship and knightly demeanor, there is no basis for assuming that the failed bon vivant would possess wisdom or even appreciate it — let alone pass it on to his son. The one arguably wise man whom Fortunatus has come to know is the merchant Alberti, a good, pious, and successful man whose upright character proves to be no defense against the

---

[18] Hans-Jürgen Bachorski makes this point, although his comment on Fortunatus's inattention to the choice of longevity is incongruous. As he stands before the Maiden of Fortune, the hero obviously cannot know that he will live to be almost eighty without choosing longevity. Bachorski, *Geld und soziale Identität im "Fortunatus": Studien zur literarischen Bewältigung frühbürgerlicher Widersprüche* (Göppingen: Kümmerle, 1983), 59.

[19] See Helmut Scheuer, "Das 'Volksbuch' *Fortunatus* (1509): Zwischen feudaler Anpassung und bürgerlicher Selbstverwirklichung," in *Literatursoziologie II: Beiträge zur Praxis*, ed. Joachim Bark (Stuttgart: Kohlhammer, 1974), 104; Bachorski, 59; Raitz, 28.

machinations of a murderous scoundrel. If anything, on the basis of his London experience Fortunatus reasonably could have concluded that the traditionally esteemed qualities of mind are of dubious value. Given the hero's past experience and given his immediate prospects as he speaks with the Maiden of Fortune, a reader is led to conclude that wisdom is no more attractive a selection than is longevity; in Fortunatus's estimation, it is a seriously compromised attribute.

Although Fortunatus's reasons for rejecting wisdom and the four other choices must be inferred, his thinking in selecting wealth is given direct expression. Before making her offer, the Maiden asks Fortunatus why he is wandering about the forest:

> sy sagt / "was geest du hie umb?" er antwurt ir und sprach / "mich zwingt armůt das ich hye umb gang unnd sůch / ob mich got beraten wölt / und mir sovil glücks verleühen das ich zeitliche narung möcht haben" (46)

> She said, "Why are you wandering about here?"
> He answered her saying, "I am forced by poverty to wander about here and see whether God will guide me and grant me the good fortune that I might have the sustenance a mortal needs."

After listing the gifts, the Maiden states her terms:

> "Da erwöle dir ains under den sechssen / unnd bedenck dich nit lang / wann die stund des glücks zu geben ist gar nach verschynen." Allso bedachte er sich nit lang und sprach / "so beger ich reichtumb / das ich alweg gelts gnůg hab" / (46)

> "Now choose one of the six and don't take long, for the time for granting good fortune passes quickly."
> So he did not take long and then said, "I'd like wealth then, so that I'll always have enough money."

Fortunatus attributes his dire condition neither to misfortune nor to stupidity. It is poverty that threatens to end his life. His prayer comprehends two possibilities: that God will provide him with food or that God will provide him with the means to buy food. Which is to say, while the hero recognizes poverty as the cause of his distress, he prays not for relief from the cause but for relief from its symptom. Reasons for the existence of the cause do not interest him in his moment of extreme jeopardy. When the Maiden identifies herself, Fortunatus can conceive of her only as an answer to his prayer for food or the money to buy food. When she makes known the six choices, only one is directly related to that for which he has prayed. When she demands haste, he does not have the time to proceed mentally from symptom to cause and from cause to speculations first about underlying reasons and then about possible future benefits of the other gifts. Because the Maiden does not offer that for which he has prayed, Fortunatus must take at least one small logical step. He takes the deductive step from "wealth" to "money for food" rather than the time-consuming series of inductive steps that separate pressing concerns of the moment from hypothetical future happiness.

The circumstances created by the author for Fortunatus's fateful decision dictate the character's choice. That structuring raises questions about authorial intent as stated in the "Preface." But first, it should be noted that Fortunatus chooses wealth not in order to luxuriate in diverse sensual pleasures, but in order to have enough money at all times. "Enough money" must be understood in the context of Fortunatus's prayer. What he seeks from his choice is relief from poverty and from the derivative fear of starvation. The text does not suggest greed, or even selfishness. In fact the contrary is the case: Fortunatus's first reaction to the gift of the magic purse is the expression of a desire to return the favor. When the Maiden requests that Fortunatus supply a dowry for the marriageable daughter of poor parents every year, he eagerly agrees. His sensitivity to the perceptions and needs of others is already well established. From the scene with the Maiden of Fortune, a reader is led to draw the inferences that Fortunatus made a reasonable choice with modest ends in view and that the youth is fair-minded and compassionate.

The chapbook author went to great lengths to make the choice of wealth over wisdom as sympathetic as possible. But one of the two stated purposes for the composition of the work is the presentation to the reader of proof that "reason and wisdom are to be sought or chosen rather than all of the treasures of this world." A decision scene consonant with that purpose would have made clear a flaw in Fortunatus's character or thinking, a failing or mistake that the reader could easily identify and reject. Instead, the motivation offered is life-threatening poverty, a condition that invites commiseration, not condemnation. The strong tension between the avowed purpose of the work and the text at the pivotal point in the plot suggests the thesis that the "Preface" is making a conspicuous, perfunctory bow to contemporary audience expectations concerning the lesson taught by the story of a rich man and his sons. Nothing in the narrative before the appearance of the Maiden contradicts the moral lesson announced since neither wisdom nor wealth determine the hero's actions in the first portion of the chapbook. In fact, the tragedy of Jeronimus Alberti supports the traditional position that wealth is transitory and unreliable as a guide to human life. But the decision scene is not the world of clear ethical choices projected by the "Preface." In the face of certain death, Fortunatus's only thought is of survival. The "Preface" speaks to the quality of life after the decision, but at the moment of truth, Fortunatus has no basis for assuming that he will live long enough to use the gift of wisdom.

The tension between "Preface" and text concerning the circumstances of Fortunatus's decision recurs as a conflict between the text and the author's final moralizing paragraph concerning the consequences of that decision. The paragraph is reproduced here:

> Bey diser hystoria ist tzu vermercken / hette der jung Fortunatus im walde betrachtlichen Weißhait / für den seckel der reichtumb / von der junckfrawen des gelücks erwölt unnd begert / sy wäre ym auch mit hauffen gegeben worden / den selben schatz ym nyemandt hett mügen enpfieren. durch welliche weißhait unnd vernunfft / er auch tzeitlich gůt / eerliche narung und grosse hab / het mügen erlangen. So aber er ym dotzumal in seiner jugent umb freüd unnd wollust willen / der weltt reichtumb und gůt am maysten liebet und geviele (als ungezweiffelt noch von manigem ain solcher seckel für alle vernuft begert wurd) schůff er im selbs und seinen sünen mye und bitterkait der gallen / und wiewol ynen etliche wenig tzeit / süß und lieblich was / nam es doch ain sollich ennd / wie ir hyerinn vernommen habt. Dem nach ain ygklicher dem solliche wal gegeben wurde / bedencke sich nit lang / volge der vernunfft und nit seinem frechen torechten gemüt / und erkyeß Weißhait für reichtumb. Als auch gethon hat Salomon / dardurch er der reichest künig der erden wordenn ist. Aber wol ist zu besorgen / die jungfraw des gelücks / die solliche wal außgibt / und Fortunato den seckel gegeben hat / sey auß unseren landen verjaget / und in dieser welt nit mer tzu finden. (194-95)

The following is to be gathered from this history: if young Fortunatus had chosen and truly desired the great wisdom offered by the Maiden of Fortune in the forest instead of the purse of wealth, it would have been given to him in full measure, and no one would have been able to deprive him of it. Through that wisdom and reason he also could have attained worldly goods, honestly earned sustenance, and many possessions. But because then in his youth he loved and took greatest pleasure in wealth and worldly things — all for the sake of happiness and pleasure — (even as without a doubt such a purse, and not reason, still would be desired by many), he brought upon himself and his sons trouble and bitter gall. And although they did have some brief and sweet time, it did finally come to the conclusion that you have now heard related. Accordingly, may each person who is given such a choice not think long about it, but let reason be his guide rather than impudent, capricious feelings, and choose wisdom rather than wealth. Solomon did just that and as a result became the wealthiest king on earth. But it is certainly to be feared that the Maiden of Fortune, who offers the choice and gave Fortunatus the purse, has been chased from our country and no longer is to be found in this world.

As should be apparent from the discussion above, the motive here attributed to Fortunatus in choosing wealth is not present in the relevant passage. "Happiness and pleasure" are far from the youth's mind as he tries to discern the straightest path to the meal that will save him. The sentence goes on to refer to contemporaries of the author who would "without doubt" choose the magic purse to satisfy their own base instincts. Of course, the absence of the motive at Fortunatus's moment of decision lessens the impact of this final address to the reader. But the address is fully in line with the pedagogical purpose announced in the "Preface." People must be taught to choose wisdom because so many are not choosing it. This traditional attitude toward wealth is stated at the two most highly visible points in the text. While the author may have been able to reconcile in his own mind the tension between the lesson announced and the example given, it is more likely that the contradiction was appreciated and allowed to remain.

The conclusion cited above contradicts the text when it refers to the supposedly disastrous consequences of Fortunatus's decision, consequences for Andolosia and Ampedo as well. In point of fact, all three men enjoy roughly sixty years of comfortable, rewarding life because of the choice. Günther Müller has determined that Fortunatus is approximately eighty years old at his death; his two sons die just short of sixty.[20] Fortunatus is about twenty years of age when he meets the Maiden of Fortune. He goes on to marry a beautiful girl who bears him sons. When he is on Cyprus, he lives in a magnificent house and pursues his favorite pastimes. He travels throughout the known world not because he must but because travel is a form of education and recreation for Fortunatus. The only sorrow that touches a (for the times) extraordinarily long life is the death of his wife, and he dies in bed shortly thereafter. Clearly, this is not a personal history characterized by "trouble and bitter gall." The happy times are long: the text

---

[20] Günther Müller, "Das Zeitgerüst des Fortunatus-Volksbuchs," in his *Morphologische Poetik: Gesammelte Aufsätze* (Tübingen: Niemeyer, 1968), 579.

refers to one twelve-year period in Famagusta given over to family life and pleasant diversions (98) and to a period of many years in which Fortunatus and Cassandra lived "in great happiness" and knew no distress (120). Müller asserts that that second period is in fact at least thirty years.[21]

The miraculous purse has nothing to do with the demise of Fortunatus; he simply follows his life's companion into death. By the same token, his death is not hastened by a lack of wisdom. Still, the concluding paragraph argues that, if Fortunatus had chosen wisdom, he could have used that wisdom to acquire wealth. This remarkable formulation is considered in detail below. It should be noted that the hero achieves the same end (possession of both gifts) by using wealth to acquire wisdom. When Fortunatus engages old Lüpoldus as a travel guide and adviser, he is "renting" intelligence and experience, that is, he is renting wisdom. In the course of subsequent travels, he gains enough wisdom of his own to be able to steal the magic hat from the Sultan's most secure treasure-vault. He displays steady prudence by keeping the secret of his purse and his hat until his dying day.

If the consequences of choosing wealth are so fortuitous for the father as to be enviable, what of the consequences for the sons? The placid, reserved Ampedo and the energetic, gregarious Andolosia are born into a home that meets all of their needs — physical, emotional, educational. Under the beneficent eyes of their parents, they are able to pursue their interests from childhood through adolescence and well into maturity. Müller estimates that the two are approximately forty-five at the death of their father.[22] Here is additional proof that the reference in the conclusion of the chapbook to the duration of happiness as "some brief and sweet time" is incongruous. Each enjoys roughly sixty years of robust health at a time in which most men probably did not attain age forty.[23] And each lives in a fashion suited to his personality. Ampedo tends the home fires while the more adventurous Andolosia seeks excitement, danger, and romance. Andolosia is the one character who encounters difficulty because of a lack of wisdom. But his life is not consumed with "trouble and bitter gall," even after he imprudently reveals the secret of the purse to Agripina. The adventures that ensue are agreeable to Andolosia, and they do not lead to an inevitable tragic conclusion. As Andolosia rides off to the ill-fated tourna-

---

[21] Müller, 590.

[22] Müller, 579.

[23] See Wolfgang Zorn, "Sozialgeschichte 1500-1648," in *Handbuch der deutschen Wirtschafts- und Sozialgeschichte: Von der Frühzeit bis zum Ende des 18. Jahrhunderts*, ed. Hermann Aubin and Wolfgang Zorn (Stuttgart: Klett, 1971), 471.

ment, all of his past difficulties have been resolved, and he is at the height of his knightly powers.

The bitterness and personal tragedy in the chapbook are concentrated in the murder of Andolosia and the suicide of Ampedo. Scenes of torture, despair, and death make for the dark conclusion of the work alluded to by the closing paragraph above. There the author asserts that Fortunatus's choice leads to "the conclusion that you have now heard related." That assertion misrepresents the text. When Counts Theodorus and Lymosy waylay Andolosia, they know nothing of a magic purse. Andolosia has aroused their hatred because his knightly skills surpass those of Theodorus and because he acts the part of a nobleman and is in fact treated like a nobleman by the royal court — to the consternation of Lymosy. Both counts view Andolosia's bearing as pretentious, his status as undeserved. It is these reactions to Andolosia that lead to tragedy; Andolosia himself is the passive victim of a kidnapping. It is Theodorus who first thinks of murdering Andolosia, who organizes the plot, and who commits the murder. His immediate motive is revenge for his defeat at the tournament. Even if Andolosia's skill is to be considered an indirect cause of his death, the source of that skill should be borne in mind. The source is family tradition, not the magic purse. The author signals the importance of the legacy of Andolosia's forbearers by using the name "Theodorus" for both the murderous count and Andolosia's grandfather. The family boasted a tradition of knightly prowess long before the purse came into its possession. Its dedication to chivalric practices and its non-aristocratic status are presented as conditions of life over which the family has no control and to which financial position is not related. Theodorus and his grandson suffer because they are in tension with the estate system. They are noble by any measure of worth — but not by birth. The friction that their presence creates within society ultimately destroys them. Fortunatus escapes their fate by rejecting the tournament as his reason for being. He comes to live for his family and his travels. That split focus would have been viewed by the aristocracy as appropriate to a wealthy townsman.

The chapbook demonstrates to real-world townsmen that wealth can lead to happiness if stratification conventions are observed. The temptation to affect an aristocratic life-style is ever present and dangerous. It is also foolish given the highly unflattering picture of the nobility presented in the text. When Counts Theodorus and Lymosy first confer, the latter reports that their hatred of Andolosia is shared by other envious Cypriot nobles (183). The reader is left with the suspicion that the actions of the two men are condoned by their peers. Apparently, the author was not concerned that that reader might himself be a nobleman; the target audience was composed of townsmen. They were to become persuaded that the use of wealth to maintain a level of representation customary in the nobility would lead to disaster. The message would have found resonance in Augsburg, the residence of the publisher and putative author. Augsburg was also home to Jakob Fugger (1459-1525), whose penchant for displaying his legendary wealth in the style of a prince is documented before the appearance of the chapbook in 1509.[24] Literary scholarship has appreciated the similarities between Fortunatus and figures such as the Fuggers and the Welsers, whose holdings enabled them to indulge in an ostentatious consumption of goods and services previously the exclusive preserve of the aristocracy.[25] While the chapbook goes so far as to show the possession of wealth to be desirable, it also emphasizes the perils of rivalry with the aristocracy.

Upon first consideration, the concluding paragraph with its chilling reference to "trouble and bitter gall" seems to reject wealth and to champion wisdom. The penultimate sentence distills that conclusion from the tale and offers it as advice to the reader. But even that sentence undercuts the traditional evaluation of the relative significance of wealth and wisdom. In the example of Solomon, wealth is presented as a necessary corollary to wisdom. His temporal power and property prove that Solomon chose correctly when he chose wisdom. Neither here nor elsewhere in the concluding paragraph is the reader provided with reasons for choosing wisdom that concern divine favor, the esteem of peers, or perduring personal satisfaction. Instead, only two reasons are advanced: wisdom is a "treasure" that cannot be stolen, and wisdom leads to "worldly goods, honestly earned sustenance, and many possessions." Of all of the motivations the chapbook might have offered for the selection of wisdom, motivations that would have confirmed the high regard for wisdom brought to a reading of *Fortunatus* by a member of the contemporary audience for literature, only permanence of possession is cited. But the reader has seen how a prudent Fortunatus is able to enjoy the benefits of the purse from late adolescence through sixty years of great activity and continual human contact to a peaceful death. The character has had enough native intelligence and has been able to develop enough wisdom to ensure permanence of possession.

---

[24] Olaf Mörke, "Die Fugger im 16. Jahrhundert: Städtische Elite oder Sonderstruktur? Ein Diskussionsbeitrag," *Archiv für Reformationsgeschichte* 74 (1983): 146-48.

[25] Concerning the profits and life-styles of the great merchant families of the time, see August Kluckhohn, "Zur Geschichte der Handelsgesellschaften und Monopole im Zeitalter der Reformation," in *Historische Aufsätze dem Andenken an Georg Waitz gewidmet* (Hannover: Hahn, 1886), esp. 669-73. See also Renate Wiemann, *Die Erzählstruktur im Volksbuch Fortunatus* (Hildesheim and New York: Olms, 1970), 241-44; Scheuer, 100-3; Raitz, 93-114.

The repudiation of Fortunatus's choice in the concluding paragraph is perfunctory and unconvincing. Its presence there and in the "Preface" suggests authorial concern that the materialism of the tale may either render publication difficult or, in the event of publication, invoke censure or proscription by the church or by local governments. An agent of such authority could be expected to focus on the beginning and the conclusion of a work under consideration for approval. The author has provided such an agent with a basis for acquiescing to the dissemination of an unaltered *Fortunatus*. Again, the presence of such thinking demonstrates the appropriateness — the etymological appropriateness — of the term "chapbook" and the logic behind the proposed resuscitation of its German cognate, "Kaufbuch."

But if considered in context, the concluding paragraph offers a concise formulation of the truth that the narrative exemplifies: wealth can purchase wisdom, which in turn can guard wealth. Together they can deliver happiness on earth and good works that will receive divine consideration on the day of judgment. Fortunatus's annual bequest in honor of the Maiden of Fortune and his foundation and ongoing support of the largest church in Famagusta bespeak a commitment to the faith. Neither Fortunatus nor his sons evince any lack of respect for Christianity or for the church. As in *Dil Ulenspiegel*, religiosity in general and the tenets of Christianity in particular are not significant themes in *Fortunatus*.

Reineke Fuchs and King Nobel still must reckon with the traditional medieval injunction against the accumulation of wealth and property. Secular authority must mediate between the inertia behind a centuries-old, feudal ethos and the rising pressure generated by an expanding social stratum that evaluates itself in temporal terms.[26] Reineke can pursue worldly goals as long as he conceals his intentions behind a traditional facade. In stark contrast, Till and the young Fortunatus concern themselves only with physical survival and with personal fulfillment. Fortunatus is no less interested in knightly activities and world travels before he has money than he is after receiving the magic purse. Till's devotion to pranks extends literally from cradle to grave. While no reader will emulate either hero, neither Till nor Fortunatus is presented as a negative example. The scant authorial criticism present is pro forma only. On the eve of the Reformation, the dominant position in human affairs occupied by wealth could be presented without apology. While brief introductions and conclusions still pay tactical homage to an idealism so faded as to be transparent, the tales of

---

[26] Raitz argues that *Fortunatus* exemplifies the equation established by the urban bourgeoisie between money and human existence itself: Raitz, 69-77.

Till and Fortunatus offer no clear metaphysical option to an audience that sees in life more pleasure than pain and that recognizes wealth as a natural guarantor of happiness.

Chapter 5

Martin Luther and the Ideal of the Christian Merchant

MARTIN LUTHER VIEWED WEALTH as a standing invitation to temptation. The intensity of the reformer's preoccupation with money and money-making as pernicious aspects of German life is evident in the fact that he took up the subject repeatedly during the hectic years bounded by the posting of the ninety-five theses and the trauma of the Peasants' War. The first extended examination of the relationship between Christian faith and contemporary materialism was entitled "Eyn Sermon von dem Wucher" ("A Sermon on Usury") when it was published late in 1519. A greatly expanded version appeared the following year under the same title. For the sake of clarity, the definitive Weimar edition of Luther's works styles the earlier, six-page effort the "(Kleiner) Sermon von dem Wucher" ("Short Sermon on Usury"), whereas the "(Großer) Sermon von dem Wucher" ("Long Sermon on Usury") refers to the twenty-four page version that Luther completed as early as December 1519.[1] To judge from the number of editions that appeared during the early years, the position of the new heresy on property and profit was well advertised. Three imprints of the "Short Sermon" have survived from 1519-21; the "Long Sermon" had gone through eleven editions by 1523.[2] The campaign against many of the commercial and financial practices of the day was extended to the famous *An den christlichen Adel deutscher Nation von des christlichen Standes Besserung* (1520) (*To the Christian Nobility of the German Nation Concerning the Reform of the Christian Estate*), in which Luther refers to the practice known as the "Zinskauf" ("the purchase of rent") as "das grossist ungluck deutscher Nation" ("the greatest misfortune of the German nation").[3] In 1524 the twelfth edition of the "Long Sermon" appeared, this time as the second half

---

[1] For a dating of the texts, see *Martin Luthers Werke: Kritische Gesammtausgabe*, Weimar edition (Weimar: Böhlau, 1888), 1.6:1-2, 33-35.

[2] *Luthers Werke* 1.6:1-2, 33-35.

[3] *Luthers Werke* 1.6:466. Subsequent references to the text will be indicated within parentheses. *Luther's Works*, ed. Helmut T. Lehmann, *To the Christian Nobility of the German Nation Concerning the Reform of the Christian Estate*, trans. Charles M. Jacobs (Philadelphia: Fortress, 1966), 44:213.

of a treatise with the title "Von Kaufshandlung und Wucher" ("Trade and Usury"). It is the first work to which scholars turn when they wish to discuss Luther's thinking in matters of both micro- and macroeconomics.[4] In the course of staking out his positions, Luther also makes known his response to the activity of Jews in trade and finance.[5] The consensus of opinion holds 1) that Luther had no clear understanding of the economic laws of his time, 2) that he was all the more out of his element in such matters because the Bible offers little guidance in what now would be termed "business ethics," and 3) that he did not later alter or expand the views contained in these early writings.[6]

Only the treatise of 1524 analyzes commercial practices extensively. What remained a relatively brief foray into the realm of economics was mounted in response to what Luther perceived to be the depredations of the "Zinskauf," a late medieval practice crucial to the circulation of money, to the granting of credit, and to the establishing of investments. That is to say, Luther's anger originally was directed against finance, not commerce. The "Zinskauf" was a later form of a practice known to the High Middle Ages as the "Rentenkauf" ("the purchase of rent"), a contract between a landowner and his tenant.[7] The tenant was obligated to return a portion of the fruits of his labor to the landowner in return for the use of the land. In the terminology of the day, the "rent" was "bought" by the landlord. In time, types of property other than land came to be acceptable forms of security for the transaction, and the "rent" changed in form from crops and livestock to money. By the Late Middle Ages, the term "Zins" was replacing "Rente." This cognate of "census" was used because the Latin noun had referred to a periodic tribute levied by Rome on the provinces. "Zins" referred to a

---

[4] Scholarship has paid surprisingly little attention to Luther's writings on economics. See Roy Pascal, *The Social Basis of the Reformation: Martin Luther and His Times* (1933: New York: Kelley, 1971), 180-93; Richard Friedenthal, *Luther* (London: Weidenfeld and Nicolson, 1970), 378-79; Bernhard Lohse, *Martin Luther: Eine Einführung in sein Leben und sein Werk* (Munich: Beck, 1981), 139. The traditional emphasis on church history and dogma doubtless has contributed to an inattention to what is a set of admittedly rudimentary, imprecise, and even contradictory views on commerce and finance. For a history of Reformation research through the mid-1960s, see Bernd Moeller, "Probleme der Reformationsgeschichtsforschung," *Zeitschrift für Kirchengeschichte* 14 (1965): 246-57.

[5] Compare Walther Bienert, *Martin Luther und die Juden: Ein Quellenbuch mit zeitgenössischen Illustrationen, mit Einführungen und Erläuterungen* (Frankfurt am Main: Evangelisches Verlagswerk, 1982), 51-55, 86-87.

[6] In addition to the works already cited, see Walther I. Brandt, "Introduction," to "Trade and Usury 1524," trans. Charles M. Jacobs and Walther I. Brandt, in *Luther's Works* (Philadelphia: Muhlenberg, 1962), 45:233-39. See also Pascal, 190.

[7] Brandt, 235-37. The rendering of both "Zinskauf" and "Rentenkauf" as "purchase of rent" is intentional. See the discussion that follows.

periodic tribute levied by Rome on the provinces. "Zins" referred to a payment of money, not goods. But contemporary understanding of the transaction remained essentially the same under the new term. Accordingly, the creditor was regarded as the "buyer" of a regular income, an income bought by extending land for another's use. The debtor was regarded as the "seller" of income derived from use of the security, whether that security was land, durable goods, or money. As a sale, the transaction was not considered a form of usury and was condoned by both church and state. As a practical matter, it was a means of establishing a financial relationship between two parties that did involve the payment of de facto interest, but that did not violate the canonical proscription of the charging of interest by contract. The old feudal concept was used as an elaborate and deceptive justification for a practice as difficult to reconcile with Christian teachings as it was essential to the development of commerce and finance.

Luther's attack on the "Zinskauf" as a practice tantamount to usury is the centerpiece of the original "Short Sermon." But the sermon begins with a broader consideration of the posture to be assumed by the faithful Christian vis-à-vis earthly goods, with specific reference to giving and lending. In the first sentence of the "Short Sermon," Luther states that guidance is to be found in the New Testament, in the fifth chapter of Matthew — the first of the three that compose the Sermon on the Mount. As the first paragraph of Luther's sermon continues, he establishes Matthew 5, 40 and 42 as the New Testament basis for his analysis of contemporary financial practices. The biblical text reads:

> 38 Yhr habt gehort, das gesagt ist, Eyn aug vmb eyn aug, eynen zan vmb eynen zan. 39 Ich aber sage euch, das yhr nitt wider streben solt dem vbel, sondern so dyr yemant eyn streych gibt auff deyn rechten backen, dem biete den andernn auch dar. 40 Vnd so ymand mit dyr rechten will, vnd deynen rock nehmen, dem laß auch den mantell. 41 Vnd so dich ymant nottiget eyn meyle, so gang mit yhm zwo. 42 Gib dem der dich bittet, vnnd wende dich nit von dem, der von dyr borgen will.
>
> 43 Yhr habt gehoret das gesagt ist. Du sollt deyn nehisten lieben vnd deynen feynd hassen. 44 Ich aber sage euch, Liebet ewere feynde, benedeyt die euch maledeyen, thut wol den die euch hassen, bittet fur die, so euch beleyden vnnd verfolgen, 45 auff das yhr kynder seyd ewers vatters yhm hymel, Denn er lest seyn Sonne auff gehen vbir die bosen vnd vbir die gutten, vnd lest regnen vbir gerechten vnd vngerechten.[8]

---

[8] *Luthers Werke* 3.6:30. 1522 version.

> 38 Ye have heard that it hath been said, An eye for an eye, and a tooth for a tooth:
>
> 39 But I say unto you, That ye resist not evil: but whosoever shall smite thee on thy right cheek, turn to him the other also.
>
> 40 And if any man will sue thee at law, and take away thy coat, let him have thy cloak also.
>
> 41 And whosoever shall compel thee to go a mile, go with him twain.
>
> 42 Give to him that asketh thee, and from him that would borrow of thee turn not thou away.
>
> 43 Ye have heard that it hath been said, Thou shalt love thy neighbour, and hate thine enemy.
>
> 44 But I say unto you, Love your enemies, bless them that curse you, do good to them that hate you, and pray for them which despitefully use you, and persecute you;
>
> 45 That ye may be the children of your Father which is in heaven: for he maketh his sun to rise on the evil and on the good, and sendeth rain on the just and on the unjust.[9]

Luther asserts that Christ establishes a hierarchy of financial transactions in the passage; the reformer's sermon begins with these words:

> Zum ersten, Ist zu wissen, das unßer herr Ihesus Christus Matt. am funfften, da er seyn volck leret, wie sie sich solten halten gegen ander yn den zeytlichen gutern, zu geben und zu leyhen, setzt er drey unterschiedliche grad.[10]

> First. It should be known that in Matthew 5 our Lord Jesus Christ sets forth three different degrees of giving and lending when he teaches his followers how they should deal with one another in the matter of temporal goods.[11]

---

[9] The Holy Bible, King James Version (Cleveland and New York: World, n.d.). Subsequent English citations are from this version.

[10] *Luthers Werke* 1.6:3. Subsequent references to the text will be indicated within parentheses.

[11] My translation, as are those subsequent translations from the "Short Sermon" that lack documentation. In vocabulary and style I have tried to emulate the translation of *Trade and Usury* by Charles M. Jacobs in *Luther's Works*, ed. Helmut T. Lehmann (Philadelphia: Muhlenberg, 1962), 45:245-310. When passages in the "Short Sermon" and *Trade and Usury* are identical, I offer Jacobs's translation.

This is one of just two quotations of Christ's words in the sermon, and those words contain no specific injunction against the charging of interest. In fact, the message of the Gospel passage concerns not the giving and lending of earthly goods but the response to actions — commonplace as well as extraordinary — taken against an individual by his fellow man. Followers of Christ are to bear in mind the world to come and the certain perdition that awaits the one who takes the eye of another. They are to pray for fellow creatures whose actions seal their own fate. Verses 38 through 42 offer examples of such actions, actions that successively diminish in repulsiveness. Verse 41 cites an event of no great inconvenience, while 42 refers to two common occurrences, begging and borrowing. The first involves little discomfort for the person approached, the second potentially none at all. Luther uses some of the elements but changes the intent of the anticlimax. He has Christ giving specific precepts concerning earthly possessions, whereas the text offers one general principle to structure one's contacts with one's errant fellow man. Luther's presentation of the three degrees of giving reads as follows:

Der erst ist, Szo yemant unß ettwas mit gewalt nimpt, solln wirs nit allein faren lassen, sondern auch bereyt sein, szo er mehr nemen wolt, dasselb auch zulassen, Und spricht alßo "wer mit dir hadernn will am gericht, das er dir den rock nehme, szo las yhm auch den mantel", das ist, solt nit widderstreben noch weeren, das er den mantell nit auch nehm. Und diß ist der hochst grad yn dißem werck. Der ander ist, das man geben soll yderman, der seyn darff und begeret, davon sagt er alßo "Wer von dir bittet, dem gib". Der dritt grad ist, das man williglich und gern leyhe odder borge an allen auffsatz odder tzinße, davon sagt er "Und wer von dyr borgen odder entleyhen will, von dem kere dich nit", das ist, vorsags yhm nicht. (3)

The first is that if anyone seizes something of ours by force, we should not only relinquish it, but be ready to let him take more if he wants to. [Our Lord Jesus Christ] says of this, "Whoever would sue you in court to take your coat, let him also have your cloak." This is the highest degree in this matter. The second is that we are to give to anyone who needs our goods or asks for them. Of this He says, "Give to him who begs from you." The third degree is that we willingly and gladly lend or borrow without charge or "Zins." Of this He says, "From him who would borrow from you, turn not away"; that is, do not refuse him.

The extent to which Luther must alter the text is particularly striking in his omission of verse 41, which cannot be read as a reference to a financial transaction. The verses before and after are presented as the establishment of a hierarchy of financial relationships, and, having established his three degrees, the reformer refers to them throughout the sermon. The third and lowest degree is derived from verse 42. While there is no reference to "Zins," interest, or any sort of surcharge in the verse, the elaboration is reasonable and the scriptural basis is provided for comparison. What is striking is that this formidable student of the Bible clearly was unable to find a strong, direct prohibition of either finance or its basis, moneylending, in the words of Christ. The only other significant use of Christ's teachings in the sermon is a reference to the presentation in Luke 6, 30-36 of the same portion of the Sermon on the Mount. The version in Luke is attractive to Luther because it uses the word "leihen" ("lend") more frequently, although in the sense "to return only that which has been borrowed." But Luke is ultimately less useful because there the focus of Christ's words, the nature of interpersonal relationships, is even clearer than is the case in Matthew.

Having delineated three types of financial relationships into which Christians may enter, Luther compares this hierarchy with the reality of the day and finds that reality sinful. The comparison would have attracted the attention of a contemporary reader, even a reader inured to formulaic condemnations of pervasive moral torpor, if only because of Luther's repeated references to his society's favorite whipping boy, the Jew. "Dißer dritte letzte grad ist der geringste, auch szo geringe, das er ym alten Testament gepoten ist dem schlechten unvolkommen volck der Juden, ja auch der ander grad ..." (3) ("This third and final degree is the lowest of all, so low that it is even required in the Old Testament of that evil, wretched people, the Jews — as the second degree is too ..."). Luther's commentary on the responses, both received and anticipated, of his fellow Germans to such severe restrictions on financial activity is informed by anti-Semitism. Here, at the beginning of the argument, the strategy is to shame Christians into adherence to an ethics at least as stringent as that of the old Hebrews. On the strength of the injunction against begging in Deuteronomy 15, 4, he adjures his co-religionists, "... billich [solt] keyn bettley unter den Christen seyn, vill weniger dan unter den Juden" (4) ("... by rights there should be no begging among Christians, much less than among Jews").

The attack on begging prepares the way for his treatment of what Luther takes to be the generally accepted practice of lending on time. The nature of the article made available by the lender is immaterial; it is the concept of interest that provokes the reformer:

Nu sehen zu, wü die bleyben, die weyn, korn, gelt und was deß ist yhrm nehsten alßo leyhen, das sie ubir das jar auß die selben zu zinßen vorpflichten odder besweren und ubir laden, das sie mehr adder eyn anders, das besser ist, widder geben müssen, dan sie geborget haben: das seyn Juddische stucklein unnd tucklein, und ist eyn unchristenlich furnehmen widder das heylig Evangelium Christi, ja widder das naturlich gesetz und recht, das der her antzeygt Luce 6. das do sagt: Was du wilt, das dir die menschen thun und lassen sollen, das thu und las du auch yhnen. (5)

Now consider where they are to be found who lend their neighbor wine, grain, money, or whatever it may be on such terms that they obligate him to pay "Zins" on it after a year; or burden or overload him with the obligation of paying back more than he has borrowed, or something else that is better than what he borrowed. These are Jewish tricks and ploys; it is an unchristian practice that goes against the holy gospel of Christ, indeed against natural law and right. The Lord points this out in Luke 6 when he says, "As you wish that men would do to you, do so to them."

The Golden Rule is then used in the sentences immediately following to demonstrate the moral bankruptcy of the charging of interest: because any person would prefer to be free of interest payments demanded by a neighbor, no person should demand such payments from a neighbor. The posture suggested is just the opposite of that supposedly manifest in the "tricks and ploys" ascribed to the Jews. The Jews oppose not only the Gospel but also the "natural law" of the Golden Rule. Those who lend money at interest are not to be excused because they are members of the clergy or because their profit goes to the church. Luther reasons that it is precisely they who should adhere scrupulously to the letter and the spirit of the ethical law against usury. "Unnd wer anderst thut, szo thut ers nit der Kirchen noch dem geystlichen gutt, sondern seynem Judischen wuchersuchtigem geytz zu besserung, er sey geleret odder ungeleret, geystlich odder weltlich" (6) ("And whoever does otherwise does so not to improve the churches or ecclesiastical property but to satisfy his Jewish usurious greed — whether he is learned or unlettered, clerical or lay").

These lines contain an old equation that writers during the several decades before Luther's emergence had allowed to fade: interest equals usury equals the sin of avarice equals de facto renunciation of Christianity and acceptance of tenets widely ascribed to the pariah faith. He who charges interest is at heart a Jew. Even in the *Narrenschiff*, the strong anti-Semitism and the use of that bigotry to scourge the Christian merchant or financier would have been out of place. If this animus had become an integral part of the program of reform, and if the secular authority that came to support Luther had affirmed it, the effect on the then blossoming German economy would have been chilling. But in the "Long Sermon," the sentence immediately above has been altered, and it is apparent that Luther has allowed practical considerations to moderate the means used to express his views, if not necessarily the views themselves. The revised version of the sentence reads: "Und wer anders thut, der thuts nit der kirchen noch geystlichen guttern zur pesserung, szondern seynem wucher suchtigem geytz, der sich schmuckt unter solchen guten namen"[12] ("He who does otherwise is doing so not to improve the churches or ecclesiastical property but for his own usury-loving greed, which decks itself out with such fine names").[13] A secular prince would have bridled at the original wording with its derogation of his nation's creators of profit and therefore national wealth. And a businessman sensitive to slight changes in the climate for commerce and finance might have reevaluated long-term goals in expectation of growing public hostility to his supposedly unethical, "Jewish" profession. Nevertheless, the equation drawn between standard business practices and the Jewish faith found considerable resonance within Luther's audience. Or at least, such was the evaluation shared by the printers of both the "Short Sermon" and the early editions of the "Long Sermon," for Jews featured prominently in the woodcuts used on the title-pages. For example, the woodcut for the first edition of the "Long Sermon" depicts a man against a largely blank background who is saying, "Bezal odder gib zinß Dan ich begere gewinß." ("Pay up or give me 'Zins,' for I need profit") (Fig. 3). He has a prominent nose, a full beard, and an armband inscribed with Hebrew characters. The facial expression conveys hostility; the gesture imperiousness. Luther was not consulted on the choice of the woodcuts that adorned his early writings; he stated only that he did not trouble himself with the selection of illustrations.[14] It was a posture from which he could disavow responsibility even as he benefitted from any increase in the circulation of the work because of an illustration that would have been appropriate for a vituperative anti-Semitic tract.

Having reminded his readers of the equation linking finance and profit with Judaism, Luther passes on to an admission that worldly goods can be acquired without sin, if such goods are purchased, awarded, or inherited.

---

[12] *Luthers Werke* 1.6:50. Subsequent references to the text will be indicated within parentheses.

[13] *Luther's Works*, ed. Helmut T. Lehmann, *Trade and Usury*, trans. Charles M. Jacobs (Philadelphia: Muhlenberg, 1962), 45:294.

[14] See Bienert, 52.

Fig. 3. Woodcut from the "Long Sermon on Usury" of Martin Luther
(from Walther Bienert, *Martin Luther und die Juden:
Ein Quellenbuch mit zeitgenössischen Illustrationen,
mit Einführungen und Erläuterungen*, 1982)

They are then free of both virtue and vice. These three permissible means of obtaining property are not to be confused with the three that the reformer educes from Matthew 5, 40 and 42. Luther presents the "Zinskauf" as a highly compromised form of the otherwise ethically neutral act of purchasing. He accepts the concept of "Zinskauf" as outlined above with the observation that circumstance can militate against the lending and giving he finds described in Matthew. Because the practice circumvents canon law, he is unable to cite ecclesiastical authority as the springboard for a general attack. Therefore, he challenges not the concept, but its abuse:

> Wan nu das geschicht an ubirtretung des geystlichen gesetzs, das man auffs hundert 4, 5, 6 gulden gibt, lest sichs tragen, doch soll altzeyt die gottis forcht sorgfeltig seyn, das sie mehr furchte, sie nehm zuvil, dan zu wenig, das der geytz nit neben der sicherheit des tzimlichen kauffs eynreysse, yhe weniger auffs hundert, yhe gottlicher und Christenlicher der kauff ist. (6)

> If this can be done without violating canon law, which provides for the payment of four, five, or six gulden on the hundred, it may be tolerated. But they should always have the fear of God in mind, and be afraid of taking too much rather than too little, so that greed may not become a factor in addition to the security of a reasonable purchase contract. The smaller the percentage the more godly and Christian the contract.[15]

The "purchase" of rents may proceed as long as participants bear in mind the constant temptation to raise interest rates. The "the ... the" construction is offered as an epigrammatic aid in resisting. In the paragraphs that follow, Luther notes that the six percent limit has been crossed all too often.

> Da solten die gewaltigen eyn sehen. Hie wirt das arm gemeyn volck heymlich auß gesogen und schwerlich unter drugckt. Drumb geschicht auch, das solch reuber und wucherer, wie die tyrannen und reuber wirdig seyn, villmals unnatürlich sterben und des gehende tods vorfallen, odder sonst schrecklich umbkommen. (6-7)

> The rulers ought to look into this. Here the poor common folk are secretly fleeced and severely oppressed. This is also why these robbers

---

[15] This passage is virtually identical to one in the "Long Sermon"; the translation is in *Luther's Works* 45:305.

and usurers often die an unnatural and sudden death, or come to some terrible end, as tyrants and robbers deserve.[16]

The reformer is urging governmental regulation of financial transactions. The control suggested would be exercised for the protection of an oppressed social group, "the poor common folk."[17] By citing that group, Luther was guaranteeing closer attention from secular rulers for his proposal that interest levels be controlled. The "Armer Heinrich" ("Poor Henry") and "Bundschuh" ("Bond of the Shoe") uprisings had provided evidence of the peasantry's willingness to meet exploitation with armed force.[18] Once aroused, the "common man" was not easily controlled: his righteous anger could turn as easily against "tyrants" as against "usurers." The self-interest of a prince was best served by moving against the excessive practices of the few in order to reduce the sense of victimization among the many. In protecting the needy from usury, the prince would also be following divine example. The last passage cited is followed by the observation: "Dan gott ist eyn richter fur die armen und durfftigen, als er vill mall ym alten gesetz sagt" (7) ("For God is a judge for the poor and needy, as he says frequently in the Old Law").[19] The prince who functions as God's representative will not have cause to fear his subjects. Luther is not just open to the idea of the regulation of potential sin by the state; he actually goads princes into accepting the responsibility even as he creates an opportunity to display his solicitousness by pointing out a source of unrest.

No such solicitousness is apparent as Luther's analysis of the "Zinskauf" proceeds to its use by the clergy and by those laymen who seek the blessing of the church. He who has implicated the faith in the sin of greed is found to be particularly dangerous: "Furwar, hatt man keyn andere sach den Wucher zu rechtfertigen, szo ist er nie ubeler geschulten, dan er will yhe die unschuldig Kirche unnd geystlickeit mit yhm zum teuffell furen und yn die sund tzihen" (7) ("If this is the best thing that can be cited in justification of usuary, it is also true that nothing worse could ever be said of it. For it is an

---

[16] *Luther's Works* 45:305-6.

[17] Concerning the expressions "der gemeine Mann" and "das gemeine Volk" at this time, see Paul Böckmann, "Der gemeine Mann in den Flugschriften der Reformation," in his *Formensprache: Studien zur Literaturästhetik und Dichtungsinterpretation* (Hamburg: Hoffman und Campe, 1966); Baeumer, "Aspekte," 16-17; John W. Van Cleve, "Converting the Common Man: German Dialogues of the Early Reformation," *Colloquia Germanica* 13, no. 2 (1980): 97-105; H.-G. Kemper, 210-45.

[18] For a brief survey, see Will Durant, *The Reformation: A History of European Civilization from Wyclif to Calvin: 1300-1564* (New York: Simon and Schuster, 1957), 293-94.

[19] *Luther's Works* 45:306.

effort to bracket the innocent church and clergy in sin with usury, and drag them down to the devil").[20] Luther finds that the blandishments of wealth have influenced not only individuals but also groups within the clergy. That much is clear from the following:

> Und, wie ich droben gesagt, wen alle welt tzehen auffs hundert nehme, szo solten doch die geystlichen stifte das gestrengist recht halten und mit furchten vier odder funff nehmen, Dan sie sollen leuchten und gutt exempell geben den weltlichen, Szo keren sie es umb, wolten freyheit haben, gottis gepott und dienst zulassen, ubell zu thun, und Wucher zu treybenn. (7)

> As I have said above, even if everybody were to charge 10 per cent, ecclesiastical institutions should still keep strictly to the law and — with fear — take 4 or 5 per cent. For they are supposed to shine and give a good example to the worldly. But they turn things around and want to be free to ignore the commandments and service of God in order to do evil and practice usury.[21]

The passage indicates an awareness of cases in which debtors of the church have been charged as much as ten percent. While Luther encourages secular authority to participate more actively in finance as a regulatory agent, he cautions the church and those connected to it against money-making as an invitation to avarice. He does not extrapolate conclusions from the experience of the church in finance that might raise doubts concerning the prospects for the state in regulation. If the possibility of graft occurred to him, he chose not to mention it. Luther was willing to trust the state, in part because he believed that he could manipulate it. A prince can be made to believe that usury is dangerous to his throne.

Luther concludes the "Short Sermon" with three paragraphs that analyze 1) the ticklish moral position of the "buyer" in a "Zinskauf" transaction, 2) the nature of that transaction, and 3) the relationship between the "Zinskauf" and usury. The "Long Sermon" concludes after the first of these, which is the least judgmental. The "buyer" does not work for his profits; he becomes rich through the labor of others while he himself easily can become lazy.

> Ist das nit wucher, szo ist er yhm fast ehnlich. Kurtzlich, es ist widder gott, Dan wo du forteyl an deynem nehsten suchst, den du nit auch

---

[20] *Luther's Works* 45:306.

[21] *Luther's Works* 45:306.

> woltest an dir yhm lassen, da ist die lieb auß und naturlich gesetz zurissen. (8)

> If that is not usury, it is mighty close to it. Briefly put, it is against God. For if you seek to take an advantage of your neighbor which you would not want him to take of you, then love is gone and natural law broken.[22]

Here again is the pronouncement that any action that violates the Golden Rule also violates natural law and divine will. One means of evasion has been left open, however, if the "buyer" can demonstrate concern for the "seller." Luther goes on to express the fear that the "Zinskauf" provides an approved, legal forum for denying the needs of one's fellow man while focusing on ever higher profit levels and avoiding honest work. The transaction itself may not be tainted by exploitation, but the behavior to which it gives rise is "eyn antzeygen des geytz odder faulheit" (8) ("a sign of greed or laziness").[23] The "buyer's" intention may well be sinful.

By concluding the "Long Sermon" at this point, the reformer leaves the ethical status of the "Zinskauf" to case-by-case evaluation. The "buyer" who can prove the purity of his motives — his concern for the "seller" — does not face automatic condemnation.

The practice itself is not questioned until the second paragraph. The first sentence cuts through the terminological mystification surrounding the "Zinskauf."

> Dan das ist eines yglichen kauffs natur und art, das der kauffer mit der war soll yn der far steen, und nit der vorkeuffer, der seyner war loß worden ist. (8)

> It is the very essence of any purchase that the buyer who has received the goods is at risk, rather than the seller, who has become free of the goods.

Luther is noting that the "seller" is expected to complete the transaction even if he has suffered losses through no fault of his own. The reformer's response is that any danger inherent in the security because of unpredictability should be the sole concern of the "buyer"; specifically, any losses accruing in this fashion, for example, as the result of drought-induced crop failure, should be absorbed by the "buyer." When they are not, he is "eyn

---

[22] *Luther's Works* 45:307.

[23] *Luther's Works* 45:308.

reuber fur gott und der welt" (8) ("a robber in the eyes of God and the world"). The crux of Luther's clever argument is that no true purchase is without risk; therefore, risk for the "buyer" must be present in the "Zinskauf." He has used the terminology of deception against itself. His analysis first takes a radical turn when it exposes the linguistic artiface upon which the transaction has been based. Of course, the continued viability of the "Zinskauf" was predicated upon the tacit acquiescence of secular and ecclesiastical authority. Public discussion of the true nature of the transaction would have brought pressure to bear on government to uphold the traditional injunction against the charging of interest.

Luther does not identify the "Zinskauf" as a form of usury: had he done so, prodding would have become censure. But of the 205 lines that constitute the "Short Sermon," 92 lines or 45% of the total concern the "Zinskauf." The strategy is to imply rather than assert — to imply broadly that the "buyer" in the transaction is perilously close to the commission of usury, and therefore, close to the sin of avarice. The concluding paragraph reduces the argument to a striking anthropomorphism designed to make a lasting impression on the reader:

> Summa, Ich acht, der zinß kauff sey nit wucher, mich dunckt aber, sein art sey, das yhm leyd ist, das er nit muß ein wucher sein, es gepricht am willen nit, und muß leyder frum seyn. (8)

> In conclusion, I am of the opinion that "Zinskauf" is not usury; but that it seems to me that because of his nature he is sorry that he must not be usury — it is not for lack of intent — and unfortunately must be upright.

After stating a conclusion — to which his argument does not lead — that the transaction is not usurious, Luther offers the opinion that the "Zinskauf" is like a continually monitored reprobate, a frustrated, would-be sinner. The final statement may be that usury in the strict sense is not present, but the implication is surely that usurious intent is. And, through adroit use of imagery and the positioning of arguments, the implication eclipses the statement.

The "Long Sermon on Usury" elaborates the positions taken in the "Short Sermon." Anti-Semitic arguments have been either tempered or eliminated, but the reflex is still present (e.g., 41). On the other hand, the language aimed at the "Zinskauf" has been sharpened to a fine edge. The "buyer" has become the "zinß herr" ("lord of 'Zins'"); the "seller," the "zinß man" (51). He who has enriched himself through extensive use of the transaction is dubbed a "zinß juncker" (55) ("Junker of 'Zins'"), whose moral standing is deemed inferior to that of the merchant since the latter at least works for his livelihood and since he subjects himself to uncertainties of transport, weather, and changing governmental policies. The Junker has a life of affluent idleness. The imagery of the epithets suggests a new feudal system based on liquidity rather than land. Luther is making it easy for his readers to transfer any resentment they may harbor against the privileged parasites of the lower aristocracy to the new lords of liquidity. Given the social unrest of the times, it is a risky strategy. The man who would turn one year later "To the Christian Nobility of the German Nation" credits himself with great rhetorical ability — unless it is that he is so intent on making the strongest possible argument that he attributes his perceptions to his audience and fails to consider the diversity of the audience and the range of possible responses. Of course, the piece does advocate greater power for the ruling nobility, but a member of the lower nobility could not have been pleased at the comparison with the overfed and underworked Junkers of "Zins."

Luther's strong response to one practice, the "Zinskauf," led to a broader assessment of finance as the institution through which money, not work, creates money. That in turn led to a consideration of the other occupation that actively and openly pursued wealth — commerce. A full-blown critique of mercantile practices first appeared in 1524 as a substantial addition to the "Long Sermon." The expanded tract appeared under the title "Von Kaufshandlung und Wucher." While the reformer's sortie against "Kaufshandlung" constituted the final element of what was to remain his most extensive analysis of economic practices, Luther's hostility to merchants is already apparent in the famous *An den christlichen Adel* (1520). Just before the conclusion of that tract, Luther catalogues the sins he finds rampant in everyday life. Finance and commerce receive particular attention. Again, Luther finds true devilry in the "Zinskauf":

> Furwar es musz der zinszkauff ein figur und antzeygen sein, das die welt mit schweren sunden dem teuffel vorkaufft sey, das zugleich zeytlich und geystlich gut uns musz geprechen, noch mercken wir nichts.
> Hie must man werlich auch den Fuckern und dergleychen geselschafften ein zawm ynsz maul legen. Wie ists muglich, das solt gotlich unnd recht zugehen, das bey eynis menschen leben solt auff einen hauffenn szo grosse kuniglich gutter bracht werdenn? Ich weysz die rechnung nicht. Aber das vorstehe ich nit, wie man mit hundert gulden mag des jarisz erwerben zwentzig, ja ein guld den andern, und das allis nit ausz der erden odder von dem fihe, da das gut nit in menschlicher witz, szondern in gottis gebenedeyung stehet. (466)

In fact, the *zynskauf* must be a sign and proof that the world has been sold to the devil because of its grievous sins and that at the same time we are losing both temporal and spiritual possessions. And yet we do not even notice it.

In this connection, we must put a bit in the mouth of the Fuggers and similar companies. How is it possible in the lifetime of one man to accumulate such great possessions, worthy of a king, legally and according to God's will? I don't know. But what I really cannot understand is how a man with one hundred gulden can make a profit of twenty in one year. Nor, for that matter, can I understand how a man with one gulden can make another — and all this not from tilling the soil or raising cattle, where the increase of wealth depends not on human wit but on God's blessing.[24]

Here the widespread dislike of the Fuggers and the other large family companies boils to the surface. He offers the companies' moneylending as the basis for referring to such businesses as beasts on which one must keep tight rein. But he shares the envy felt by the less affluent when contemplating the regal life-style of the Fuggers and their peers.[25] In the text the traditional injunction against the concept of interest is justified by a comparison with agriculture and animal husbandry, activities through which man receives tangible forms of divine grace. Such property is not to be confused with property acquired in the absence of God's blessing. Luther goes on to admit that as a theologian, his understanding of such matters is certainly limited; still, he maintains that the practice is to all appearances evil. And one more thing is certain:

> Das weysz ich wol, das viel gotlicher weere acker werck mehren und kauffmanschafft myndern, und die viel besser thun, die der schrifft nach die erden erbeytten und yhr narung drausz suchen, wie zu uns und allen gesagt ist in Adam "vormaledeyet sey die erde, wen du drynnenn erbeytist, sie sol dir distel unnd dornen tragen, und in dem schweysz deynis angesichts soltu essenn dein brot". Es ist noch viel lanndt, das nit umbtrieben und geehret ist. (466-67)

I know full well that it would be a far more godly thing to increase agriculture and decrease commerce. I also know that those who work on the land and seek their livelihood from it according to the Scriptures do far better. All this was said to us and to everybody else

---

[24] *Luther's Works* 44:213-14.

[25] Mörke, 141-62.

in the story of Adam, "Cursed be the ground when you work it; it shall bear you thistles and thorns, and in the sweat of your face you shall eat your bread." There is still a lot of land lying unworked and neglected.[26]

From the paragraph emerges a bucolic vision of a simple, self-sufficient, rural society of farmers and herdsmen who have little use for money and the luxuries it procures. The closing reference to the ready availability of land for purposes sanctioned in Genesis indicates a genuine belief that the vision can become reality. Of course, in light of the rapid centralization of population, commerce, and finance just before and during Luther's lifetime, this belief is hopelessly romantic. It attests to the extent of Luther's naivete in matters of economic policy: the charge to Adam cannot be carried out in an increasingly urban society. The realm of "Fuggers and similar companies" requires governmental regulation because it is not the same realm apportioned to man after the original fall from grace. Luther's advice to the prince is therefore to act in God's stead. But the individual is better advised to place himself under the Creator's direct guidance in an environment far from the treacherous financial practices and consumer-mentality of the city.

That not all of his contemporaries shared Luther's view that life in the country remained innocent is apparent in the presentation of rural people offered in *Dil Ulenspiegel*. The same materialistic goals are pursued by isolated peasants and by urban artisans. In the absence of an alternative ethos such as Luther's, the reader was left to accept a status quo tolerable in large measure because it encompasses ironic deflation in the person of the rogue type, who acts as a release mechanism for the pressure that periodically develops in a society in stasis. Luther has no need of a Till. The case for reform is stronger if the extent of reform is, or at least seems to be, smaller. By attributing avaricious practices to city-dwellers, Luther limits his critique and asserts the existence of an alternative that the reader will recognize immediately. The older way of life is supposedly the better way of life; the reformer urges a return to the country and subsistence farming, to hard physical labor and the biblical prescription for human life.

"Von Kaufshandlung und Wucher" begins with a categorical rejection of worldly things supported by reference to St. Paul (Romans 13, 12) Luther asserts that this teaching is so clear that even some merchants have understood it and have recognized deceit in the common practices of their profession. The argument in the first paragraph of the treatise is structured so as to introduce a powerful indictment of the profession based on biblical authority. But the most condemnatory comment that Luther can cite is the

---

[26] *Luther's Works* 44:214.

observation in Ecclesiasticus that it is difficult for merchants to avoid sin (Ecclesiasticus 26, 28). He attempts to lead the reader quickly past that ambivalent statement:

> ... zu besorgen ist, es gehe hie zu wie der Ecclesiasticus sagt, Das kauffleut schwerlich on sunde seyn mügen: Ja ich acht, es treffe sie der spruch S. Pauli 1, Timo. ult. "Der geytz ist eyne wurtzel alles ubels ..."[27]

> It is to be feared that the words of Ecclesiasticus apply here, namely, that merchants can hardly be without sin. Indeed, I think St. Paul's saying in the last chapter of the first epistle to Timothy fits the case, "The love of money is the root of all evils ..."[28]

He then adds the immediately preceding verse (1 Timothy 6, 9) with its warning that those who strive to be wealthy fall into the devil's clutches. As a group, the three allusions may well seem to constitute scriptural rejection of commerce as tantamount to sin and damnation. But the profession actually is mentioned by name only in Ecclesiasticus — that is, in a book of the same Apocrypha that Luther was to present in 1536 as not the equal of the canon.[29] In the first paragraph, then, Luther uses his rhetorical ability and adjusts his attitudes concerning the canon in order to cast commerce in a bad light at the beginning of his analysis of the profession. Simple pragmatism dictated the strategy in view of Luther's belief that commerce is necessary and that it has been and still can be practiced honorably. He saves these concessions for the third paragraph:

> Das kan man aber nicht leucken, das keuffen und verkeuffen eyn nottig ding ist, des man nicht emperen und wol Christlich brauchen kan sonderlich ynn den dingen, die zur nott und ehren dienen. Denn also haben auch die Patriarchen verkaufft und gekaufft vieh, wolle,

---

[27] *Luthers Werke* 1.15:293. Subsequent references to the text will be indicated within parentheses.

[28] *Luther's Works* 45:245.

[29] Martin Luther, "Vorrede auff die Propheten," in *Die Propheten alle Deudsch* (Wittenberg: Hans Lufft, 1636), ii. Luther creates a straw man, the arrogant "Meister Klügel," who has memorized the Bible and who views the Apocrypha as "eitel faul todt gewesche." Luther's long defense asserts repeatedly that Christians "sollen ... die Propheten mit ernst und nutz lesen und gebrauchen." Inescapable is the inference that many Lutherans viewed the noncanonical writings with suspicion and that an argument based on the Apocrypha would have been far weaker than one based on the Bible.

getreyde, butter, milch und ander gueter. Es sind Gotts gaben, die er aus der erden gibt und unter die menschen teylet. (293)

It cannot be denied that buying and selling are necessary. They cannot be dispensed with, and can be practiced in a Christian manner, especially when the commodities serve a necessary and honorable purpose. For even the patriarchs bought and sold cattle, wool, grain, butter, milk, and other goods in this way. These are gifts of God, which he bestows out of the earth and distributes among mankind.[30]

Of course, the mercantile activity ascribed to the patriarchs cannot be reconciled with the vision of bucolic self-sufficiency in *An den christlichen Adel*. The reformer has come to realize that his monkish attitudes concerning the necessities of life will not be shared by his readers, even as they were not held by the ancient Israelites. Because merchants provide what long tradition has considered essential, their presence must be accepted; but the scope of their activity should be limited.

Luther's proposed limits are primarily microeconomic: the mores of individual traders and companies are subjected to intense criticism. Pricing policies concerned Luther greatly. But he does venture several macroeconomic observations immediately after the grudging recognition that trade has a legitimate, traditional function in society:

Aber der auslendische kauffs handel, der aus Kalikut und Indien und der gleychen wahr her bringt, alls solch kostlich seyden und golltwerck und wurtze, die nur zur pracht und keynem nutz dienet und land und leutten das gellt aus seuget, sollt nicht zu gelassen werden, wo wyr eyn regiment und fursten hetten. (293-94)

But foreign trade, which brings from Calcutta and India and such places wares like costly silks, articles of gold, spices — which minister only to ostentation but serve no useful purpose, and which drain away the money of land and people — would not be permitted if we had proper government and princes.[31]

The suggestion is completely impractical. Is it directed only against transoceanic trade? Transcontinental trade? When does a trade route become unacceptably long? And what items are to be excluded? Of those cited,

---

[30] *Luther's Works* 45:246.

[31] *Luther's Works* 45:246.

jewelry and silk met the nobility's need to demonstrate its status; the market in such goods was permanent. Spices were used to preserve foods as well as to enhance flavor; still, Luther finds it easy to begin a list of unnecessary luxury goods. The statement can be read as an indictment of all foreign trade, a reading supported by the expression of concern about the flow of capital out of the country. But unlike Sebastian Brant, Luther is concerned about the effect of a practice on the individual and the nation rather than about its financial soundness. He expresses the fear that foreign trade eventually will reduce the Germans to a race of paupers:

> Gott hatt uns deutschen dahyn geschlaudert, das wyr unser gollt und sylber mussen ynn frembde lender stossen, alle wellt reych machen und selbst bettler bleyben. Engeland sollt wol weniger gollts haben, wenn deutsch land yhm seyn tuch liesse, und der könig von Portigal sollt auch weniger haben, wenn wyr yhm seyne wurtze liessen. Rechen du, wie viel gellts eyne Messe zu Franckfurt aus deutschem land gefurt wird on nott und ursache, so wirstu dich wundern, wie es zu gehe, das noch eyn heller ynn deutschen landen sey. (294)

> God has cast us Germans off to such extent that we have to fling our gold and silver into foreign lands and make the whole world rich, while we ourselves remain beggars. England would have less gold if Germany let her keep her cloth; the king of Portugal would have less if we let him keep his spices. Count up how much cash is taken out of Germany, without need or reason, from a single Frankfurt fair, and you will wonder how it happens that there is still a heller left in German hands.[32]

Reference to trade with England in cloth woven from raw materials produced on the continent suggests that Luther is in fact thinking of all trade across the borders of Germany. Frankfurt and its fair constitute a symbol of such pernicious commerce. It is there that German financiers and merchants conspire against their countrymen:

> Franckfurt ist das sylber und gollt loch, da durch aus deutschem land fluesst, was nur guillet und wechst, gemuntzt odder geschlagen wird bey uns. Were das loch zugestopfft, so durfft man itzt der klage nicht horen, wie allenthalben eytel schuld und keyn gellt, alle land und stedte mit zinsen beschweret und ausgewuchert sind. (294)

[32] *Luther's Works* 45:246-47.

Frankfurt is the gold and silver drain through which everything that springs and grows — or is minted or coined — here, flows out of Germany. If that hole were stopped up we should not now have to listen to the complaint that there are debts everywhere and no money, that all lands and cities are burdened with *zinss* payments and milked dry by usury.[33]

The image is that of a gaping hole in a wall built to protect Germans from a hostile outside world. The concern about the departure of liquidity ("everything minted or coined") would be appreciated by protectionist economists of the present day. His opposition to the export of raw materials ("everything that springs and grows") resonates with the simple tenet that a nation is best advised to import raw materials, employ its population in manufacturing, and then export finished goods. But defensible as such observations may have been, the idea that the elimination of the Frankfurt nexus somehow would eliminate foreign commerce and finance, or more generally, that the elimination of all involvement in foreign business would be salutary — the idea was so impractical that Luther may have realized that he was in danger of appearing ridiculous. He closes this line of reasoning abruptly and with forced jocoseness: "Aber las gehen, es wil doch also gehen, Wyr deutschen mussen deutschen bleiben, wyr lassen nicht ab, wyr mussen denn" (294) ("But let that pass; it will go that way anyhow. We Germans must always be Germans; we never stop until we have to").[34] Nevertheless, it is clear that he feels the same animus against foreign trade that is so strongly expressed in the earlier sermons against the practice mentioned here again — the "Zinskauf."

The great bulk of Luther's analysis of trade concerns professional mores and matters of conscience. He charges that one universally accepted rule-of-thumb is tantamount to avarice:

> Erstlich haben die kauffleut unter sich ein gemeyne regel, das ist yhr heubtspruch und grund aller fynantzen, da sie sagen "Ich mag meyne wahr so thewr geben alls ich kan." Das hallten sie fur eyn recht, da ist dem geytz der raum gemacht und der hellen thur und fenster alle auffgethan. Was ist das anders gesagt denn so viel: Ich frage nichts nach meynem nehisten?" (294)

> First. Among themselves the merchants have a common rule which is their chief maxim and the basis of all their sharp practices, where

---

[33] *Luther's Works* 45:247.

[34] *Luther's Works* 45:247.

they say: "I may sell my goods as dear as I can." They think this is their right. Thus occasion is given for avarice, and every window and door to hell is opened. What else does it mean but this: I care nothing about my neighbor?[35]

Time and again in the balance of the treatise, Luther returns to the incompatibility of the profit motive and love of one's neighbor. It is a perception that he cannot reconcile either with biblical precedent or with his need for simple pragmatism.

> Was sollt nu gutts ym kauffhandel seyn? was sollt on sunde seyn, wo solch unrecht das heubtstuck und regel ist des gantzen handels? Es kan damit der kauffhandel nichts anders seyn denn rawben und stelen den andern yhr gutt. (294-95)

> How can there be anything good then in trade? How can it be without sin when such injustice is the chief maxim and rule of the whole business? On such a basis trade can be nothing but robbing and stealing the property of others.[36]

Here in pure form is the underlying antipathy that leads to a litany of treacherous practices, a list that fills eight of the twenty-one pages devoted to trade. Most of the practices are assessed as manifestations of greed in individuals. Luther rails against the sale of merchandise in installments at a higher total price, against inflation induced by intentionally inadequate supply, against price reduction as a means of eliminating competition, against buying low and selling high, against price-fixing arrangements among individuals. He points to tricks such as the addition of water weight and artificial colors to foodstuffs as well as the placement of choice wares on top and the control of lighting over displays to create inaccurate positive impressions among buyers. The diatribe against these and other instances of unfeeling exploitation of the defenseless consuming public, "der gemeyn man" ("the common man") who lives from year to year on a constant income, then passes on to abuses committed by companies. They are supposedly nothing but monopolies that carry out the abuses of unscrupulous individuals on a grand scale, with impunity, and without discretion.[37]

---

[35] *Luther's Works* 45:247.

[36] *Luther's Works* 45:247-48.

[37] Wolfgang Landgraf is incorrect when he asserts that Luther sides with individual capitalists and against the large companies that hinder the development of individually owned and operated firms. Luther is in fact hard pressed to find anything positive to say

Companies are charged with an attempt to use worldly goods to create in corporate wealth a form of permanence in a world that is impermanent, transient by divine plan. They have attempted to create permanent profit:

> ... sie habens funden und troffen, das sie důrch ferliche, unsichere, zeitliche wahr sichern, gewissen und ewigen gewinst treyben. Aber daruber mus gleichwol alle wellt gantz aus gesogen werden und alles gellt ynn yhren schlauch sincken und schwemmen. (312)

> ... they have found a way to make safe, certain, and continual profit out of unsafe, uncertain, and perishable goods; though because of it all the world must be sucked dry and all the money sink and swim in their gullets.[38]

The sin charged is pride: only God can create permanence. In their attempt, the owners of trading companies are ruining the lives of their fellow creatures. Luther then varies the theme of pride by asserting that merchants use their companies to control kings and emperors by controlling the flow of goods and capital. Not only does he charge that international traders have become de facto kings, but he also finds that recognized authority often works with if not for such merchants. The inference to be drawn is that commerce is eroding social stratification. Luther is suggesting that it is time that princes reassert their primacy. He then concludes his consideration of companies with the observation that, because honor and justice cannot coexist with the companies, participation in company activity is unthinkable for anyone who wishes to keep a clear conscience.[39]

The independent entrepreneur can avoid the many temptations of his occupation if he exercises restraint when he takes profits and if he remains true to his Christianity when he practices his trade. Luther admits that each man must earn a living and that no one works without compensation. He also observes that merchants expose themselves to physical danger in their travels and to financial hazards beyond their control. Both the roads and the elements can add unexpected expense. He is willing to include risk incurred in the calculation of profit. But he would prefer that prices and therefore profit levels be set by boards appointed by the princes. What he suggests

---

about trade, let alone about merchants of the sort to which this East German biographer refers as "der aufstrebende kapitalistische Unternehmer," Landgraf, *Martin Luther: Reformator und Rebell: Biographie* (Berlin: Verlag Neues Leben, 1981), 227.

[38] *Luther's Works* 45:271.

[39] For a discussion of critics of the companies who wrote before Luther, see Kluckhohn, 668-70.

would have represented an early step toward an administrative bureaucracy of the kind that became increasingly common in the late seventeenth century. Luther would gladly assign the regulation of greed to such agencies of government. But he quickly concedes that such an arrangement is not now and will not soon become common practice. Therefore, when the individual merchant is left to his own devices, he should hold to price levels customary for his wares at the markets he frequents. Such an individual will be able to practice the requisite self-discipline if he keeps in mind the ideal of the Christian merchant.

Just before he begins to excoriate sinful commercial practices that he has seen or of which he has heard, Luther sketches the mores that would guide a paragon among merchants. The Christian merchant buys and sells either with cash or by barter; he neither accepts nor extends credit. He relies not on conditions that will exist in the future but only on God. If he wishes to lend money, he does so only to Christians. In addition, he lends no more than an amount he does not need. Finally, he does not become surety for another; instead, he makes a free gift of money. To follow these precepts is to practice the profession honorably:

> Das mocht eyn recht Christlicher kauffman seyn, den wurde Gott auch nicht lassen, weyl er yhm also feyn trawet und frölich mit seynem ferlichen nehisten wagt und handelt. (303)

> Such a man would be a true Christian merchant; God would not forsake him, because he trusts properly in Him and cheerfully takes a chance in dealing with his untrustworthy neighbors.[40]

Luther's paragon would have been unsuccessful in business because of the unwillingness to attempt to foresee future conditions, to project a future reality and then respond to that projection in the present. It goes without saying that without this keystone the edifice of commerce comes crashing down. In fact the ideal of the Christian merchant is as romantic as the suggestion that financiers renounce their profession and return to the land and to the labor ordained in Genesis. Nevertheless, the very attempt to construct an ideal that is compatible with conservative Christian beliefs forms the centerpiece of a halting and ultimately unconvincing effort to legitimate commerce, an effort based on pragmatic rather than theological considerations. A demand for the total proscription of commercial and financial activity would have been the reformer's initial, natural response to the "Zinskauf" when that practice first drew his attention to economic issues.

---

[40] *Luther's Works* 45:260.

But even in 1519, Luther was too practical to follow his instincts blindly. In his final treatment of money-making activity, the section of the tract from 1524 that concerns "Kaufshandlung," Luther indicates a desire to incorporate real-world conditions into his analysis. But he is unable to do so. He leaves the door open to commerce and finance — as he defines them. But the mores and practices proposed cannot be reconciled with the economic conditions of the day. When they looked to Luther for guidance in their responses to the pursuit of wealth, his followers were to find only ambivalence, veiled hostility, and the "Christian merchant."

Chapter 6

Hans Sachs asks, "Ist das gůt Ewangelisch?"

OF LUTHER'S FOLLOWERS, THE man of letters whose reputation has proved most resilient is Hans Sachs (1494-1576). The ambivalent response of the reformer to money-making activity finds literary reflection in one of the four prose dialogues written by Sachs in 1524, "Ein Dialogus des inhalt ein argument der Römischen wider das Christlich heüflein; den Geytz, auch ander offenlich laster etc. betreffend" ("A Dialogue Containing an Argument Used by the Romans Against the Christian Congregation Concerning Greed and Other Flagrant Sins"). Luther's ideal of the Christian merchant represents a failed attempt to reconcile his conviction that trade and finance leave man open to the blandishments of hell with his realization that those areas of activity cannot be eliminated. He makes the attempt for the sake of those who wish to be Christian despite their ethically dubious occupations. Of course, by 1524 Luther identified the true Christian as he who followed the new teachings and rejected the leadership of the Roman church. The portion of "Von Kaufshandlung und Wucher" ("Trade and Usury") that analyzes commerce was written after the Diet of Worms, after the schism became a public issue for the Empire. Hence, although Luther does not discriminate among Christians either in the original "Short Sermon" or in "Von Kaufshandlung und Wucher," his words in the latter are intended for adherents of the reformed faith. The Christian merchant is in fact the Lutheran merchant. The extent of his survey of unethical commercial practices suggests that Luther had observed such behavior among his converts. His expectation is that a merchant who calls himself a Lutheran will recognize himself in the tract and will take steps to effect change. Failure to move against manifestations of greed will invoke censure from the leadership of the faith. Luther wrote "Von Kaufshandlung und Wucher" in the summer of 1524;[1] the Sachs dialogue was published on September 29, 1524. The dialogue repeats the warning of the treatise, and the intended reader is the same, but the nature of the censure has been changed.[2] Sachs exchanges

---

[1] *Luthers Werke* 1.15:280-81.

[2] For a list of borrowings from "Von Kaufshandlung und Wucher," see Bernd Balzer, *Bürgerliche Reformationspropaganda: Die Flugschriften des Hans Sachs in den Jahren 1523-1525* (Stuttgart: Metzler, 1973), 145, 215.

critique from within for attack from without, from the enemy, from the Catholic priesthood.

By his mid-teens, Hans Sachs was serving his apprenticeship under a master shoemaker while learning the art of a Meistersinger under the tutelage of Lienhardt Nunnenbeck.[3] The youth had attended one of the Latin schools in his native Nuremberg. But the training of a medieval craftsman took precedence, and in 1511 the new journeyman set out on the sort of extended tour then considered an integral part of the education of a future master. He returned home a year before Luther posted the famous ninety-five theses, married before the end of the decade, and set himself up in business as a master shoemaker. By 1520 his literary career was also underway; in addition to the religious "Meistersang," he had tried his hand at the popular song and the sententious "Spruchgedicht" ("epigrammatic poem"), and he had experimented with the genre with which his name would become synonymous, the "Fastnachtspiel" ("shrovetide play"). But a hiatus in productivity occurred during the early 1520s when Sachs focused his intellectual energies on an extensive study of the writings of Luther and the other reformers. As of 1522 his library included some forty theological publications. The three-year silence ended with the publication of a "Spruchgedicht" that established Hans Sachs as the bard of the early Reformation, a status recognized far beyond the towers of Nuremberg. The seven hundred verses of "Die Wittenbergisch Nachtigall" (1523) ("The Nightingale of Wittenberg") attack both the practices and the defenders of the Roman church and then present a few tenets of the new faith in simplified form. The easy lyricism of the rhymed couplets contrasts with both the message and the earnestness of Sachs's spiritual commitment, creating a tension that a contemporary would have found difficult to ignore. The animal allegory was an established, popular vehicle for examining the public and private morality of society's leaders. The appearance of the Good Shepherd raises the sort of social analysis present in *Reynke de Vos* to a higher, anagogical plane. Sachs tries to guide reception not only by keeping the allegory transparent but also by incorporating explication of the text into the text.

On the heels of his success with "Die Wittenbergisch Nachtigall," Sachs reached for an established genre that allowed him to present both the positions and the problems of Lutheranism with greater clarity, that is, without the cautious literary device of allegory. In 1524 he published four prose dialogues, one of which examines the relationship between the

---

[3] A short biography with references to detailed studies can be found in Barbara Könneker, *Hans Sachs* (Stuttgart: Metzler, 1971), 1-10. See also Ingeborg Spriewald, "Der Bürger ergreift das Wort: Luther und die Reformation im Werk von Hans Sachs," *Weimarer Beiträge* 29, no. 2 (1983): 1911-13.

pursuit of wealth and both major factions of the divided faith. The dialogue was enjoying a sudden burst of popularity as Sachs worked on his contributions — fifty or more "gesprächbüchlein" appeared from 1520 to 1525.[4] The dialogue would have been particularly attractive during this period of intellectual controversy and political tension because of its structure: truth emerges from the clash of differing points of view, truth that is accepted by reasonable and therefore sympathetic dialogue-participants — and, of course, by the reader. Plato, Augustine, and Duns Scotus had used dialectical argumentation in order to make the naturally passive reader an active participant in the distillation of truth. Petrarch (in *De remediis utriusque fortunae* and *De vera sapientia*) pressed the genre into the service of Humanism, an adaptation that became tradition in the hands of Hutten and Erasmus. The admixture of pure entertainment always present in the dialogue was increased in the 1520s through the frequent appearance of a central character who either speaks for or considers himself an example of the common man. Typically, the common man is a Lutheran thoroughly versed in the scriptures who demonstrates the truth of his beliefs to a Catholic interlocutor who often enjoys high social rank. The popularity that such "gesprächbüchlein" could achieve is manifest in the publishing history of the most famous dialogue *Karsthans* (1521) ("Field-hoe Johnny"), of which some ten thousand copies were available by 1525.[5]

In 1524 Sachs experimented with the archetypical form of the Protestant dialogue in his "Disputation zwischen einem Chorherren vnd Schuchmacher, darinn das wort gottes vnnd ein recht Christlich wesen verfochten würdt" ("Disputation between a Canon and a Shoemaker in which the Word of God and a Truly Christian Bearing are Advocated"). As the shoemaker is delivering a pair of shoes to the canon, he makes a veiled reference to "Die Wittenbergisch Nachtigall." The churchman is incensed immediately, and a lively debate ensues. The Lutheran craftsman proves to be not only more familiar with biblical authority, but also more concerned about the condition of Christianity than is his conversation partner. The canon, who is bested at every turn, must seek refuge in evasion, sarcasm, and threats. Standard Lutheran charges against the Roman hierarchy remain unanswered. It soon becomes apparent that the shoemaker is well equipped to serve as his own priest, whereas the canon should not be entrusted with sacerdotal duties of

---

[4] For more information about Reformation dialogues, see Werner Lenk, "Einleitung," to *Die Reformation im zeitgenössischen Dialog: 12 Texte aus den Jahren 1520 bis 1525*, ed. Werner Lenk (Berlin: Akademie-Verlag, 1968), 9-43. The estimate of fifty "gesprächbüchlein" appears on page 30.

[5] For this and other estimates of the availability of the dialogues, see Hannelore Winkler, "Zum soziologischen Aspekt von Flugschriften aus der Zeit der Reformation," *Beiträge zur Geschichte der deutschen Sprache und Literatur* (Halle) 94 (1974): 37-49.

any kind. A second dialogue that fits the pattern easily is entitled "Ein gesprech von den Scheinwercken der Gaystlichen vnd jren gelübten, damit sy zůverlesterung des blůts Christi vermaynen selig zů werden" ("A Conversation Concerning the False Good Works and Oaths of the Priesthood, by which They Presume to Attain Salvation even as They Malign the Blood of Christ"). The Lutheran craftsmen Hans and Peter fall into conversation with a monk, a conversation that soon considers the worth of cloister life. Once again, the representative of the Catholic Church is unable to rebut the standard Lutheran critique of the priesthood as a caste of social parasites; but unlike the canon, Sachs's monk leaves the craftsmen with a promise to consider carefully what they have said. All openmindedness aside, the existence of monastic orders has been shown to be a drain on society.

Each of the two remaining dialogues constitutes a departure from the pattern of Lutheran attack and Catholic retreat. Both call into question attitudes and practices within the Lutheran community that diminish the movement in the eyes of potential converts. Hostility to those whose Catholicism remains unshaken emerges as a problem in "Ain gesprech eins Ewangelischen christen mit einem Lutherischen. Darinn der ergerlich wandel etzlicher, die sich Lutherisch nennen, angezaigt vnd bruderlich gestrafft wirdt" ("A Conversation of an Evangelical and a Lutheran Christian in which the Vexing Transformation Undergone by Many who Call Themselves Lutheran is Analyzed and Chastised in the Spirit of Brotherhood"). Once again Sachs uses the craftsmen Hans and Peter, but in this dialogue the latter has decided that eating meat on Friday constitutes a confession of faith. He is ready to come to blows with his father-in-law, a devout Catholic who keeps the traditional day of fasting. The older, wiser Master Hans mediates the dispute by cautioning his coreligionist not to confuse secondary rites with the essentials of the faith and not to affront and alienate fellow Christians. While the fraternal spirit to which the title alludes is present throughout, Peter's vehemence has been cited as evidence of the incendiary nature of religious disputes at the time.[6] The passion of a Thomas Müntzer was not restricted to a small number of zealots or to a few isolated locations. Still, the source of the dispute here *is* relatively unimportant; the attention of scholars has been drawn to the other atypical work, a work that deals with wealth and profit.[7]

---

[6] Ingeborg Spriewald, "Einleitung," to *Die Prosadialoge von Hans Sachs*, ed. Ingeborg Spriewald (Leipzig: VEB Bibliographisches Institut, 1970), 27.

[7] An analysis of profit and wealth in this dialogue would have been appropriate in Anne-Kathrin Brandt, *Die "tugentreich fraw Armut": Besitz und Armut in der Tugendlehre des Hans Sachs* (Göttingen: Gratia, 1979). Unfortunately, the author cites the existence of other studies of the interrelated topics "Luther," "Sachs," "Christianity," and "Bible" as grounds for withholding any thoughts she may have (85).

"Ein Dialogus des inhalt ein argument ..." is usually referred to as the "Romanusdialog" after the more assertive of the two characters. In the accompanying woodcut, Father Romanus in his monk's cowl stands before the counting table of the wealthy Reichenburger (Fig. 4). With an expression of forbearance, the cleric points to a full sack of coins with one hand while extending the other toward his conversation partner as if to invite open, thoughtful discussion. Reichenburger, resplendent in fur hat and collar, scowls with agitation and defensiveness. One hand clutches the edge of the table while the other hovers stiffly just behind the money as if to avoid painful contact. It is a title-page calculated to catch the attention of the potential reader by confounding expectations which, by 1524, would have been brought to a dialogue written by a Lutheran spokesman. How could the writer of "Die Wittenbergisch Nachtigall" place a Roman monk in such a commanding position?

Sachs increases the confusion by beginning the dialogue in the familiar pattern. Romanus has come to discuss a mutual business concern, an errand that prompts Reichenburger to make a sarcastic reference to the avarice widely imputed by Lutherans to the Catholic clergy:

> Ich wolt fürwar wenen, jr wöltet ewer klaydt der geytzigkait (geystligkait solt ich sagen) hierinn bey mir abziehen, vnd wolt ein Christ werden, seyt jr also vnversehens vnd eynig zů mir herein schleicht.[8]
>
> I actually was about to believe that you meant to put aside the gown of a greedy man — I mean a clergyman — here at my house and become a Christian. For you have slipped into my place so unexpectedly and all alone.

The priest has just two speeches before these barbs are sent in his direction, and nothing in the two could possibly give offense. That is to say, Reichenburger initiates the confrontation. It is an aggressiveness that Lutheran readers had come to expect of their spokesmen. The charge of avarice has such well established precedent in Luther's writings that Reichenburger must resort to a second charge in order to achieve the intensity of attack expected by readers since Luther's tracts of 1520. The denial of the monk's Christianity is from the same rhetorical arsenal as the identification of the Pope as the Antichrist. The reader who smiled in anticipation of a scathing litany of

---

[8] Hans Sachs, "Ein Dialogus des inhalt ein argument der Römischen wider das Christlich heüflein; den Geytz, auch ander offenlich laster etc. betreffend," in *Die Prosadialoge des Hans Sachs*, ed. Spriewald, 124-25. Subsequent references to the text will be indicated within parentheses. The English translations are mine.

Fig. 4. Woodcut from the "Romanusdialog" of Hans Sachs (from Hans Sachs, *Die Prosadialoge*, 1970)

Catholic misdeeds would have been startled by Romanus's reaction, however. He responds in kind:

> Ich wil mein kutten noch wol lenger tragen, der miltigkait halben, so ir newen Ewangelischen übet vnd treybet vnder einander, vnd jr seyt mir nůr zů lieb darzů, wölt euch sunst anders antwůrten. (125)
>
> I probably shall keep wearing my habit a long time considering the generosity that you new Evangelicals practice among one another. If you were not so dear to me, I would give you a different kind of answer.

Sarcasm meets with sarcasm as the accusation is turned back on the accuser. In order to understand the author's purpose, a reader must pay close attention to what Romanus says and what he does not say. He implies that he will remain true to the old faith because he finds repulsive the behavior that he has observed among many Lutherans. It is critical to note that Sachs has the priest object not to the new teachings, but to the ethics of the new congregation.

When Reichenburger urges his visitor to speak on without fear of giving offense, he hears the observation that a Lutheran looks to the size of his own purse first and only later to the welfare of his neighbor. To the rejoinder that no Protestant has at his disposal money-making practices that bear comparison with offerings and indulgence sales, Romanus responds that in the confessional he has heard terrible tales about practices common in trade, finance, and litigation. The intimation stops Reichenburger in his tracks; he asks the monk to tell what he has heard, however unpleasant it may be.

It is at this point that Sachs turns his back on reader-expectations brought to a Protestant dialogue and leads his audience into terra incognita. As an inducement he offers a mixture of residual reverence for the integrity of a Catholic institution, the confessional, with simple voyeurism, the chance to eavesdrop on one's neighbor. In the course of the exchange concerning the first invidious practice cited by the monk, Romanus firmly establishes his as the stronger position. Under consideration is preemption, here the practice of acquiring the right to buy large quantities of storable commodities for future sale. The businessman Reichenburger defends preemption as a service to society: during war of famine, or in the dead of winter, necessary supplies will always be on hand. The monk responds that not all merchants who practice preemption content themselves with modest profit levels; many buy huge quantities in order to sell high during hard times. In conceding the point, Reichenburger indicates his belief in Luther's concept of the Christian merchant: "Fürkauffen in solcher maß ist nicht ein Christlicher handel, es thů gleich wer da wöl!" (127) ("Preemption on that scale is not Christian commerce — regardless of who does it!"). In retreat, Reichenburger falls back on the word for "Christian" to avoid singling out the Lutheran businessman. Romanus responds to that tactic with a rhetorical question that then becomes a refrain at the conclusion of each point on his list of avaricious practices. In response to the query "Ist das gůt Ewangelisch" ("Is that truly Evangelical"), Reichenburger can manage only a sorrowful "Ey" and a few words of pained agreement that the behavior described is unacceptable.

The breaches of ethics cited include cornering the market, adding worthless weight, using inaccurate scales, charging excessive interest via the "Zinskauf," and selling on time at high rates of interest. One accusation of abuse that does elicit a defense of business practices concerns the alleged exploitation of workers. Romanus observes:

> Weyter regirt der geytz gewaltigklich vnter den kauffherren vnd verlegern, die da drucken jre arbeyter vnd stückwercker; wenn sie jnen jr arbeyt vnd pfenwerdt bringen oder haim tragen, da thadeln sie jn jr arbeyt auffs hinderst. Dann steet der arm arbeyter zitrent bey der thür mit geschloßnen henden, stilschweygent, auff das er des kauffherren huld nit verlier, hat etwann vor gelt auff die arbeyt entlehent, alßdann rechent der kauffherr mit jm, wie er wil. Büst der arm sein aygen gelt ein zů seiner arbeyt, dann frewt sich der reich des gůten wolflen kauffs, maynt er hab jm recht gethan. (128-29)

> In addition avarice holds powerful sway over the merchants and entrepreneurs who oppress their employees and pieceworkers. When they bring them their work and wares or when they take it home, they disparage their work to their faces. Then the poor worker stands by the door trembling, hands closed, and keeping still so that he will not lose the merchant's favor. He may have borrowed money against the work, and now the merchant does with him as he pleases. If the poor man loses his own money through his work, the rich man is pleased at the good, profitable transaction and believes that he has done right by him.

The image of hapless workers trembling as they await payment from hard-hearted and tight-fisted merchants is too much for Reichenburger. He responds as employers traditionally have responded:

Ir sagt aber nicht darbey, wie stoltz die arbayter seind. So man jr bedarff, kan man jns nicht genůg bezalen vnd kan dannocht niemant nichts von jn bringen. (129)

But you have not mentioned how arrogant the workers are. When one needs them one cannot pay them enough, and no one can get anything out of them.

Workers are over-assertive and under-productive. Romanus overwhelms this objection with references to the miserable living conditions endured by laborers and piece-workers, conditions that only worsen during the winter. The businessman has no defense to offer against descriptions of widespread starvation among workers and their children.

This passage has been of great interest to Marxist scholars. Ingeborg Spriewald, the director of the "Working Group for German Literature of the 15th-17th Centuries" at the Academy of Sciences of the German Democratic Republic, summarizes the principal intention of the work in these terms: "Basically it concerns the position and social condition of the worker in the merchant-financed manufacturing of early capitalism, in which the options and limits of the new evangelical teaching vis-à-vis the abusive conditions and indigence of working people are brought up."[9] While the relative significance of Romanus's point concerning oppression can be argued, the depth of Sachs's concern for the working poor is beyond question. By having Reichenburger protest the charge, Sachs highlights this by-product of the pursuit of profit. The reader's attention is riveted on the pathetic scene of cringing workers and cold, crying children. At the same time, Sachs serves the self-interest of those who sit atop the guild system as master craftsmen. Spriewald has pointed out that the growth of merchant-financed manufacturing was a menace in the eyes of a master such as Hans Sachs.[10] The "putting-out system" or "domestic system" offered merchants a way to circumvent the guilds by supplying piece-workers with raw material and then merchandizing the finished goods, a process that effectively circumvented organized labor.[11] In addition to his anger at the exploitation of the poor, Sachs expresses fear of what proved to be a step toward the factory system of the Industrial Revolution.

Romanus laments the fact that he sees usury, avarice, and crass exploitation wherever he turns, and when Reichenburger defends the well-to-do or

---

[9] Spriewald, "Der Bürger," 1916. My translation — JVC.

[10] Spriewald, "Der Bürger," 1917-18.

[11] See George Unwin, *Industrial Organization in the Sixteenth and Seventeenth Centuries* (1904; New York: Kelley, 1971), 3-4, 216-19.

questions the behavior of the poor, he meets with stinging refutation. When the businessman notes that many poor debtors gamble and whore their money down the drain, the monk first responds that such cases fall under the purview of secular authority (135). He then resumes the offensive with the assertion that many a lender has no need of immediate payment and therefore has no excuse for pressuring debtors. Reichenburger must finally concede each point as Romanus buttresses his arguments with quotations from the Bible. At the conclusion of his litany, Romanus delivers the longest speech of the dialogue, a summary that uses no fewer than fifteen quotations from the Bible (135-37).

The long speech marks the conclusion of the first structural unit of the dialogue. By this point, roughly halfway through the work, the Protestant reader has grown accustomed to Sachs's daring experiment with genre stereotypes and reader- or listener-expectations. The harangue is positioned so as to meet with little resistance. But the reader who has been lulled into passive acceptance and a sense of security concerning the structure of the dialogue has been led down the garden path. After the speech, in his moment of greatest distress, Reichenburger begins a second structural unit by changing the subject of the conversation from avarice to wealth. He sees no chance for victory as long as current economic conditions remain the point at debate because he will have to continue to affirm the existence of both abject poverty and excessive profit. That is to say, as long as the discussion is restricted to current economic conditions, the monk will have the upper hand.

Reichenburger escapes the cul-de-sac with a metaphysical leap. Sachs cannot close the work with his Lutheran vanquished; in the second section of the work, each character scores debating points. The businessman's strategy is apparent in his first words of response to the summarizing speech: "Ein warhaffter Christ waiß wol, das er nůr ein schaffner ist vber das zeytlich gůt vnd das man nichts mit jm eingrebt.... Wir haben nichts in die welt bracht: darumb offenbar ist, wir werden nichts drauß bringen" (137) ("A true Christian knows well that he is only a steward of temporal things and he will be buried with nothing.... We bring nothing into this world; therefore it is obvious that we shall take nothing out of it"). All irony aside, the man in the fur hat is falling back on the traditional teaching of contemptus mundi. This allows Sachs to move his analysis from objective conditions to questions of volition and intent. Although Reichenburger serves his own self-interest by raising new, subjective issues at this point in the conversation, his concerns are fully consistent with his membership in a church that holds that a layman must serve as his own priest. Reichenburger asserts that those who try to become wealthy fall prey to temptation and court eternal damnation. All possessions are transitory: "Derhalb ein warer Christ nicht sorgfeltig ist umb das zeytlich, das er vil schetz samel..." (137) ("Therefore a true Christian does not pay great attention to temporal things, to the acquisition of great riches ..."). This position makes possible a convenient corollary: "Wo aber einem recht gewunnen gůt zů steet, in erbfal, heyrat oder mit gerechten kauffhendeln, solt derselbig darumb nicht got anhangen mögen?" (138) ("But if one is entitled to property that has been obtained justly — through inheritance, marriage, or through honest commerce — should such a person not be able to devote himself to God for that reason?"). If one is committed to the disciplined avoidance of acquisitiveness, any unintended accrual of assets will not affect one's chances for salvation. Wealth is not in itself sinful, and the young man who uses a dowry or an inheritance to engage in "honest commerce" is not necessarily paving a private road to hell. Sachs's term "gerechtes kauffhendeln" is consonant with Luther's concept of the Christian merchant, and, like Luther, Sachs emphasizes the difficulty of any attempt to attain that ideal. He has Romanus cast doubts on the significance of volition. Although the monk does not go so far as to argue that wealth and property are inherently evil, he implies that, as a practical matter, they might as well be. He uses quotations from Christ that describe wealth as an idol (Matthew 6, 21-24 and 13, 3-22). Reichenburger responds with Christ's comment in Mark 10, 24 that it is difficult for those who place their trust in wealth to enter heaven. He then cites the Old Testament patriarchs as examples of wealthy men who nevertheless trusted only in God and never in mammon. Faced with this argument, Romanus must finally concede that attitudes, not assets, lead either to salvation or to damnation (139).

Sachs is showing himself to be as politically astute as Luther: continued support from wealthy Lutherans was essential to the fledgling movement. Despite Catholicism's long-standing opposition to profit and interest, such entrepreneurs and their forbearers had accumulated holdings and therefore political power. While the "Romanusdialog" does not encourage business activity, it does attempt to improve the moral standing of wealth and the wealthy. At the same time, the dialogue attempts to guide the well-to-do toward Lutheran ethics by citing example after example of unacceptable behavior. While wealth officially will be tolerated, it is to be used within strictly observed limits. Because the Catholic Church held to a policy of condemnation and proscription in matters of finance, Rome was not in a position to exert such control. The example set by worldly fifteenth-century popes and by practices such as the sale of indulgences contained an implicit tolerance of conflict between church teachings and church mores. The pious Catholic received mixed signals, or so Hans Sachs presents the situation.

When Romanus accepts Reichenburger's volitional litmus test for the wealthy, there is no indication in the text that a major theological point has been carried. But in fact, a thoughtful and critical monk has affirmed the new faith's response to material possessions and to individual as opposed to ecclesiastical responsibility for personal salvation. The larger inference to be drawn is that a priest who questions the ethics but not the teachings of Lutheranism is open to further persuasion. Finally, of course, the strength of the arguments of the new faith will be apparent if those arguments are not undercut by rampant hypocritical behavior among Lutherans.

The balance of the dialogue examines unethical behavior attributed to both sides. Romanus charges that rich Lutherans are unconcerned about the plight of the poor — to which the businessman responds that those who do not work should not expect compensation. Here Reichenburger directs his comments at the Catholic clergy, whom he views in the same light as do Hans and Peter in "Ein gesprech von den Scheinwercken der Gaystlichen...." Eventually he must concede that selfishness and greed are not unknown within the Lutheran congregation. Many have come to understand the importance of generosity and charity since the Gospel has been preached clearly, but others have yet to mend their sinful ways. Of the members of the new community of faith, they are the least Christian (145).

The significance attached by Sachs to the presence of avarice within his church emerges from Romanus's final substantive speech:

> Ich hab noch kain lust zů ewerm hauffen, weyl also rutzigs vnd reüdigs durcheinander geet. Wenn aber ein hyrt vnd ein schaffstal wurdt, alßdann wölt ich mein kutten an zaun hencken vnd zum hauffen tretten. (148-49)

> I still have no desire to join your number because it is such a mangy, snot-nosed mess among you. But if you ever have a shepherd and a fold, I shall hang my habit on a fence and join your number.

In view of the readiness with which Romanus has made significant doctrinal concessions, no irony should be read into the second sentence. The first reiterates the response of this earnest, pious Catholic to the proselytizing campaign waged by Lutherans. He is repulsed by what he perceives to be a complete lack of order within a congregation whose members share a "mangy," "snot-nosed" aspect. "Rutzigs vnd reüdigs" implies both impurity and immaturity. As an evaluation by a member of the entrenched church hierarchy, it is predictable. By offering it, Sachs makes two points: lack of internal discipline is costing the new movement converts, and patterns of upright, mature behavior must be offered to the Lutheran congregation. At the same time he suggests that organizational discipline is all that is holding Catholicism together. When Romanus goes on to set forth the conditions for his conversion, he uses traditional imagery to imply that the new church should be organized as is the old. The Good Shepherd's place on earth was assumed by Peter and his heirs in Rome; their charge was to keep the sheep in a fold — that is, in a disciplined, united congregation. Lutheranism lacks both leadership and organization, and the lack retards its spread. In 1524 the charge of inappropriate behavior by a congregation coupled with that of irresponsible leadership would have prompted a reader to think of Andreas Karlstadt, Thomas Müntzer, and their followers. And of course, any implication that leadership has been wanting reflects on Luther himself. Reichenburger responds to Romanus's final words with an admonition not to delay the conversion too long. The criticism goes unanswered. Because the primary subject of the dialogue is unbridled greed within the Lutheran congregation, it is only logical to conclude that Sachs faults Protestant leadership for giving the wealthy a free hand. Ethical standards of the sort suggested by Reichenburger must be promulgated, and compliance must be monitored.

Close attention to the arguments in the "Romanusdialog" can clarify a question that has divided recent Sachs scholarship, the question of authorial intention. As already indicated, Marxist analysis has emphasized Sachs's pointed references to social grievances, particularly in Romanus's speeches. Writing in 1970, Ingeborg Spriewald asserts that Sachs's determination to castigate such abuses undermined his effort to refute Catholic charges of rampant avarice within the Lutheran congregation.[12] Spriewald goes on to imply that the extent of the treatment of social conditions testifies to a subconscious affinity for radical leaders like Karlstadt and Müntzer.[13] In an article that appeared thirteen years later, Spriewald finds firmer ground by abandoning the search for unstated affinities; but because she still believes that the purpose of the dialogue is a repudiation of Catholic charges, she finds it astounding that Romanus's points in the first section go unanswered.[14]

Spriewald's original analysis, which appeared in the introduction to her excellent edition of Sachs's prose dialogues, opened two avenues of research. The idea that Sachs intended to pen a defense of Lutheranism against the rival faith is taken up with variations by Bernd Balzer (1973). He maintains that Romanus is being used as a mouthpiece for radical Protestantism. Sachs supposedly hopes that Reichenburger will seem stable and reasonable by comparison — and therefore attractive to moneyed interests,

---

[12] Spriewald, "Einleitung," 20.

[13] The argument is as weak and forced as is indicated here. Spriewald, "Einleitung," 25-26. Enthusiasm (page 26: "?!") has replaced logic.

[14] Spriewald, "Der Bürger," 1916.

whose support was needed.[15] Barbara Könneker has demolished Balzer's reading on the grounds that it assumes elaborate reasoning of a sort that Hans Sachs does not require of his audiences in other texts and that a sixteenth-century reader or listener would not have had the sophistication necessary to reject the arguments of the earnest, persuasive Romanus.[16] Finally, it escapes Könneker that Balzer's concept of a sympathetic Reichenburger cannot be reconciled with Sachs's statement of intention in a dedication that has attracted little scholarly notice.

The other avenue of research opened by Spriewald leads to an image of Sachs as an early champion of workers' rights. Klaus Wedler goes so far as to try to forge a link between the dialogue and Gerhart Hauptmann's *Die Weber*; in the process he misrepresents the title of Sachs's piece as "Dialog wider den Geiz und andere öffentliche Laster."[17] While the reach from 1524 to 1892 is only naive, the act of changing a title to match an interpretation is reprehensible. That interpretation distills Sachs's intention as to shame capitalists into more responsible, humane behavior toward their totally dependent workforce. Sachs supposedly does not criticize that dependency, but views it as part of a "divinely justified exploitation."[18] Wedler's basis for the attribution of such an attitude is the acceptance by both Romanus and Reichenburger of the concept of "property that has been obtained justly" (138). Hence, the avenue of inquiry into the concept of Sachs as a spokesman for the oppressed leads to the predictable conclusion that the writer actually was speaking for the interests of his own elevated social level.

Spriewald's enduring position that the "Romanusdialog" pursues contradictory goals — the discussion of abusive practices employed by Lutherans and the defense of Lutherans against the charge of employing abusive practices — is accepted by Jürgen Schutte in what remains the most extensive examination of scholarly response to the prose dialogues.[19] His thesis is that Sachs wishes to persuade employers either to monitor the

---

[15] Balzer, 147.

[16] Könneker, *Die deutsche Literatur der Reformationszeit*, 156.

[17] Klaus Wedler, "Klassenkampf und Bündnisproblematik in den Flugschriften, Fastnachtspielen und Zeitgedichten des Hans Sachs," in *Der Bauer im Klassenkampf: Studien zur Geschichte des deutschen Bauernkrieges und der bäuerlichen Klassenkämpfe im Spätfeudalismus*, ed. Gerhard Heitz, Adolf Laube, Max Steinmetz, Günter Vogler (Berlin: Akademie-Verlag, 1975), 310-11.

[18] Wedler, 312.

[19] Jürgen Schutte, "'Was ist vns vnser freyhait nutz / wenn wir ir nicht brauchen durffen': Zur Interpretation der Prosadialoge," in *Hans Sachs: Studien zur frühbürgerlichen Literatur im 16. Jahrhundert*, ed. Joachim Bumke, Thomas Cramer, Gert Kaiser, Horst Wenzel (Berne: Lang, 1978), 71.

quality of their workers' lives or to allow the state to do so; that is, Schutte sees an attempt to find middle ground between those employer-employee relationships determined solely by profit margin and those determined solely by Christian love. He argues, "The dialogue controversy presented, whose explosiveness lies exclusively in social rather than confessional confrontation, aims from the beginning — both in form and in content — at a compromise...."[20] Schutte's use of the verb for "lies" is both typical and revealing. Had he used the past tense in order to specify sixteenth-century intention and reception, he would have been at odds with the author's statement of intent in the dedication. But by using the present tense, he unconsciously reveals the point at which analysis of the "Romanusdialog" has broken down. The recent interest in Reformation literature has been focused on social and economic determinants. Here, the resultant tendency to neglect confessional issues is particularly apparent. For Sachs's audience the "explosive" dimension of this dialogue would have been the act of criticizing Lutheranism from within less than seven years after the posting of the ninety-five theses. Sachs's conclusion that public discussion of Lutheran avarice via the dialogue was required attests to the degree of importance attached to the elucidation of a defensible Lutheran position on wealth.

Close attention to the course of the debate between Romanus and Reichenburger reveals the structure of Sachs's attempt to stake out such a position. Censure from a Catholic monk in the first section of the dialogue establishes authorial credibility. Lutheranism has a problem that is both serious and widely discussed. When the precise nature of the problem is presented in sharp relief, the few excuses offered are shown to be unacceptable. The first section stands as the mea culpa of an entire congregation. The second then offers support for the pursuit of profit subject to the oversight of the purified faith. The Lutheran businessman Reichenburger first wins acceptance for the concept of honest commerce. Then he removes any ethical stigma associated with material goods by establishing the moral neutrality of wealth acquired through marriage or inheritance and by using the example of the Old Testament patriarchs to specify individual volition as *the* source of avarice.

The dedication of the "Romanusdialog" indicates authorial intent while conveying a sense of urgency and preparing readers for what will be for many an uncomfortable discussion. Just beneath the accompanying woodcut stands a reference to Ephesians 5, 3, and beneath the reference, the verse itself: "Hůrerey vnd vnrainigkait / oder geytz / laßt nit von euch gesagt werden / wie den heyligen zů steet" (Fig. 4) ("But fornication, and all

---

[20] Schutte, 71. My translation — JVC.

uncleanness, or covetousness, let it not be once named among you, as becometh saints"). After three sentences of personal greetings and dedication, Sachs describes the content of the dialogue in this way:

> Des inhalt ist ein Argument, so vnnsere Römische mit hoher stimm außschreyen auff der Cantzel vnd wo sie raum haben, die Ewangelischen leer zu lestern, fürnemlich mit dem verfluchten geytz, nachmals mit andern offenlichen lastern, welche noch (got erbarms) in vollem schwanck bey vns geend von den, so Christum noch nicht warhafftig im geyst erkent haben, als wer darumb die leer falsch. Mit disputieren vnd schreyben haben sie wenig eer erlanget, noch vil weniger mit jren vngezelten hinderdücken, fallen nun auff das sündig leben, welches ich hoff, werdt kurtzer zeyt fallen durch den hall der Ewangelischen Pusaun, wie die Statmaur Hiericho, Josue 6. (123-24)

> The content is an argument that our Romans shout at the top of their lungs from the pulpit and wherever else they have a forum in order to decry Evangelical teachings primarily on the basis of the accursed greed, in addition to other flagrant vices, that are still (God have mercy!) in full swing among those of us who have not yet truly accepted Christ — as though the teachings were therefore false. In public debate and in their writings they gained little glory — and even less with their countless treacheries. Now they have hit upon this sinful way of life, which I hope will fall before the blast of the Evangelical trumpet, like the wall of the city of Jericho, Joshua 6.

While the Bible verse refers to the appearance of impropriety, Sachs twice concedes the existence of avarice in Lutheran ranks. After this highly visible concession, the direction of the first section of the dialogue should come as no surprise. That Romanus does not attempt to refute Lutheran teachings is fully consonant with the dedication's assertion that the Catholic side has prevailed neither in debate nor in print; that is to say, its theology is inferior. The opposition supposedly has abandoned the restatement of its weak theology in favor of the censure of flawed ethics that all have observed in the new congregation. Sachs is laying out a mission to be undertaken by his contemporary Lutheran writers, a mission in which the "Romanusdialog" will play a role. The printed word is to serve as did Joshua's trumpet.

Sachs conveys the urgency of the situation not only through the imagery of war, but also through the suggestion that Catholics have begun to use ethical censure as a means of opening Lutheran theology to ridicule. The improper behavior of a portion of the Lutheran community undermines the new articles of faith. Here is a stratagem imputed to Catholics that Sachs chooses not to exemplify with Romanus. Nervous expectations that the monk will refute the religious practices and beliefs of his dialogue partner remain unfulfilled. Sachs was not about to supply Catholic spokesmen with arguments. But to the extent that it left Lutheran readers apprehensive about the well-being of their church, Sachs's dialogue would have fostered solidarity within the group, a consensus of opinion that would have brought pressure to bear on wayward members. With his dialogue Sachs intends to change the behavior of such Lutherans. The quotation from Ephesians affirms the importance of the impression one makes on others, and the dialogue is seeking a basis for disciplining from without those Lutherans whose intentions are good but whose will power is deficient. The last words of the dedication are taken from Matthew 26, 41: "Der geyst ist willig, aber das fleysch ist schwach" (124) ("The spirit is willing, but the flesh is weak"). The words spoken in Gethsemane recognize the imperfection of man just before the most ardent disciple Peter renounces Christ. With the first section of his dialogue, Sachs shows that this famous observation of Christ is applicable to Lutherans; the second section suggests appropriate responses to the innate weakness.

The "Romanusdialog" marks a change of direction in the history of the literary treatment of wealth and money-making. Gone is the uncritical acquisitiveness of *Fortunatus*. The plot of that chapbook contradicts its opening and closing paragraphs with their traditional bows before the concept of *turpe lucrum*. By contrast, the dedication of the "Romanusdialog" is not at odds with the text. Instead, Sachs first states his intentions with the piece and then presents a debate whose structure is a calculated attempt to carry out those intentions. He and Luther approach the problem of wealth in the same three-step fashion: both 1) argue that wealth is dangerous by suggesting that it coexists with sin, 2) accept the existence of customs (inheritance, dowry) and professions based on the accrual of liquidity by referring to scriptural precedent and/or by making unsupported assertions of the historical and practical utility of such constructs as property that has been obtained justly, honest commerce, and the Christian merchant, and 3) urge the adoption of measures and attitudes that will control the acquisitive urge. The amount of pure hostility with which Lutheranism responded to those who had or pursued wealth is reflected in the structure of the dialogue: the first section with its litany of the forms of avarice constitutes half of the text.

Such hostility had precedence in Reformation literature. In the most famous dialogue *Karsthans* (1521), the negative character Murner refers to himself as a miser.[21] He goes on to assert that a poor priest is an unhappy

---

[21] "Karsthans," in *Die Reformation im zeitgenössischen Dialog*, ed. Lenk, 72.

priest and states the hope that the common people will not learn that much discord arises from the greed of clerics. Unbridled self-enrichment is one of the characteristics of his social "betters" that prompt the Lutheran peasant Karsthans to cry his fateful refrain "Wo ist myn pflegel?" ("Where is my flail?"). In the sequel *Gesprech biechlin neüw Karsthans* (1521) (*Field-hoe Johnny: A New Dialogue*), Karsthans paints the following picture of the priesthood for his discussion partner, the famous knight Franz von Sickingen:

> Sie wöllent aber yetzunt niergen hin zů predigen, sunder bleyben sie da heimet, pflegen gůter rů vnd alles lustes, heissen vns in gelt vnd gůt zů huß bringen, vnd wenn wir nit zu irer zeyt damit kommen, bannen sie vns....[22]

> But nowadays they do not want to go anywhere to preach; instead, they stay home, pursue relaxation and all of the pleasures, order us to bring our money and possessions to them at home, and if we do not come within the time that they have set, they place us under the ban....

The Lutheran practice of charging the Catholic clergy with avarice in polemical pieces such as these was intended as a device for discrediting the second estate as parasitic and irreligious. A natural and perhaps at first actively desired side-effect was the attraction of the attention of readers to the dangers of avarice itself. Traditionalism in matters touching the problematic topic of wealth and the deadly sin of covetousness had to be reconciled with the need for support from wealthy and powerful Lutherans. The compromise position of the new church offered the entrepreneur legitimacy and acceptance upon his acquiescence to strict moral guidance. Sachs's Reichenburger may continue to count his money *and* hope for heaven if only he will hold to the precepts distilled during his conversation with the doubting monk. His every action should be tested in advance with Romanus's pointed question. "Ist das gůt Ewangelisch?" must be asked of each decision made in the pursuit of profit.

---

[22] "Gesprech biechlin neüw Karsthans," in *Die Reformation im zeitgenössischen Dialog*, ed. Lenk, 95. The translation is mine.

Chapter 7

Historia von D. Johann Fausten: The Problem Redux

DURING THE EARLY YEARS of the Reformation, Martin Luther and Hans Sachs affirmed the traditional theological response to wealth and its pursuit. They did so not with the intention of excoriating an evil but with the hope of controlling a reality while giving it doctrinal legitimacy. The solution to the problem of wealth offered in *Dil Ulenspiegel* and *Fortunatus* was anathema to upright Lutherans. Their solution, the Christian merchant, was a bold step and, in its boldness, a characteristic step for the young movement. But Luther was not averse to taking two steps forward and one step back when a particularly daring position created political difficulties. When the peasants whose support he had needed in 1520 rose in revolt in 1525, he was ready with condemnations of their "murderous" activity. Does Lutheranism's first solution to the problem of wealth also change? Or does literature produced during the formation of the Lutheran orthodoxy continue to promulgate the original, rather sophisticated position?

The *Historia von D. Johann Fausten* (1587), the *Faustbuch*, is an attractive work to test for the durability of the Luther/Sachs line. It was published more than half a century after the partial consolidation of Protestantism accomplished by the Augsburg Confession of 1530. Authorship of the chapbook has been attributed to a university educated apologist for the Lutheran orthodoxy whose name is still unknown.[1] The story of Faust is well-known internationally because the *Faustbuch* introduced into the written tradition subject matter that has proved to be resilient and adaptable. Whether they have read Thomas Mann, Goethe, Christopher Marlowe, or the chapbook, educated people know of Faust. The history of its reception validates the assertion that the *Faustbuch* is the most important German chapbook of the sixteenth century.[2]

---

[1] For a discussion of the author, see Barbara Könneker, "Faust-Konzeption und Teufelspakt im Volksbuch von 1587," in *Festschrift Gottfried Weber*, ed. Heinz Otto Burger and Klaus von See (Bad Homburg: Gehlen, 1967), 160-61. For a Marxist savaging, see Günter Albrecht, Joachim G. Boeckh, Kurt Böttcher, Klaus Gysi, Paul Günter Krohn, *Geschichte der deutschen Literatur: Von 1480 bis 1600* (Berlin: Volk und Wissen Volkseigener Verlag, 1961), 419.

[2] Albrecht et al., 417.

The most familiar critical edition of the *Faustbuch* was prepared by Robert Petsch and published in 1911.[3] The text has six divisions: a dedication to the court officials Caspar Kolln and Hieronymous Hoff by the printer/publisher Johann Spies, a foreword by the author, and the tale itself in four sections, the final three of which are supplied with titles. Short chapters bearing summarizing titles compose each narrative section; the first details Faust's family circumstances, upbringing, and education. It relates the young man's growing interest in "speculation" in the natural sciences and in magic and then describes the appearance of Mephistopheles and the signing of a pact with the Devil. The second narrative section reports conversations between Faust and his new servant Mephistopheles concerning the nature of the universe. Faust's activities as an astrologer and calendar-maker are duly recorded, as are his journeys throughout the known world. The third section comprises comic episodes that result from Faust's contact with representatives of estates high and low. The chronologically arranged episodes are presented either in single chapters or in groups of chapters; successive episodes are usually unrelated. The loose structure of the third section resembles that of *Dil Ulenspiegel*. The final narrative section describes the last of Faust's allotted twenty-four years, commencing with the composition of a will and concluding with Faust's terrible death and its immediate aftermath.

The full title of the *Faustbuch* contains an unambiguous statement of authorial intent (Fig. 5). It may be translated "The History of Dr. Johann Faust, the well-known magician and practitioner of the black arts: How he made a pact with the devil for a specified period of time; what strange adventures he then saw, arranged, and carried out himself until he finally received his well deserved wages. Largely drawn together from his own remaining papers as a horrifying lesson, a revolting example and a sincere warning for all arrogant, insolent, and godless people, and then set into print." The second sentence specifies the ethical message of the work and the means by which that lesson is to be taught. Pride, intellectual arrogance, and loss of faith are not sins that afflict the entire population. The sentence applies to a group within that population; it is aimed at errant and potentially errant members of that group. References to the fictive papers in Faust's estate and to the process of preparing the work for publication follow a formula for establishing authorial credibility. They also suggest that the reader, writer, and main character come from similar circumstances. Educated Germans make up the small group within the general population

---

[3] *Das Volksbuch vom Doctor Faust: Nach der ersten Ausgabe, 1587*, ed. Robert Petsch, 2nd ed. (Halle: Niemeyer, 1911). Subsequent references to the text will be indicated within parentheses. Unless noted otherwise, the translations are mine — JVC.

HISTORIA

Von D. Johañ

Fausten/ dem weitbeschreyten
Zauberer vnnd Schwartzkünstler/
Wie er sich gegen dem Teuffel auff eine be-
nandte zeit verschrieben/ Was er hierzwischen für
seltzame Abentheuwer gesehen/ selbs angericht-
tet vnd getrieben/ biß er endtlich sei-
nen wol verdienten Lohn
empfangen.

Mehrertheils auß seinen eygenen hin-
derlassenen Schrifften/ allen hochtragenden/
fürwitzigen vnd Gottlosen Menschen zum schrecklichen
Beyspiel/ abscheuwlichen Exempel/ vnd treuw-
hertziger Warnung zusammen gezo-
gen/ vnd in den Druck ver-
fertiget.

IACOBI IIII.

Seyt Gott vnderthänig/ widerstehet dem
Teuffel/ so fleuhet er von euch.

CVM GRATIA ET PRIVILEGIO.

Gedruckt zu Franckfurt am Mayn/
durch Johann Spies.

M. D. LXXXVII.

Fig. 5. Title page of the first edition of the *Faustbuch*

that is threatened by the sins that destroyed Faust.[4] It is the presence of arrogance within that group that has motivated the author to shock the self-important sinners into self-critical reflection. The use of the word for "all" indicates that the author deems the number of such sinners large enough to warrant issuance of a printed warning.

The chapbook's long title challenges an educated townsman to watch for manifestations of intellectual arrogance in Faust and to compare them with the reader's own conduct and attitudes. What shape does the character's arrogance take? The reader is to search the text for answers to that question, a search that proceeds on the assumption that an unassailable personal ethics is attainable. The printer/publisher Spies supports that optimistic position in a dedication that follows the title page and takes the form of a letter. The salutation is instructive: "Den ehrnhafften, Wolachtbaren vnnd Fürnemmen Caspar Kolln, Churfürstlichem Meyntzischen Amptschreibern, Vnd Hieronymo Hoff, Renthmeistern in der Graffschafft Königstein, meinen insonders gunstigen lieben Herrn vnd Freunden" (3) ("To the honorable, estimable, and distinguished Caspar Kolln, Secretary to the Elector of Mainz, and Hieronymus Hoff, Treasurer of County Königstein, my particularly devoted dear gentlemen and friends"). Spies then comments briefly on his motivation in printing the tale and thanks his two friends for their moral support. Kolln and Hoff were pursuing careers in the service of absolute rulers, one secular and one ecclesiastical. Together with the entrepreneur Spies himself, they constitute a microcosm of the educated target audience, readers busily advancing their careers but still hoping to remain "honorable," "estimable," and "distinguished." Spies presents his two friends as paragons of personal integrity. Although the publisher states his intention of honoring two old school friends, the effect of his two-page piece is to mitigate the impact of the title with its promise of "a horrifying lesson, a revolting example, and a sincere warning." Spies writes that he has looked for a way to do something for his friends and that he first thought of presents of money. But that idea was abandoned when he recalled their common financial status: "durch Gottes Segen an zeitlicher Nahrung vnd leiblichen Gütern dermassen geschaffen vnd begabet ..., daß sie meiner hierin nit bedürffen..." (5) ("provided for and granted through God's grace with daily sustenance and temporal possessions to such a degree ... that they do not need my help in this ..."). It follows that, if one or both of the friends was (were) experiencing financial difficulty, Spies would be able to help. All three are in comfortable circumstances.

---

[4] For a discussion of the development of the educated, non-aristocratic stratum in the second half of the sixteenth century, see Zorn, 481-85.

Spies's dedication indicates the social position of the reader to whom the message of the *Faustbuch* is directed. The "Vorred an den Christlichen Leser" ("Foreword to the Christian Reader") then summarizes that message and specifies authorial intent:

> In Summa, der Teuffel lohnet seinen Dienern, wie der Hencker seinem Knecht, vnnd nemmen die Teuffelsbeschwerer selten ein gut Ende, wie auch an D. Johann Fausto zusehen, der noch bey Menschen Gedächtnuß gelebet, seine Verschreibung vnnd Bündtnuß mit dem Teuffel gehabt, viel seltzamer Abenthewr vnd grewliche Schandt vnd Laster getrieben, mit fressen, sauffen, Hurerey vnd aller Vppigkeit, biß jm zu letzt der Teuffel seinen verdienten Lohn gegeben, vnd jm den Halß erschrecklicher weiß vmbgedrehet. Damit ist es aber noch nich gnug, sondern es folgt auch die ewige Straff vnnd Verdammnuß, daß solche Teuffelsbeschwerer endtlich zu jrem Abgott dem Teuffel in Abgrund der Hellen fahren, vnd ewiglich verdampt seyn müssen. (9)

> In sum, the devil pays his servants as the hangman pays his bondman; those who conjure the devil seldom come to a good end. This can be seen in the case of Dr. Johann Faust, who lived as many who are still alive can remember, who had his agreement and pact with the devil, carried on many an adventure, shameful deed, and vice including gluttony, drunkenness, whoring, and all manner of debauchery until the devil finally gave him his well deserved wages and twisted his neck in the most horrifying way. But even that does not suffice — on the contrary, there follow eternal punishment and damnation when such conjurers of the devil finally must go to their idol the devil in the abyss of hell and be damned for eternity.

The godless arrogance cited in the complete title of the chapbook is to take the form of conjuring the Devil. This particular form of pride will lead in two directions: to a luxurious, dissolute life-style and then to a horrible death and eternal damnation. Of course, many sixteenth-century Germans would have been entertained when contemplating such behavior and such consequences. But if the basis for entertainment was broad, that for edification was narrow. It safely can be assumed that relatively few people of 1587 had ever attempted to conjure the Devil or, more generally, "speculate" in the sciences. The then familiar concept of pride the mortal sin would have had far greater potential applicability, but few readers could have been expected to find themselves guilty of an arrogance as self-aware, as mocking as that of Faust. Still, the use of the title page to issue a warning does indicate a desire on the part of a deeply concerned author to change patterns of behavior deemed both invidious and widespread.

Faust's death and the anticipation of the gruesome scene certainly stood to make an impression on the reader, but a lasting impression was possible only if the reader could imagine himself in Faust's position. Simple empathy with Faust the man was not sufficient; the reader had to recognize as his own the thoughts, interests, and behavior patterns of the conjurer. Of the major plot elements cited in the summary — the pact, the life-style, and the damnation — it was the life-style that had the potential to unsettle the contemporary reader. The enjoyment of earthly pleasures adumbrated here and detailed in the narrative was a manifestation of pride available only to those in comfortable circumstances, to men like Spies and his two friends. Such a reader was to search himself for Faust's love of earthly things and therefore for Faust's overweening egocentrism. In the *Faustbuch*, the mortal sin of pride is inextricably bound to the trappings of wealth.

The preface concludes with another statement of intent:

> Damit aber alle Christen, ja alle vernünfftige Menschen den Teuffel vnd sein Fürnemmen desto besser kennen, vnnd sich darfür hüten lernen, so hab ich mit Raht etlicher gelehrter vnd verstendiger Leut das schrecklich Exempel D. Johann Fausti, was sein Zauberwerck für ein abscheuwlich End genommen, für die Augen stellen wöllen, Damit auch niemandt durch diese Historien zu Fürwitz vnd Nachfolge möcht gereitzt werden, sind mit fleiß vmbgangen vnnd außgelassen worden die *formae coniurationum*, vnnd was sonst darin ärgerlich seyn möchte, vnnd allein das gesetzt, was jederman zur Warnung vnnd Besserung dienen mag. (10)

> But in order that all Christians, indeed all reasonable people may get to know the devil and his undertakings better and learn to protect themselves, I would like to set before the eyes of the world with the assistance of a number of learned and wise people the horrifying example of Dr. Johann Faust and the vile outcome of his sorcery; in order that no one might be tempted to insolence and emulation through these histories, the conjuring spells have been avoided and omitted with diligence — in addition to anything else that might be vexing — and only that has been set down which might serve everyone as a warning and a call for improvement.

The chapbook author wishes to change behavior for the better through education. In particular the strategic placement of the words for "learn" and "improvement" make this intention more apparent here than it is in the intense and even shocking title. The long sentence above assumes a readership of "all reasonable people" that includes all Christians and suggests that that entire audience has something to learn about the Devil and his devices in order to better protect itself. The intellectual abilities of the projected audience are considerable if it can be described as reasonable; its expectations of a book are high if the author feels obliged to consult with "learned people" during composition. The otherwise formulaic reference to authorities would have had immediacy for those like Spies and his friends who had had contact with university instructors and whose subsequent careers involved regular contact with others who had had university schooling. One effect of this sentence is to buttress the inference to be drawn from the summary that the average Christian would do well to search for the Faust within him. Another effect is to obviate inappropriate responses to the title page. To the reader who expected a precise report of the conjurer's procedure, the author offers the excuse that details have been omitted so that no one is tempted to imitate Faust. This evasion is necessary if the reader's attention is to be focused on broad moral issues raised by the pact rather than on sensational specifics of the plot.

The reader is duly reminded of broad issues within the body of the narrative, and such reminders are more elaborate at points in the plot that are particularly significant or dramatic. For instance, the pact that Faust writes out in his own warm blood is reproduced as the sixth chapter. Immediately beneath the signature appears the title of the seventh chapter: "Wider D. Fausti Verstockung, ist dieser Verß vnd Reymen wol zusagen" (22) ("It is well to say these verses and rhymes as a counter to Dr. Faust's obduracy"). The title indicates that the author is about to specify the nature of Faust's obduracy and draw conclusions of benefit to the reader. The chapter is in verse:

> Wer sein Lust setzt auff stoltz vnd Vbermuht,
> Vnnd darinnen sucht sein Freuwd vnd Muht,
> Vnd alles dem Teuffel nach thut,
> Der macht vber jhne ein eygen Ruht,
> Vnd kompt endtlich vmb Seel, Leib vnd Gut.
>   Item:
> Wer allein das Zeitlich betracht,
> Vnd auff das Ewig hat kein acht,
> Ergibt sich dem Teuffel Tag vnd Nacht,
> Der hab auff seine Seel wol acht.
>   Item:
> Wer sich das Feuwer muhtwillig läßt brennen,
> Oder wil in einen Brunnen springen,

> Dem geschicht recht, ob er schon nicht kan entrinnen.
> (22)
>
> He who sets his heart on pride and arrogance,
> And therein seeks spirit and joy,
> And imitates the devil in all things,
> He makes a cane for use on himself,
> And finally loses soul, body, and property.
> Further:
> He who considers only the temporal,
> And pays no attention to the eternal,
> Surrenders to the devil every day,
> He should pay close heed to his soul.
> Further:
> He who lets the fire burn on purpose,
> Or wishes to jump into the well —
> It serves him right, if he cannot escape.

The lines borrow heavily from Brant's *Narrenschiff*, specifically, from the short mottos that precede the woodcuts for Chapters 3, 43, and 45.[5] The motto for Chapter 3 reads as follows: "Wer setzt sin lust vff zyttlich gůt / Vnd dar jnn sůcht sin freyd vnd můt / Der ist eyn narr jnn lib vnd blůt"[6] ("Who sets his heart on earthly ware / And seeks his joy and comfort there, / Inveterate foolishness his share").[7] The first line of the *Narrenschiff* motto focuses attention on the symptom, whereas the same line in the *Faustbuch* features the underlying cause. Still, the *Faustbuch* reader is threatened with the loss of property as well as the loss of body and soul.

In the second *Faustbuch* strophe, the polarity of the temporal and the eternal reinforces the message that Faust's obduracy results in disastrous consequences — in this earthly realm as well as in the next. The point is worth emphasizing since the reader otherwise might fail to look for similarities between his life and Faust's. If similarities exist that are rooted in Faustian arrogance, the property of the first strophe that is lost at death will be lost not only to the decedent but to all family members.

The possibility of a pauper's death would have caught the attention of Spies, his friends, and their educational and occupational peers — all the

---

[5] Compare Peter Suchsland, "Anmerkungen," to *Deutsche Volksbücher in drei Bänden: Dritter Band: Historia von Doktor Johann Fausten, Histori von den vier Heymonskindern* (Berlin: Aufbau, 1975), 330.

[6] Brant, *Narrenschiff*, 6.

[7] Brant, *Ship of Fools*, trans. Zeydel, 66.

more since reports about the historical Faust circulating at the end of the sixteenth century mentioned books as the only remaining personal effects.[8] In fact, the *Faustbuch* deviates from reports concerning the circumstances of the conjurer's death. That change reflects a desire to deepen the impact of the story on the chapbook's target audience. But before proceeding to Faust's "middle-class death," an analysis of the problem of wealth as it appears in the chapbook must detail the manner in which wealth is presented through other characters and through Faust himself.

The first sentence of the *Faustbuch* establishes the financial status of characters as a matter of great concern to the author. Not only does it serve as a point of reference for all stages of Faust's development but it also provides a durable model for the conjurer's approach to survival in a free-enterprise economy: he will depend upon the munificence of others:

> Doctor Faustus ist eines Bauwern Sohn gewest, zu Rod, bey Weinmar bürtig, der zu Wittenberg ein grosse Freundschafft gehabt, deßgleichen seine Eltern Gottselige vnnd Christliche Leut, ja sein Vetter, der zu Wittenberg seßhafft, ein Bürger, vnd wol vermögens gewest, welcher D. Fausten aufferzogen, vnd gehalten wie sein Kind, dann dieweil er ohne Erben war, nam er diesen Faustum zu einem Kind vnd Erben auff, ließ jhn auch in die Schul gehen, *Theologiam* zu studieren, Er aber ist von diesem Gottseligen Fürnemmen abgetretten vnd Gottes Wort mißbraucht. (11)

> John Faustus, born in the town of Rhode, lying in the province of Weimer in Germanie, his father a poor husbandman, and not able to bring him up: but having an uncle at Wittenberg, a rich man and without issue, took this J. Faustus from his father, and made him his heir, in so much that his father was no more troubled with him, for he remained with his uncle at Wittenberg, where he was kept at the University in the same city to study Divinity. But Faustus being of a naughty mind and otherwise addicted, applied not his studies, but took himself to other exercises.[9]

Had the child followed the traditional life's path of one born into such circumstances, he would have remained a peasant's son ready to shoulder an ever increasing financial burden as he and his father aged. Faust's life

---

[8] Hans Henning, "Faust als historische Gestalt," *Jahrbuch der Goethe-Gesellschaft* 21 (1959): 112, 132.

[9] *The History of the Damnable Life and Deserved Death of Doctor John Faustus*, trans. William Rose (London: Routledge, 1930), 65.

turns away from this norm because his parents are willing to put the future financial needs of the childless relative before their own need for a son's help with farming. That willingness is at least in part a product of the difference in social levels. The wealthy relative wishes to ensure that the fruits of his labor will remain in the family after his death, but, beyond that, his heir must be able to manage the legacy successfully. The requisite acumen is to be gained through formal schooling underwritten by the uncle. When the relative's death is later reported, the narrator describes him as "fromm" (24) ("pious"). In the sentence above, he is presented as having played the role of parent to the young Faust, and the text goes on to praise parents and friends as pious and desirous of the very best for the gifted Faust (11). That is to say, the text presents Faust's urban relative as not only wealthy and pious but also as willing to extend both his wealth and his moral example to help a poor, uneducated young kinsman from a lower estate. Other wealthy men who appear in the text — the Pope, members of the aristocracy, and Faust himself — are depicted in greater and less flattering detail. The uncle would have been familiar to a burgher of the late sixteenth century, to a burgher like Spies, as the ideal townsman — upright, devout, and generous, but also successful, pragmatic, and wealthy. The presence of this character in the first sentence of the chapbook makes it impossible to read the work as an aggressive attack on wealth and the wealthy. Generosity can proceed from wealth, and an irreproachable Christian ethics can be obeyed and taught by the wealthy.

Faust leaves behind the uncle's comfortable but pious home to see the world with his demonic companion. Soon he passes through Rome, which is described as the residence of a self-indulgent prince:

Er kam auch vnsichtbar für deß Bapsts Pallast, da sahe er viel Diener vnd Hoffschrantzen, vnd was Richten vnd Kosten man dem Bapst aufftruge, vnd so vberflüssig, daß D. Faustus darnach zu seinem Geist sagte: Pfuy, warumb hat mich der Teuffel nicht auch zu einem Bapst gemacht. Doct. Faustus sahe auch darinnen alle seines gleichen, als vbermut, stoltz, Hochmut, Vermessenheit, fressen, sauffen, Hurerey, Ehebruch, vnnd alles Gottloses Wesen deß Bapsts vnd seines Geschmeiß, also, daß er hernach weiters sagte: Ich meynt, ich were ein Schwein oder Saw deß Teuffels, aber er muß mich länger ziehen. Diese Schwein zu Rom sind gemästet, vnd alle zeitig zu Braten vnd zu Kochen. (60)

... he and his Spirit made themselves invisible, and came into the Pope's Court, and privy chamber where he was, there saw he many servants attendant on his holiness, with many a flattering Sycophant carrying of his meat, and there he marked the Pope and the manner of his service, which he seeing to be so unmeasurable and sumptuous; fie (quoth Faustus), why had not the Devil made a Pope of me? Faustus saw notwithstanding in that place those that were like to himself, proud, stout, wilful, gluttons, drunkards, whoremongers, breakers of wedlock, and followers of all manner of ungodly exercises: wherefore he said to his Spirit, I thought that I had been alone a hog, or pork of the devil's but he must bear with me yet a little longer, for these hogs of Rome are already fattened, and fitted to make his roast-meat....[10]

There is a clumsy redundancy in "proud, stout, wilful." It is as though a simple reference to the sin that Faust and the Pope supposedly share is insufficient; the gravity of the offense to God must be emphasized, if only through repetition. The four German synonyms for pride are followed by four immoral activities that result from pride, activities in which Faust engages even before he begins his world tour. Not only is the Pope's household an insult to Christian decency, but his very person radiates luxury. When Faust subsequently visits the court of the Turkish emperor, he performs self-levitation: in the splendid attire and jewelry of a Pope (68). Of course, by 1587 the Pope had become a traditional target for Lutheran writers. Still, the author's decision to emphasize the opulence of the Vatican reflects a readiness to rely on the old concept of *turpe lucrum*. That reliance was necessitated in part by the economy of the text: in this section of the chapbook, the author is offering a travelogue, a breathless, whirlwind tour. Stops along the way must be presented very briefly. Casting the Pope as a man of decadence suggests that the author trusted that the concept of filthy lucre would again merge easily with the standard Lutheran caricature of the leader of the opposing church. This reliance on old attitudes appears in the same work that uses only the word for "pious" to describe the character of the wealthy uncle — as if the word for "well-to-do" could be an ethically neutral adjective in a text that refers to the wealthy of Rome as swine and vermin.

Ambiguity concerning wealth emerges not just from an analysis of extreme opposites, the burgher of Wittenberg and the prince of Rome, but also from consideration of the moneyed aristocracy. On one hand, the nobility enjoys the creature comforts of life at court. When Faust visits a noble residence, he frequently is offered a seat at a large banquet.[11] He is treated with great respect before he performs his feats of magic, and he

---

[10] *History of Faustus*, trans. Rose, 127.

[11] For example, pages 76, 81, and 87.

receives a generous reward for his efforts.[12] On the other hand, the chapbook does not depict such courts as small reflections of the negative example set by Rome. Wealth is indeed present, but so too are conjugal love, attentive child-rearing, and simple courtesy. While members of other social strata often try to get the better of Faust, the nobility usually treats him in a manner appropriate to the provider of a highly valued service. Faust's talents appear in an especially flattering light when he conjures forth exotic food and drink for the pregnant Countess of Anhalt — a feat that is particularly timely because it is performed in the dead of winter (89-90). The woman's condition is certain to elicit the sympathy of the reader.

It is worthy of note that the *Faustbuch* does not derogate the one wealthy segment of the population, a segment that enjoyed great visibility. The nobility offered a large target for criticism, but little is forthcoming. Faust's dependence on the rewards given for his entertaining feats holds to the pattern for financial survival established in the home of his uncle. Faust's own financial history constitutes a significant response to the problem of wealth.

As Faust's association with Mephistopheles begins, the conjurer has just fallen heir to his uncle's estate. That inheritance includes the house (24) and those unspecified holdings that a reader of the day would have attributed to a man described as a well-to-do burgher (11). Accordingly, young Faust is able to maintain a comfortable life-style after leaving the university. His dabblings in astrology and herbal healing and his readings in the black arts are inexpensive pastimes. The pleasures of the flesh become Faust's first concern only after signing of the pact. On receiving that signature, his new masters fill the house with terrible sights and sounds. In the midst of the chaos, the Devil offers his first gift:

Bald geschichts, daß ein grosser Nebel in der Stuben wirdt, daß D. Faustus vor dem Nebel nicht sehen kundte, so bald aber der Nebel vergienge, lagen vor jhme zween Säck, der ein war Goldt, vnd der ander Silber. (23)

Hereupon fell a mist in the hall, that Faustus saw no light, but it lasted not, and so soon as it was gone, there lay before Faustus two great sacks, one full of gold, the other full of silver.[13]

Faust is given wealth in its most seductive form, liquidity that is easily converted into the coin of any realm. In the chapters that immediately

---

[12] Pages 82, 90, and 105.

[13] *History of Faustus*, trans. Rose, 78.

follow, Mephistopheles takes care to accustom the conjurer to a sinful life by providing at no cost first food and drink and then beautiful women. Faust is described as leading an "Epicurean life" and as giving no thought either to the passage of time or to the reality of heaven and hell (25). Not only does he have all of the pleasures that money can buy, but he has the money, too. Thanks to the sin of pride, he has come to embody many of the negative characteristics associated with wealth and the wealthy. Faust is wallowing in wanton luxury. If the conjurer had been allowed to remain in this state for the full twenty-four years, the author of the chapbook would have run the risk of playing the tempter's role himself. At least that perception of the writer might have gained currency within his reading public. The mounting anxiety of the final year and the horror of the damnation scene still would have remained, but the less pious might have been tempted to balance the message of the final section of the narrative against the pleasures of the first three sections. More than two decades of economic stability at the highest level of prosperity and sensual pleasure might have seemed relatively attractive.

But Faust does not remain in this happy state. Instead, the reader soon observes instability: four years after signing the pact, Faust has no money. This state of affairs is reported shortly after the beginning of the third section of the chapbook. His travels concluded and his interest in Mephistopheles's evasive responses to his questions waning, Faust has become a regular houseguest at noble residences, where he provides evening entertainment. Chapter 37 recounts such a visit and concludes with mention of a handsome honorarium (82). All the more jarring is the beginning of Chapter 38, the first sentence of which reads:

> Man spricht, Ein Vnhold vnnd Zauberer werden ein Jahr nicht vmb drey Heller reicher, das widerfuhr dem Doctori Fausto auch, die Verheissung war groß mit seinem Geist, aber viel erlogen ding, wie dann der Teuffel ein Lügen Geist ist, Wurffe Doctori Fausto für die Geschicklichkeit, darmit er durch jhnen begabet seye, Darmit solte er sich selbsten zu Reichthumb schicken, dann jhme dardurch kein Gelt zerrinnen wûrde, so seyen auch seine Jar noch nicht auß, sondern die Versprechung mit jhme erstrecke sich erst auff vier Jahr nach dem Außgang seiner Verheissung, da er mit Gelt vnd Gut kein Mangel haben würde. (83)

> It is said that the fiend and the sorcerer will not wax three penny richer in a year, and even so did it come to pass with Doctor Faustus. Much had been promised by his spirit, but much had been lies, for

the Devil is the spirit of lies. Mephistopheles had once reproached Doctor Faustus, saying:

With the skill where with I have endowed thee thou shouldst acquire thine own wealth. Such arts as mine and thine can scarcely lose thee money. Thy years are not yet over. Only four years are past since my promise to thee that thou wouldst want neither for gold nor for goods.[14]

If Mephistopheles must now counsel his charge how to obtain money, Faust's financial condition has suffered serious reversals since the days of excess immediately after the signing of the pact. That decline is presented as predictable since it is generally known that miscreants never prosper and that the Devil always lies. Positioned in the middle of a long series of adventures, these simple folk truths expressed in prosaic language snap the reader back to reality. Suddenly that reader must compare what the text describes with late sixteenth-century religious and economic norms. Up to this point, both the main character and the reader have been led to suspend critical evaluations of the adventures and to be entertained by the ever-changing variety of experiences. Abruptly, such naive response is shattered by folk truths that have the same "distancing" function as the placards of Brechtian theater. Faust's carefree days are over, and the reader's voyeuristic experience with wild immorality is also at an end. The steady financial support begun by the uncle and continued by the Devil has been stopped. From this point on, Faust is to use his powers and abilities to support the life-style to which he has been accustomed.

Faust's financial history proceeds from the stability of the home of his uncle to boundless opulence and then to instability and even indebtedness. Just after the sobering exchange with Mephistopheles, Faust sets out to go feasting with friends only to discover that he has no cash. He goes to a Jewish moneylender to borrow funds and eventually swindles the Jew. His new vocation as a confidence man is profiled further in the following chapter, "D. Faustus betreugt einen Roßtäuscher" (84-85) ("Dr. Faust Tricks a Horse Trader"). The man who once basked in the status of a wealthy, pious burgher has become the peer of society's outcasts. The response of a reader to the chapter with the moneylender would have been complex. On one hand, Faust could have been admired for proving more clever than the (stereotypically) clever Jew; he might have been applauded for beating the Jew at the Jew's game — larcenous money-making. On the other hand, Faust could have been deplored for having fallen to the level of horse traders,

---

[14] *The History of Doctor Johann Faustus*, trans. H.G. Haile (Urbana: University of Illinois Press, 1965), 86.

moneylenders, and Jews. The chapbook author is using anti-Semitism as a weapon against his central character even though that character is not a Jew. Scholarly evaluations of Faust's financial circumstances go astray when they consider only the sensualist of the early chapters.[15] It could be argued that Faust's ethical reflexes remain constant; but it must be conceded that his behavior and his activities change at this point in the text. Financial stability does return to Faust, but only toward the end of his allotted time. In the twenty-second year of the pact, he receives a gift of gold and silver worth several thousand gilders from Mephistopheles (108). The reader is left to draw the conclusion that for most of the twenty-four years, Faust has to support himself by swindling members of the lower social levels and by entertaining the nobility. The sin of pride has led to a life of financial insecurity.

The presentation in the *Faustbuch* of techniques employed by the Devil was designed to touch a responsive chord in the financially stable townsman. The strategy employed in teaching the lesson about pride was not without risk. Faust's fall from the status of a burgher occurs so early in the twenty-four-year period that the approach of death and damnation potentially has less effect on readers like Spies and his friends. It might have been difficult to feel touched by the death of a social misfit. For his death to trouble such men, Faust must rejoin their ranks shortly before the final act of the tragedy. His status as a burgher must be reasserted.

The late gift of the "treasure" of gold and silver enables Faust to die as a man of property. The final section of the chapbook relates events during the last year of the pact, and the first item on the conjurer's agenda is to set his affairs in order. Accordingly, the first chapter of the section describes Faust's sole heir, the rascally famulus Wagner. The young delinquent has accompanied his benefactor on Faust's journeys and has participated in the various adventures and swindles. When the text reports that Faust refers to Wagner as his son, the reader is reminded of Faust's uncle and the earlier adoption. Of course, the second is a caricature of the first, but moneyed readers would have been able to recall instances in which sole heirs did not deserve their legacies. Faust's estate, as itemized in the chapter, would not have been viewed as inherently evil since a portion of it came from the uncle and since other items were not associated with Faust's sinful ways. The description of the will goes into some detail:

---

[15] For example, Ulrich Stadler, "Notiz über den 'Faustus,'" *Argument-Sonderbände* 3 (1976): 157-58. Rainer Dorner sees Faust as pursuing the goals of "Erkenntnis, Besitz und Macht"; but surely, after the low-point at the beginning of chapter 38, Faust must concentrate on simple self-sufficiency. Dorner, *"Doktor Faust": Zur Sozialgeschichte des deutschen Intellektuellen zwischen frühbürgerlicher Revolution und Reichsgründung (1525-1871)* (Kronberg: Scriptor, 1976), 17.

Als sich nu die zeit mit D. Fausto enden wolte, berüfft er zu sich einen Notarium, darneben etliche Magistros, so offt vmb jnen gewest, vnd verschaffte seinem Famulo das Hauß, sampt dem Garten, neben deß Gansers vnd Veit Rodingers Hauß gelegen, bey dem Eysern Thor, in der Schergassen an der Ringmawren. Item, er verschaffte jhme 1600. Gůlden am Zinßgelt, ein Bawren Gut, acht hundert gůlden wert, sechs hundert Gülden an barem Gelt, eine gülden Kette, drey hundert Cronen werth, Silbergeschirr, was er von Höfen zu wegen gebracht, vnnd sonderlich auß deß Bapsts vnd Türken Hoff, biß in die tausend Gůlden wert, Sonsten war nit viel besonders da an Haußraht, dann er nicht viel daheym gewohnet, sondern bey Wirten vnd Studenten Tag vnd Nacht gefressen vnd gesoffen. (110)

When the time agreed upon for Faust was coming to an end, he summoned a notary and several masters who had spent time with him and bequeathed his famulus the house and garden next to the Gansers and Veit Rodinger's house, which are near the Iron Gate on Scherr Street on the Ring-Wall. Furthermore, he bequeathed him 1600 guilders lent out for "Zins," a farm worth 800 guilders, 600 guilders in cash, a gold chain worth 300 crowns, silver service worth nearly 1000 guilders that he had taken from courts he had visited — in particular the courts of the Pope and the Turk. Otherwise, there were not many household items there because he had not spent much time at home; instead, he had spent his days and nights at taverns eating and drinking with students.

The estate comprises several forms of equity in addition to cash: two parcels of real estate, one of which presumably has been producing income, an interest-yielding investment ("Zinßgelt"), jewelry, and a large amount of silver service. Even that last item — tainted as it is by the larcenous method of its acquisition — even the presence of the silver service would have been somewhat forgivable in the eyes of many readers since the two courts specified as Faust's primary victims were the courts of two enemies of Lutheranism, the rulers of the Roman Catholic Church and of the Ottoman Empire.

In fact, the estate is itemized in order that the reader can empathize with Faust's position, if not with the life story that has left him in that position. It is the will at the beginning that makes the last section of the text a death and damnation scenario that a moneyed townsman could take to heart. The will represents the remnant of a sense of responsibility to a dependent (albeit undeserving) successor: Faust wishes to guarantee Wagner the financial stability that the conjurer had known and then lost. Faust may be an inveterate sinner, but, despite twenty-three years of contact with the Devil, he retains an understanding of the milieu in which he grew up, an appreciation of the security that it can offer, and a determination to assert the rights and meet the final responsibilities of a free townsman. The chapbook author had to create these motivations out of thin air because the three contemporary reports of the circumstances of the historical Faust's death (by Melanchthon, Johannes Gast, and Johannes Müller for the chronicle of Baron von Zimmer) do not so much as mention a will.[16] In those reports, Faust is described as an elderly man who dies during yet another journey. Each report emphasizes the terrible state of the corpse, and one notes the presence of books in the dead man's room. In sharp contrast, the chapbook character laments the fact that he must die while he is still young and full of life (112). He meets his end at an inn just half a mile from Wittenberg, after spending his final days in the old house. The closing monitory address to his students (118-20) again displays Faust's sense of responsibility to those dependent on him. The grotesque death of an aged vagabond, a walking curiosity, has given way to the shocking fate of a famous neighbor who chose the wrong path in his youth and who now must forfeit "the prime of life." Thanks to the decision to spend the night at the inn, Faust's house, assets, and books are not affected by hell's savage assault.

The effect of the changes made in the death scenario is the conversion of an entertaining tale of at least passing interest to all into a tragic biography of immediacy to the members of one social stratum. The intent was to disturb, rather than merely titillate, a reader who was to recognize some of himself in Faust. And the tragic action continues after Faust's death. Wagner's misspent youth and his participation in the years of swindling and riotous living lead the reader to expect that the conjurer's intention to provide security for his ward will be frustrated. Faust's legacy in Wagner's hands will suffer a fate similar to that of the legacy of the uncle in Faust's hands — but at a lower social and intellectual level. Wagner is also assigned a demonic companion, but it is an ape rather than the dark monk Mephistopheles (111). The heir himself will commence independent life with the property of a burgher, but he lacks the education and experience required to gain entry into society's higher strata, or even to maintain his inheritance. The reader can only assume that the "wicked, depraved knave" (110) will fritter away his holdings on mindless pleasures and pranks. Originally a beggar boy, Wagner has come to understand wealth as a gift from hell. That attitude is fully in line with traditional medieval teaching, but it is held by a completely unsympathetic character. Rejection of the famulus by the reader entails rejection of the attitude even as approbation of the uncle entails

---

[16] Henning, 112, 129, 132.

acceptance of the Lutheran position that he represents, the position that piety and wealth can coexist. The probable loss of the fortune built by the uncle is to be viewed as lamentable. The stability of a pious burgher has given way to the instability of an empathetic sinner — which in its turn will give way to the dissipation of a repulsive miscreant. Both the family's ethics and its finances deteriorate from one generation to the next.

The *Faustbuch* was first published during the period of emergence of a Lutheran orthodoxy that was to exert a powerful influence on the cultural life of Germany for several centuries. Still to be addressed then is the question of whether the response to the problem of wealth in the *Faustbuch* differs substantially from the response of Luther and Sachs during the seminal years of the movement.

The answer is a qualified "yes" because, although wealth is a significant motivation in its plot, the *Faustbuch* has no stones to throw at the traditional means of acquiring property. Faust's money-making activities are to be viewed as immoral, if interesting and at times humorous, but the chapbook author does not use Faust's adventures as pretexts for comments on the sinfulness of riches. This is particularly noticeable because the writer *is* determined to have his readers draw conclusions about philosophical and metaphysical "speculation." That is apparent in the title page. Therefore, brief statements concerning the evils of earthly goods would not have constituted a change in the manner in which the author approaches the reader. Stylistic integrity would have been retained. Such statements are not present because there is no longer an underlying hostility to wealth whatever its form. The pious uncle is presented as the norm, not the ideal. As a purely practical matter, a work written for men like the uncle, men like Spies and his friends, cannot reject the professional and commercial pursuits that have put such men in a position not just to read, but actually to buy books.

Nevertheless, elements of Luther's animus are still present. After all, money is proffered by the Devil as a reward for signing the pact. One of Mephistopheles' primary concerns, at least in theory, is that his charge be supplied with the wherewithal to experience every earthly diversion. And the text presents many familiar secondary characters whose negative reputations result from their avarice — characters ranging in status from the Pope to the Jewish moneylender.

But it is in the portrayal of Faust himself that the chapbook makes its clearest statements about the importance of money in a supposedly Christian society. The conjurer surrenders his soul in the expectation of answers to all of his questions. The Devil accepts those terms only to substitute gradually the possibility of financial stability for cosmic revelation. The result is the declassing of a townsman. With no money in his pocket, Faust has no time for speculation; he travels from place to place relying on happenstance and personal notoriety to stave off penury. Itinerancy and regular impoverishment constitute a bond with a group found in the lowest stratum of medieval society, the homeless of the day (the "fahrendes Volk"), who, along with non-resident beggars and the Jews, had no point of entry into established society. Max Baeumer has written that the members of this group were looked upon either as the poor or as the rabble and that they had neither religious nor social status even though they were considered a constituent layer in urban social stratification.[17] While the standing of the peasantry varied from region to region, the pariah status of this urban group was universal. Of course, Faust's fame and his inherited holdings prevent complete descent to this lowest level, but his unwillingness to analyze and control his finances puts his rank as a burgher in jeopardy. Inability is not the problem — this is a man who can get the better of a horse trader. Hell relies not on wealth but on Faust's flawed attitude toward wealth to maintain its control over the conjurer. Faust's eagerness to speculate and his devotion to sensuality have a common source in the sin of pride.

On one hand, the traditional assumption affirmed by Luther of a bond between *vanitas* and wealth is still held. On the other hand, professional money-making is tacitly accepted if an entrepreneur has advanced himself through diligence tempered with piety and if he has used his holdings to help those less fortunate than himself. The character Reichenburger is still suspect in the eyes of Hans Sachs; later in the century, the uncle can be a paragon, the pinnacle of virtuous success from which his adoptive son falls. Writing the will after twenty years of depredation is the first of a series of virtuous actions of the condemned man. Faust takes additional steps to control his legacy when he consults with his heir and when he remonstrates with his students.

The *Faustbuch* returns to the problem of wealth only to leave it unresolved. Opposing images of the townsman before his comfortable house and the Devil behind his bags of silver and gold are recalled at crucial junctures in Faust's story. The Pope is repulsive in part because he wallows in his possessions, but Faust is sympathetic in part because he gives such careful thought to his estate. Luther had used the ambivalence toward wealth that he himself had resuscitated to legitimate his proposal of governmental controls on acquisitiveness. Rather than weighing the *vanitas* analysis of wealth against the legitimation of wealth through the concept of pious diligence, Luther uses the former to improve the latter. He neither illuminates nor settles the old problem of wealth; he uses it. Likewise Sachs never leads the reader to expect Reichenburger to renounce his affluence and his

---

[17] Baeumer, "Gesellschaftliche Aspekte," 17.

faith and to don a sackcloth. The only outcome of a complete victory for his opponent would be a modification of what are presented as customary practices in order to induce greater social responsibility. That same sense of social responsibility motivates Faust's uncle. His act of taking in a poor peasant's son combines Christian caritas with financial self-interest. In effect, the uncle has solved the problem of wealth.

It is Faust's pride that gives new life to the tension between faith and acquisitiveness — a development that burghers of the late sixteenth century would have thought unfortunate. One side effect of Faust's speculations is the reemergence of the concept of *turpe lucrum* — Mephistopheles holding bags of silver and gold. Men who would have seen the uprightness of their personal and professional lives confirmed in the uncle would have been dismayed to contemplate slippage in that esteem, slippage induced by the arrogance of an outsider with visible ties to the propertied estate. In rejecting the values and objectives of his adopted social level, Faust endangers it. If other non-conformists follow Faust's pattern, the self-confidence of that social level, self-confidence so apparent in Spies's introduction, will be shaken. Townsmen will be forced back into the defensive posture personified by Reichenburger half a century earlier. The Fausts of the world must be rejected; their very existence compromises the ethical legitimacy of what later was to become the middle class.

The reader of the *Faustbuch* was to find a "horrifying lesson" and a "sincere warning" directed against moral transgressions: debauchery, impious speculation, pride, commerce with the Devil. Previous interpretations have concentrated on questions raised by the presence of those sins, and properly so. Attention to the text's response to the problem of wealth suggests that an additional, somewhat more subtle transgression concerned the author: insensitivity to decorum. That insensitivity was particularly dangerous in a townsman because the conventions for propriety that incorporated the pursuit of wealth were still new and therefore fragile. Mavericks were in a position to smash the Lutheran construct of decorum appropriate for a moneyed townsman. As a work of social commentary, the *Faustbuch* brings an easily recognizable type of maverick into sharp relief, shows the effects that his behavior has on his family, raises the specter of a reactive return to the concept of *turpe lucrum* with a concomitant undermining of the townsman's position, and thereby suggests the necessity of identifying and ostracizing such mavericks. If readers like Spies and his friends tolerate the Fausts among them, the fate of the conjurer will overtake their entire stratum. The manure pile of the final chapter will become the final resting place of financial integrity, familial responsibility, civic respectability — and personal salvation.

Conclusion

I HAVE WRITTEN THIS study in an attempt to help the modern reader scale the wall that surrounds the literature of Luther's Germany. The metaphor will be familiar to those who regularly mediate between things German and a non-German culture. In their performance of that task, American Germanists tend to focus on familiar writers and canonical works in order to convey most accurately what Robert Weimann has called the "present meaning" of older literature:

> What *is* the object of the literary historian as critic?
> ... To ask the question is ... to suggest that the historian's task (and the pastness of the work) cannot be separated from the critic's task (and the work of art as a present experience). Obviously, we cannot afford to isolate these two necessary aspects: merely to do the former is to fall back into some kind of antiquarianism; merely to do the latter is to run all the risks of misunderstanding and distortion that the New Criticism was guilty of so often.[1]

As a German Shakespearean, Weimann is familiar with the mediation between cultures that carries implications for the temporal mediation that he is discussing. Scholars as talented as he will be able to bring the reflexes of the historian and those of the critic into a state of creative tension. The discipline at large will be able to strike a similar balance because of the complementary tendencies of "foreign" and "native" Germanics. The latter branch grows in the direction of historicism ("antiquarianism") because it serves a German public that knows its great writers and their works. "Foreign" Germanics grows in the direction of formalism because those who cultivate it function as critics in the classrooms and therefore tend to function as critics in their scholarship.

The American tendency is evident here in the selection of wealth as the theme and in the selection of familiar writers and canonical works as the subject matter. During the 1980s Americans seemed to pursue wealth more openly and with fewer apologies than during the two preceding decades, and the national change of heart, whether real or imagined, has occasioned much comment. Both as an analogous debate and as a source of arguments

---

[1] Robert Weimann, *Structure and Society in Literary History: Studies in the History and Theory of Historical Criticism* (Charlottesville: University Press of Virginia, 1976), 47.

for modern debaters, Germany's discussion of the problem of wealth during the sixteenth century is pertinent to the late twentieth-century discussion in the United States. But Weimann's concern about possible misunderstanding and distortion must be borne in mind, for literature as a medium of discussion during the Reformation differs from literature as it is written and read today.

The function of literature has changed. Two developments that separate us from the literary world of the sixteenth century are the replacement of rational suasion by emotional appeal as the goal of literary expression and the division of literature into categories according to artistic worth, whether inherent or assigned. German Romanticism added a complication when it coined the term "Volksbuch." For a century and a half, scholarship wallowed in a mire of nationalistic and racist responses to the new mythology of the "Volk." The English equivalent "chapbook" has no such dubious past, and the etymological root "chap-" identifies the literature in question as a retail commodity. The arrival of literature in the marketplace made possible what we have come to call "literary life." With this in mind, I have proposed that the cognate "Kaufbuch" be given a new meaning: A work of utilitarian fictional literature printed on movable type, bound in book format, and sold on the retail market to the general reading public during the late fifteenth, sixteenth, and early seventeenth centuries.

Responses to the problem of wealth very strikingly during the time in which the "Kaufbücher" were written. Sebastian Brant asserts the traditional view of the medieval church when he teaches that the acquisition of wealth and property makes possible transitory happiness in this world even as it makes certain that death will bring damnation. Avarice is still one of the mortal sins; it can subvert not just an individual, but a family and even a social level. Brant tries to strike fear into the heart of his townsman neighbor by pointing to a familiar type — the once proud burgher of whom the pursuit of wealth has made a fool who begs on street-corners. But the *Narrenschiff* does not send a consistent message. Brant suspends his campaign when he considers those whose diligence and determination in professional or business activities has produced wealth.

The pervasive defensiveness and the occasional ambivalence of the *Narrenschiff* suggest that Brant knew that he was engaged in a futile attempt to halt the advance of an opposing analysis of wealth. The chapbook *Reynke de Vos* offers that analysis. The fox is successful because he understands that self-aggrandizement is the linchpin of his society, a society that the chapbook author finds amusing, not horrifying. Although the author does not affirm the thinly veiled materialism of King Nobel's realm, neither does he hold up traditional Christian morality as the alternative. The shift from rule by force toward meritocratic rule would have been welcomed by the townsman of

1500. He saw his social, economic, and moral environment reflected not only in *Reynke de Vos* but also in *Dil Ulenspiegel* and *Fortunatus*. *Dil Ulenspiegel* analyzes late medieval materialism from below — from the perspective of a non-conformist who has regular brushes with penury and starvation. *Fortunatus* brings the opposite perspective; Fortunatus, whose wealth gives him the status of a prince, touches the lives of others from above. A semblance of objective analysis is possible in both works because each central character maintains ironic distance from his social status: Till because he embodies the rogue type that stands apart from the occupational groups that constitute society's lower levels, and Fortunatus because he and the reader remember his humble beginnings. In neither chapbook does the author castigate the hero's world for its materialism, and in neither is the hero offered as a negative example.

Martin Luther's writings on money-making practices evince a profound hostility to commerce, finance, and the pursuit of wealth in general. But while his reflexes resemble Brant's, his position in the early 1520s as the leader of a developing movement entailed some subordination of personal attitudes to the survival of the new polity. Luther responded to the challenge first by railing against money-making practices, then by suggesting the need for greater governmental control, and finally by offering the ideal of the Christian merchant as a compromise to those followers who were also businessmen. Hans Sachs puts his critique of the wealthy into the mouth of a Catholic monk in order to capture the attention of his Lutheran audience. To Luther's arguments he adds the appeal to members of the new congregation that they not discredit their faith through questionable business practices. The pursuit of profits must be subjected to scrupulous oversight.

Acceptance of the wealthy Lutheran had been tentative in 1524, but it seemed permanent by 1587. That much is apparent in the *Faustbuch* with its presentation of the fall of a Lutheran family from the pious burgher who "adopts" Faust to the speculator and sympathetic confidence man himself and finally to Faust's "son," the repulsive scoundrel Wagner. Of the many warnings issued by the chapbook, one is directed against Faust's addiction to the pleasures of the flesh — that is, against an extreme form of the same egocentric devotion to one's physical well-being that Sachs's monk sees in his Lutheran interlocutor. Faust's behavior has the potential of reopening the discussion of wealth and its pursuit as a problem and, in the process, resurrecting the medieval concept of *turpe lucrum*. The author of the *Faustbuch*, who saw no inherent conflict between piety and wealth in the person of Faust's "father," feared the return of the concept. It was in the self-interest of well-established Lutherans to reject non-conformists like Faust.

The patina of six decades had not made Luther's solution to the problem attractive. Then as now, the ancient animus against disproportionate wealth could be stimulated too easily. And then as now, the politic, or at least pragmatic response to that possibility was silence. To address the problem was to open Pandora's box. Before modern American readers rush to find the stance of the *Faustbuch* author cowardly, they should consider their response to and participation in the "affluent eighties." Cultural condescension may be unavoidable if we find ourselves in an ethically superior position. If not, we would do well to view the response of the chapbook either as a stimulus to find satisfactory contemporary solutions to the problem or as a warning posted above a box that is still too dangerous to be opened.

Bibliography

Albrecht, Günter, Joachim G. Boeckh, Kurt Böttcher, Klaus Gysi, and Paul Günter Krohn. *Geschichte der deutschen Literatur: Von 1480 bis 1600*. Berlin: Volk und Wissen Volkseigener Verlag, 1961.

Arendt, Dieter. "Eulenspiegel: Sprachwitz und Widerstand." *Kürbiskern* 2 (1977): 108-16.

—. *Eulenspiegel — ein Narrenspiegel der Gesellschaft*. Stuttgart: Klett-Cotta, 1978.

Aust, Hugo. "Zum Stil der Volksbücher: Ein Problemaufriß." *Euphorion* 78, no. 1 (1984): 60-81.

Bachorski, Hans-Jürgen. *Geld und soziale Identität im "Fortunatus": Studien zur literarischen Bewältigung frühbürgerlicher Widersprüche*. Göppingen: Kümmerle, 1983.

Baeumer, Max L. "Gesellschaftliche Aspekte der 'Volks'-Literatur im 15. und 16. Jahrhundert." In *Popularität und Trivialität*. Ed. Jost Hermand and Reinhold Grimm. Frankfurt am Main: Athenäum, 1974.

—. "Sozialkritische und revolutionäre Literatur der Reformationszeit." *Internationales Archiv für Sozialgeschichte der deutschen Literatur* 5 (1980): 169-233.

—. "Die sozialen Verhältnisse und der sozialkritische Charakter der Volksliteratur im braunschweigischen Raum zur Zeit des *Dyl Vlenspiegel*." *Eulenspiegel-Jahrbuch* 25 (1985): 33-47.

Bainton, Roland H. *Here I Stand: A Life of Martin Luther*. 1950. New York: New American Library, 1964.

—. *The Age of the Reformation*. Princeton: Van Nostrand, 1956.

Balzer, Bernd. *Bürgerliche Reformationspropaganda: Die Flugschriften des Hans Sachs in den Jahren 1523-25*. Stuttgart: Metzler, 1973.

Bausinger, Hermann. *Formen der "Volkspoesie."* 2nd ed. Berlin: Schmidt, 1980.

Becker, Eva D. *Der deutsche Roman um 1780.* Stuttgart: Metzler, 1964.

Benz, Richard. *Die deutschen Volksbücher: Ein Beitrag zur Geschichte der deutschen Dichtung.* Jena: Diederichs, 1913.

Bienert, Walther. *Martin Luther und die Juden: Ein Quellenbuch mit zeitgenössischen Illustrationen, mit Einführungen und Erläuterungen.* Frankfurt am Main: Evangelisches Verlagswerk, 1982.

Böckmann, Paul. "Der gemeine Mann in den Flugschriften der Reformation." In his *Formensprache: Studien zur Literaturästhetik und Dichtungsinterpretation.* Hamburg: Hoffman und Campe, 1966.

Bollenbeck, Georg. "Das 'Volksbuch' als Projektionsformel: Zur Entstehung und Wirkung eines Konventionsbegriffes." In *Mittelalter — Rezeption: Gesammelte Vorträge des Salzburger Symposions "Die Rezeption mittelalterlicher Dichter und ihrer Werke in Literatur, bildender Kunst und Musik des 19. und 20. Jahrhunderts."* Ed. Jürgen Kühnel, Hans-Dieter Mück, and Ulrich Müller. Göttingen: Kümmerle, 1979.

—. *Till Eulenspiegel: Der dauerhafte Schwankheld: Zum Verhältnis von Produktions- und Rezeptionsgeschichte.* Stuttgart: Metzler, 1985.

Brandt, Anne-Kathrin. *Die "tugendreich fraw Armut": Besitz und Armut in der Tugendlehre des Hans Sachs.* Göttingen: Gratia, 1979.

Brandt, Walther I. "Introduction." "Trade and Usury." *Luther's Works.* Trans. Charles M. Jacobs, and Walther I. Brandt. Philadelphia: Muhlenberg, 1962.

Brant, Sebastian. *[Das] Narrenschiff.* Ed. Friedrich Zarncke. Leipzig: Wigand, 1854.

—. *The Ship of Fools.* Trans. Edwin H. Zeydel. 1944. New York: Dover, 1962.

Bruford, Walter Horace. *Germany in the Eighteenth Century: The Social Background of the Literary Revival.* 1935. Cambridge: Cambridge University Press, 1968.

Burger, Heinz Otto. *Renaissance Humanismus Reformation: Deutsche Literatur im europäischen Kontext.* Bad Homburg: Gehlen, 1969.

Cannon-Geary, Irene. "Trends in Literary Research: New Developments in GDR Reception of the Sixteenth Century in Germany." *German Quarterly* 55, no. 3 (1982): 370-86.

The Compact Edition of the Oxford English Dictionary. Oxford: Oxford University Press, 1971.

Davies, Clifford S.L. "Die bäuerliche Gemeinde in England (1400-1800)." In *Aufstände, Revolten, Prozesse: Beiträge zu bäuerlichen Widerstandsbewegungen im frühneuzeitlichen Europa.* Ed. Winfried Schulze. Stuttgart: Klett-Cotta, 1983.

Dilthey, Wilhelm. *Das Erlebnis und die Dichtung: Lessing, Goethe, Novalis, Hölderlin.* Leipzig: Teubner, 1906.

Dorner, Rainer. *"Doktor Faust": Zur Sozialgeschichte des deutschen Intellektuellen zwischen frühbürgerlicher Revolution und Reichsgründung (1525-1871).* Kronberg: Scriptor, 1976.

Duden: Das große Wörterbuch der deutschen Sprache in sechs Bänden. Mannheim: Bibliographisches Institut, 1978.

Durant, Will. *The Reformation: A History of European Civilization from Wyclif to Calvin: 1300-1564.* New York: Simon and Schuster, 1957.

Eichborn, Reinhart von. *Der kleine Eichborn: Wirtschaft und Wirtschaftsrecht.* Hövelhof: Siebenpunkt, 1981.

Engelsing, Rolf. *Analphabetentum und Lektüre: Zur Sozialgeschichte des Lesers in Deutschland zwischen feudaler und industrieller Gesellschaft.* Stuttgart: Metzler, 1973.

—. *Der Bürger als Leser: Lesergeschichte in Deutschland 1500-1800.* Stuttgart: Metzler, 1974.

—. *Zur Sozialgeschichte deutscher Mittel- und Unterschichten.* 2nd ed. Göttingen: Vandenhoeck & Ruprecht, 1978.

Entner, Heinz, and Werner Lenk. "Literatur und Revolution im 16. Jahrhundert: Zu einigen Aspekten der Renaissancekultur." *Weimarer Beiträge* 5 (1970): 139-62.

Entner, Heinz, Horst Heintze, Helga Militz, Ingrid Schiewek, Ingeborg Spriewald, Monika Walter, and Robert Weimann. *Realismus in der Renaissance: Aneignung der Welt in der erzählenden Prosa*. Berlin: Aufbau, 1977.

Erffa, Dagmar von. *Wirtschaftslexikon*. Munich: Humboldt, 1976.

Foerste, William. "Von Reinaerts Historie zum Reinke de vos." *Niederdeutsche Studien (Münstersche Beiträge zur niederdeutschen Philologie)* 6 (1960): 105-46.

Fortunatus: Studienausgabe nach der editio princeps von 1509. Ed. Hans-Gert Roloff. Stuttgart: Reclam, 1981.

Friedenthal, Richard. *Luther*. London: Weidenfeld and Nicolson, 1970.

Frey, Winfried, Walter Raitz, and Dieter Seitz. *Einführung in die deutsche Literatur des 12. bis 16. Jahrhunderts: Band 3: Bürgertum und Fürstenstaat — 15./16. Jahrhundert*. Opladen: Westdeutscher Verlag, 1981.

Fuhrmann, Horst. *Deutsche Geschichte im hohen Mittelalter: Von der Mitte des 11. bis zum Ende des 12. Jahrhunderts*. Göttingen: Vandenhoeck & Ruprecht, 1978.

Geering, Traugott. *Handel und Industrie der Stadt Basel: Zunftwesen und Wirtschaftsgeschichte bis zum Ende des 17. Jahrhunderts*. Basle: Schneider, 1886.

"Gesprech biechlin neüw Karsthans." *Die Reformation im zeitgenössischen Dialog: 12 Texte aus den Jahren 1520-25*. Ed. Werner Lenk. Berlin: Akademie-Verlag, 1968.

Görres, Johann Joseph von. *Die teutschen Volksbücher: Nähere Würdigung der schönen Historien-, Wetter- und Arzneybüchlein, welche theils innerer Werth, theils Zufall, Jahrhunderte hindurch bis auf unsere Zeit erhalten hat*. Vol. 3 of *Joseph Görres gesammelte Schriften*. Ed. Wilhelm Schellberg. Cologne: Gilde, 1926.

Goossens, Jan. "Reynaerts und Reynkes Begegnung mit dem Affen Martin." *Niederdeutsches Wort* 20 (1980): 73-84.

Grimm, Jacob, and Wilhelm Grimm. *Deutsches Wörterbuch*. Leipzig: Hirzel, 1854-1961.

Grimminger, Rolf. "Aufklärung, Absolutismus und bürgerliche Individuen: Über den notwendigen Zusammenhang von Literatur, Gesellschaft und Staat in der Geschichte des 18. Jahrhunderts." In *Deutsche Aufklärung bis zur französischen Revolution*. Ed. Rolf Grimminger. Vol. 3 of *Hansers Sozialgeschichte der deutschen Literatur vom 16. Jahrhundert bis zur Gegenwart*. Ed. Rolf Grimminger. Munich: Hanser, 1980.

Habermann, Paul, and Wolfgang Mohr. "Deutsche Versmaße und Strophenformen." *Reallexikon der deutschen Literaturgeschichte*. 2nd ed. Berlin: de Gruyter, 1958.

Hadley, Michael. *Romanverzeichnis: Bibliographie der zwischen 1750-1800 erschienenen Erstausgaben*. Berne: Lang, 1977.

Hankamer, Paul. *Deutsche Gegenreformation und deutsches Barock: Deutsche Literatur im Zeitraum des 17. Jahrhunderts*. 1935. Stuttgart: Metzler, 1964.

Haug, Wolfgang Fritz. "Die Einübung bürgerlicher Verkehrsformen bei Eulenspiegel." *Argument-Sonderband* 3 (1976): 4-27.

Heeroma, Klaas. "Henric van Alckmaer: Versuch einer neuen Würdigung." *Niederdeutsches Jahrbuch: Jahrbuch des Vereins für niederdeutsche Sprachforschung* 93 (1970): 16-35.

Henning, Hans. "Faust als historisches Gestalt." *Jahrbuch der Goethe-Gesellschaft* 20 (1959): 107-39.

Hildebrandt, Hans Hagen. "Sozialkritik in der List Till Eulenspiegels: Sozialgeschichtliches zum Verständnis der Historien von Till Eulenspiegel (1971)." In *Eulenspiegel-Interpretationen: Der Schalk im Spiegel der Forschung 1807-1977*. Ed. Werner Wunderlich. Munich: Fink, 1979.

Hilton, R.H. *The English Peasantry in the Late Middle Ages: The Ford Lectures for 1973 and Related Studies*. Oxford: Clarendon, 1975.

The History of the Damnable Life and Deserved Death of Doctor John Faustus. Trans. William Rose. London: Routledge, 1930.

The History of Doctor Johann Faustus. Trans. H.G. Haile. Urbana: University of Illinois Press, 1965.

Hoffmann, Konrad. "Wort und Bild im 'Narrenschiff.'" In *Literatur und Laienbildung im Spätmittelalter und in der Reformationszeit: Symposion Wolfenbüttel 1981*. Ed. Ludger Grenzmann and Karl Stackmann. Stuttgart: Metzler, 1984.

Honegger, Peter. *Ulenspiegel: Ein Beitrag zur Druckgeschichte und zur Verfasserfrage*. Neumünster: Wachholtz, 1973.

Huizinga, Johan. *Herbst des Mittelalters: Studien über Lebens- und Geistesformen des 14. und 15. Jahrhunderts in Frankreich und in den Niederlanden*. Stuttgart: Kröner, 1969.

"Karsthans." *Die Reformation im zeitgenössischen Dialog: 12 Texte aus den Jahren 1520 bis 1525*. Ed. Werner Lenk. Berlin: Akademie-Verlag, 1968.

Kellenbenz, Hermann. "Gewerbe und Handel." In *Handbuch der deutschen Wirtschafts- und Sozialgeschichte: Von der Frühzeit bis zum Ende des 18. Jahrhunderts*. Ed. Hermann Aubin and Wolfgang Zorn. Stuttgart: Klett, 1971.

—. *Deutsche Wirtschaftsgeschichte: Von den Anfängen bis zum Ende des 18. Jahrhunderts*. Munich: Beck, 1977.

Kemper, Hans-Georg. *Deutsche Lyrik der frühen Neuzeit: Band 1: Epochen- und Gattungsprobleme: Reformationszeit*. Tübingen: Niemeyer, 1987.

Kemper, Raimund. "Zur Beurteilung des Sebastian Brant." *Leuvense Bijdragen* 73, no. 1 (1984): 1-31.

Kluckhohn, August. "Zur Geschichte der Handelsgesellschaften und Monopole im Zeitalter der Reformation." In *Historische Aufsätze dem Andenken an Georg Waitz gewidmet*. Hannover: Hahn, 1886.

Könneker, Barbara. *Wesen und Wandlung der Narrenidee im Zeitalter des Humanismus: Brant — Murner — Erasmus*. Wiesbaden: Steiner, 1966.

—. "Faust-Konzeption und Teufelspakt im Volksbuch von 1587." In *Festschrift Gottfried Weber.* Ed. Heinz Otto Burger and Klaus von See. Bad Homburg: Gehlen, 1967.

—. *Hans Sachs.* Stuttgart: Metzler, 1971.

—. *Die deutsche Literatur der Reformationszeit: Kommentar zu einer Epoche.* Munich: Winkler, 1975.

Körner, Josef. "Erlebnis — Motiv — Stoff." In *Vom Geiste neuer Literaturforschung: Festschrift für Oskar Walzel.* Ed. Julius Wahle and Victor Klemperer. Potsdam: Athenaion, 1924.

Kohlschmidt, Werner. *Geschichte der deutschen Literatur vom Barock bis zur Klassik.* Stuttgart: Reclam, 1965.

Kokott, Hartmut. *"Reynke de Vos."* Munich: Fink, 1981.

Krause, Joachim. *Der deutsche Buchhandel: Kurze Geschichte und Organisation.* Düsseldorf: Buchhändler heute, 1975.

Kreutzer, Hans Joachim. *Der Mythos vom Volksbuch: Studien zur Wirkungsgeschichte des frühen deutschen Romans seit der Romantik.* Stuttgart: Metzler, 1977.

Kreuzer, Helmut. "Trivialliteratur als Forschungsproblem: Zur Kritik des deutschen Trivialromans seit der Aufklärung." In his *Veränderung des Literaturbegriffs: Fünf Beiträge zu aktuellen Problemen der Literaturwissenschaft.* Göttingen: Vandenhoeck & Ruprecht, 1975.

Krogmann, Willy. "Ulenspiegel." *Die deutsche Literatur des Mittelalters: Verfasserlexikon.* Ed. Karl Langosch. Berlin: de Gruyter, 1953.

Ein kurtzweilig Lesen von Dil Ulenspiegel. Ed. Wolfgang Lindlow. Stuttgart: Reclam, 1968.

Landgraf, Wolfgang. *Martin Luther: Reformator und Rebell: Biographie.* Berlin: Verlag Neues Leben, 1981.

Langosch, Karl. "Nachwort." *Reineke Fuchs: Das niederdeutsche Epos "Reynke de Vos" von 1498 mit 40 Holzschnitten des Originals.* Trans. Karl Langosch. Stuttgart: Reclam, 1975.

Lenk, Werner. "Einleitung." *Die Reformation im zeitgenössischen Dialog: 12 Texte aus den Jahren 1520 bis 1525.* Ed. Werner Lenk. Berlin: Akademie-Verlag, 1968.

Leuscher, Joachim. *Deutschland im späten Mittelalter.* Göttingen: Vandenhoeck & Ruprecht, 1975.

Liepe, Wolfgang. "Volksbuch." *Reallexikon der deutschen Literaturgeschichte.* Ed. Paul Merker and Wolfgang Stammler. Berlin: de Gruyter, 1928.

Lindow, Wolfgang. "Nachwort." *Ein kurtzweilig Lesen von Dil Ulenspiegel.* Ed. Wolfgang Lindow. Stuttgart: Reclam, 1968.

—. "Der Narr und sein Publikum: Einige Anmerkungen zur Rolle des Titelhelden im Volksbuch vom Eulenspiegel (1971)." In *Eulenspiegel-Interpretationen: Der Schalk im Spiegel der Forschung 1807-1977.* Ed. Werner Wunderlich. Munich: Fink, 1977.

Lohse, Bernhard. *Martin Luther: Eine Einführung in sein Leben und sein Werk.* Munich: Beck, 1981.

Ludwig, Karl. *Kurze Geschichte des Buchhandels in Deutschland.* 3rd. ed. Düsseldorf: Jung, 1964.

Lütge, Friedrich. *Deutsche Sozial- und Wirtschaftsgeschichte: Ein Überblick.* 3rd ed. Berlin: Springer, 1966.

Luther, Martin. *Die Propheten alle Deudsch.* Wittenberg: Hans Lufft, 1536.

—. *Martin Luthers Werke: Kritische Gesammtausgabe* (Weimar Edition). Weimar: Böhlau, 1883-1966.

—. *Luther's Works.* Ed. Helmut T. Lehmann. St. Louis: Concordia, 1955-date.

Mackensen, Lutz. *Die deutschen Volksbücher.* Leipzig: Quelle und Meyer, 1927.

Manger, Klaus. *Das "Narrenschiff": Entstehung, Wirkung und Deutung.* Darmstadt: Wissenschaftliche Buchgesellschaft, 1983.

Marx, Karl, and Friedrich Engels. *Die deutsche Ideologie*. Vol. 3 of their *Werke*. Ed. Institut für Marxismus-Leninismus beim ZK der SED. Berlin: Dietz, 1958.

Mischler, Beat. *Gliederung und Produktion des "Narrenschiffes" (1494) von Sebastian Brant*. Bonn: Bouvier, 1981.

Moeller, Bernd. "Probleme der Reformationsgeschichtsforschung." *Zeitschrift für Kirchengeschichte* 14 (1965): 246-57.

—. *Deutschland im Zeitalter der Reformation*. Göttingen: Vandenhoeck & Ruprecht, 1977.

Mörke, Olaf. "Die Fugger im 16. Jahrhundert: Städtische Elite oder Sonderstruktur? Ein Diskussionsbeitrag." *Archiv für Reformationsgeschichte* 74 (1983): 141-62.

Mottek, Hans. *Wirtschaftsgeschichte Deutschlands: Ein Grundriß*. Berlin: VEB Deutscher Verlag der Wissenschaften, 1964.

Müller, Günther. *Geschichte der deutschen Seele: Vom Faustbuch zu Goethes Faust*. Freiburg: Herder, 1939.

—. "Das Zeitgerüst des Fortunatus-Volksbuchs." In his *Morphologische Poetik: Gesammelte Aufsätze*. Tübingen: Niemeyer, 1968.

Müller, Jan-Dirk. "Poet, Prophet, Politiker: Sebastian Brant als Publizist und die Rolle der laikalen Intelligenz um 1500." *LiLi: Zeitschrift für Literaturwissenschaft und Linguistik* 10, no. 37 (1980): 102-27.

—. "Gattungstransformation und Anfänge des literarischen Marktes." *Textsorten und literarische Gattungen: Dokumentation des Germanistentages in Hamburg vom 1. bis 4. April 1979*. Berlin: Schmidt, 1983.

Nadler, Josef. *Buchhandel, Literatur und Nation in Geschichte und Gegenwart*. Berlin: Junker and Dünnhaupt, 1932.

Pascal, Roy. *The Social Basis of the Reformation: Martin Luther and His Times*. 1933. New York: Kelley, 1971.

A Pleasant Vintage of Till Eulenspiegel, Born in the Country of Brunswick. How He Spent His Life. 96 of His Tales. Trans. Paul Eugene Oppenheimer. Diss. Columbia University, 1970.

Prang, Helmut. *Formgeschichte der Dichtkunst.* Stuttgart: Kohlhammer, 1968.

Raitz, Walter. *Zur Soziogenese des bürgerlichen Romans: Eine literatursoziologische Analyse des "Fortunatus."* Düsseldorf: Bertelsmann, 1973.

—. *"Fortunatus."* Munich: Fink, 1984.

Reineke Fuchs: Das niederdeutsche Epos "Reynke de Vos" von 1498 mit 40 Holzschnitten des Originals. Trans. Karl Langosch. Stuttgart: Reclam, 1975.

Reinke de Vos. Ed. Friedrich Prien and Albert Leitzmann. 3rd ed. Halle/Saale: Niemeyer, 1960.

Reuter, Hans-Heinrich, and Werner Rieck. *Geschichte der deutschen Literatur: Vom Ausgang des 17. Jahrhunderts bis 1789.* Berlin: Volk und Wissen Volkseigener Verlag, 1979.

Reynard the Fox. [Trans. Dietrich Wilhelm Soltau.] 1826. Boston: Estes, 1901.

Ritter, Gerhard. *Studien zur Spätscholastik: Via antiqua und via moderna auf den deutschen Universitäten des 15. und 16. Jahrhunderts.* Heidelberg: Winter, 1921-27.

Roloff, Hans-Gert. "Anfänge des deutschen Prosaromans." *Handbuch des deutschen Romans.* Ed. Helmut Koopmann. Düsseldorf: Bagel, 1983.

Rupprich, Hans. *Die deutsche Literatur vom späten Mittelalter bis zum Barock: Erster Teil: Das ausgehende Mittelalter, Humanismus und Renaissance, 1370-1520.* Vol 4. Part 1 of *Geschichte der deutschen Literatur von den Anfängen bis zur Gegenwart.* By Helmut de Boor and Richard Newald. Munich: Beck, 1970.

Sachs, Hans. "Ein Dialogus des inhalt ein argument der Römischen wider das Christlich heüflein; den Geytz, auch ander offenlich laster etc.

betreffend." *Die Prosadialoge von Hans Sachs.* Ed. Ingeborg Spriewald. Leipzig: VEB Bibliographisches Institut, 1970.

Schenda, Rudolf. "Bilder vom Lesen — Lesen von Bildern." *Internationales Archiv für Sozialgeschichte der deutschen Literatur* 12 (1987): 82-106.

Scheuer, Helmut. "Das 'Volksbuch' *Fortunatus* (1509): Zwischen feudaler Anpassung und bürgerlicher Selbstverwirklichung." In *Literatursoziologie II: Beiträge zur Praxis.* Ed. Joachim Bark. Stuttgart: Kohlhammer, 1974.

Schmidt, Peter. "Buchmarkt, Verlagswesen und Zeitschriften." In *Zwischen Absolutismus und Aufklärung: Rationalismus, Empfindsamkeit, Sturm und Drang: 1740-1786.* Ed. Ralph-Rainer Wuthenow. Vol. 4 of *Deutsche Literatur: Eine Sozialgeschichte.* Ed. Horst Albert Glaser. Reinbek: Rowohlt, 1980.

Schutte, Jürgen. "'Was ist vns vnser freyhait nutz / wenn wir ir nicht brauchen durffen': Zur Interpretation der Prosadialoge." In *Hans Sachs: Studien zur frühbürgerlichen Literatur im 16. Jahrhundert.* Ed. Joachim Bumke, Thomas Cramer, Gert Kaiser, Horst Wenzel. Berne: Lang, 1978.

Schwitalla, Johannes. *Deutsche Flugschriften 1460-1525: Textsortengeschichtliche Studien.* Tübingen: Niemeyer, 1983.

Spengler, Walter Eckehart. "Volksbuch." In *Reallexikon der deutschen Literaturgeschichte.* Ed. Klaus Kanzog and Achim Masser. 2nd ed. Berlin: de Gruyter, 1982.

Sprandel, Rolf. "Sozialgeschichte 1300-1500." In *Handbuch der deutschen Wirtschafts- und Sozialgeschichte: Von der Frühzeit bis zum Ende des 18. Jahrhunderts.* Ed. Hermann Aubin and Wolfgang Zorn. Stuttgart: Klett, 1971.

Spriewald, Ingeborg. "Einleitung." *Die Prosadialoge von Hans Sachs.* Leipzig: VEB Bibliographisches Institut, 1970.

—. *Vom "Eulenspiegel" zum "Simplicissimus": Zur Genesis des Realismus in den Anfängen der deutschen Prosaerzählung.* Berlin: Akademie-Verlag, 1978.

—. "Der Bürger ergreift das Wort: Luther und die Reformation im Werk von Hans Sachs. "*Weimarer Beiträge* 29, no. 2 (1983): 1908-27.

Spriewald, Ingeborg, Heinz Entner, Werner Lenk, and Hildegard Schnabel. *Grundpositionen der deutschen Literatur im 16. Jahrhundert*. Berlin: Aufbau, 1976.

Stadler, Ulrich. "Notiz über den 'Faustus.'" *Argument-Sonderbände* 3 (1976): 156-61.

Steiner, Gerhard. "Zur Exegese des Volksbuchs von Till Eulenspiegel." *Acta Litteraria Academiae Scientiarum Hungaricae* 2 (1959): 251-75.

Suchsland, Peter. "Anmerkungen." *Deutsche Volksbücher in drei Bänden: Dritter Band: Historia von Doktor Johann Fausten, Histori von den vier Heymonskindern*. Berlin: Aufbau, 1975.

Szövérffy, Josef. "Das Volksbuch: Geschichte und Problematik." *Der Deutschunterricht* 14, no. 2 (1962): 5-28.

Trunz, Erich. "Nachwort." Johann Wolfgang von Goethe. *Gedichte und Epen I*. Vol. 1 of *Goethes Werke* (Hamburg Edition). 12th ed. Munich: Beck, 1981.

Ungern-Sternberg, Wolfgang von. "Schriftsteller und literarischer Markt." In *Deutsche Aufklärung bis zur französischen Revolution*. Ed. Rolf Grimminger. Vol. 3 of *Hansers Sozialgeschichte der deutschen Literatur vom 16. Jahrhundert bis zur Gegenwart*. Ed. Rolf Grimminger. Munich: Hanser, 1980.

Unwin, George. *Industrial Organization in the Sixteenth and Seventeenth Centuries*. 1904. New York: Kelley, 1971.

Van Cleve, John. "Converting the Common Man: German Dialogues of the Early Reformation." *Colloquia Germanica* 13, no. 2 (1980): 97-105.

—. "Two Priests for Reineke Fuchs." *Neophilologus* 65, no. 2 (1980): 239-46.

Das Volksbuch vom Doctor Faust: Nach der ersten Ausgabe, 1587. Ed. Robert Petsch. 2nd ed. Halle/Saale: Niemeyer, 1911.

Walzel, Oskar. *Leben, Erleben und Dichten: Ein Versuch*. Leipzig: Haessel, 1912.

Weber, Ernst, and Christine Mithal. *Deutsche Originalromane zwischen 1680 und 1780: Eine Bibliographie mit Besitznachweisen*. Munich: Schmidt, 1983.

Wedler, Klaus. "Klassenkampf und Bündnisproblematik in den Flugschriften, Fastnachtspielen und Zeitgedichten des Hans Sachs." In *Der Bauer im Klassenkampf: Studien zur Geschichte des deutschen Bauernkrieges und der bäuerlichen Klassenkämpfe im Spätfeudalismus*. Ed. Gerhard Heitz, Adolf Laube, Max Steinmetz, and Günter Vogler. Berlin: Akademie-Verlag, 1975.

Weimann, Robert. *Structure and Society in Literary History: Studies in the History and Theory of Historical Criticism*. Charlottesville: University Press of Virginia, 1976.

Widmann, Hans. "Geschichte des deutschen Buchhandels." *Der deutsche Buchhandel: Wesen — Gestalt — Aufgabe*. Ed. Helmut Hiller and Wolfgang Strauß. Hamburg: Verlag für Buchmarkt-Forschung, 1968.

Wiemann, Renate. *Die Erzählstruktur im Volksbuch Fortunatus*. Hildesheim and New York: Olms, 1970.

Winkler, Hannelore. "Zum soziologischen Aspekt von Flugschriften aus der Zeit der Reformation." *Beiträge zur Geschichte der deutschen Sprache und Literatur* (Halle) 94 (1974): 37-51.

Wis, Marjatta. "Zum deutschen 'Fortunatus': Die mittelalterlichen Pilger als Erweiterer des Weltbildes." *Neuphilologische Mitteilungen* 63, no. 1 (1962): 5-55.

—. "Nochmals zum 'Fortunatus'-Volksbuch: Quellen- und Datierungsprobleme." *Neuphilologische Mitteilungen* 66, no. 2 (1965): 199-209.

Wiswe, Hans. "Sozialgeschichtliches um Till Eulenspiegel (1971)." *Eulenspiegel-Interpretationen: Der Schalk im Speigel der Forschung 1807-1977*. Ed. Werner Wunderlich. Munich: Fink, 1979.

Witton, Niclas. "Die Vorlage des Reinke de Vos." In *Reynaert Reynard Reynke: Studien zu einem mittelalterlichen Tierepos*. Ed. Jan Goossens and Timothy Sedmann. Cologne and Vienna: Böhlau, 1980.

Wolf, Herbert. *Martin Luther: Eine Einführung in germanistische Luther-Studien*. Stuttgart: Metzler, 1980.

Wunderlich, Werner. *"Till Eulenspiegel."* Munich: Fink, 1984.

—. "Till Eulenspiegel: Zur Karriere eines Schalksnarren in Geschichte und Gegenwart." *Monatshefte* 78, no. 1 (1986): 38-47.

Zeydel, Edwin H. *Sebastian Brant*. New York: Twayne, 1967.

Zorn, Wolfgang. "Sozialgeschichte 1500-1648." *Handbuch der deutschen Wirtschafts- und Sozialgeschichte: Von der Frühzeit bis zum Ende des 18. Jahrhunderts*. Ed. Hermann Aubin and Wolfgang Zorn. Stuttgart: Klett, 1971.

Index

Aeneas Sylvius (Pope Pius II) 26
Albrecht, Günter 155, 179
Alckmer, Hinrek van 63, 64, 183
Alexandria 100
Anhalt 166
Apocrypha 128
Arendt, Dieter 96, 97, 179
Aschersleben 89
Aubin, Hermann 20, 106, 184, 189, 192
Augsburg 20, 98, 108
Augustine 139
Aust, Hugo 15, 16, 179

Bachorski, Hans-Jürgen 101, 179
Baeumer, Max L. 3, 4, 5, 121, 173, 179
Bainton, Roland H. 179
Balzer, Bernd 21, 137, 149, 150, 179
Bark, Joachim 101, 189
Basle 24, 26, 43, 182
Bausinger, Hermann 4, 180
Becker, Eva D. 3, 180
Benz, Richard 9, 10, 11, 12, 180
Bible 25, 112, 114, 116, 128, 132, 139, 140, 146
Bienert, Walther 112, 118, 119, 180
Boeckh, Joachim G. 155, 179
Böckmann, Paul 121, 180
Böttcher, Kurt 155, 179
Bollenbeck, Georg 9, 90, 97, 180
"Bond of the Shoe" uprising 121
Boor, Helmut de 76, 188
Bote, Hermen 83, 85-97, 98, 109, 110, 127, 155, 156, 177, 179, 180, 183, 184, 185, 186, 188, 189, 190, 191, 192
Brandon (St. Brandon) 91
Brandt, Anne-Kathrin 140, 180
Brandt, Walther I. 112, 180
Brant, Barbara Picker 24
Brant, Diebold 24
Brant, Sebastian 19, 23-61, 77-78, 80, 81, 83, 85, 117-18, 130, 162, 176, 177, 180, 184, 186, 187
Braunschweig 85, 86, 94, 179
Brecht, Bertolt 168
Brentano, Clemens 4
Brittany 99
Bruford, Walter Horace 3, 180
Bumke, Joachim 150, 189
Burger, Heinz Otto 155, 181, 185

Calcutta 129
Calvin, John 121, 181
Cannon-Geary, Irene 5, 6, 181
China 100
Churchyard, Thomas 98
Constantinople 99
Cramer, Thomas 150, 189
Crates 30, 45
Croesus 29, 30, 40
Crotus Rubeanus 27
Cusanus, Nicolaus 26
Cyprus 99, 100, 105

Dante Alighieri 2
Davies, Clifford S.L. 181
Denmark 94

Deuteronomy, Book of 116
Dibdin, Thomas Frognall 16
Dil Ulenspiegel 83, 85-97, 98, 109, 110, 127, 155, 156, 177, 179, 180, 183, 184, 185, 186, 188, 189, 190, 191
Dilthey, Wilhelm 2, 181
Dorner, Rainer 169, 181
Duden: *Das große Wörterbuch der deutschen Sprache in sechs Bänden* 18
Duke Ernst 12
Duns Scotus 139
Durant, Will 121, 181

Ecclesiasticus, Book of 128
Egypt 100
Eichborn, Reinhart von 18, 181
Engels, Friedrich 6, 187
Engelsing, Rolf 3, 4, 181
England 99, 100, 130, 181, 183
Entner, Heinz 182, 190
Ephesians, Book of 151, 152, 153
Epicurus 167
Erasmus, Desiderius 27, 139, 184
Erffa, Dagmar von 18, 182
Eugen Diederichs (publishing company) 9

Famagusta 99, 100, 106, 109
Faust, Georg 163, 171, 183
Fischart, Johann 24
Flanders 99, 101
Foerste, William 63, 64, 182
Fortunatus 38, 83, 85, 86, 97-110, 153, 155, 177, 179, 182, 187, 188-89, 191
France 99
Frankfurt am Main 130, 131
Frey, Winfried 182
Friedenthal, Richard 112, 182
Fugger family 21, 108, 125-26, 187

Fuhrmann, Horst 5, 182

Gast, Johannes 171
Geering, Traugott 26, 182
Genesis, Book of 127, 134
German Democratic Republic 5, 6, 181
Gesprech biechlin neüw Karsthans 154, 182
Gethsemane 153
Glaser, Horst Albert 3, 189
Görres, Johann Joseph von 8, 9, 10, 11, 12, 13, 14, 16, 182
Goethe, Johann Wolfgang von 2, 155, 181, 190
Goossens, Jan 63, 64, 72, 183, 192
Greece (ancient Greece) 6
Grenzmann, Ludger 25, 184
Grieninger, Johannes 85
Grimm, Jacob 4, 18, 78, 183
Grimm, Reinhold 4, 179
Grimm, Wilhelm 4, 18, 78, 183
Grimminger, Rolf 3, 183, 190
Gysi, Klaus 155, 179

Habermann, Paul 24, 183
Hadley, Michael 3, 183
Haile, H.G. 168, 184
Hankamer, Paul 183
Haug, Wolfgang Fritz 89, 183
Hauptmann, Gerhart 150
Heeroma, Klaas 64, 183
Heinrich II (Holy Roman Empire) 42
Heintze, Horst 182
Heitz, Gerhard 150, 191
Henning, Hans 163, 171, 183
Herder, Johann Gottfried 4, 8
Hermand, Jost 4, 179
Hessia 94
Heynlin, Johannes 26
Hildebrandt, Hans Hagen 90, 183

Index 195

Hiller, Helmut 18, 191
Hilton, R.H. 6, 7, 183
Histori von den vier Heymonskindern 162, 190
Historia von D. Johann Fausten 2, 98, 155-74, 177, 183, 184, 185, 187, 190
Hölderlin, Johann Christian Friedrich 2, 181
Hoff, Hieronymous 156, 158
Hoffmann, Konrad 25, 184
Honegger, Peter 85, 184
Horace 61
Huizinga, Johan 8, 184
Hutten, Ulrich von 27, 139

India 100, 129
Ireland 99
Israelites 57, 129

Jacobs, Charles M. 111, 114, 118
Jethro 49
Joshua, Book of 152

Kaiser, Gert 150, 189
Kanzog, Klaus 14, 189
Karlstadt, Andreas 149
Karsthans 139, 153, 184
Kaysersberg, Geiler von 27
Kellenbenz, Hermann 20, 21, 184
Kemper, Hans-Georg 25, 27, 121, 184
Kemper, Raimund 44, 184
Klemperer, Victor 2, 185
Klopstock, Friedrich Gottlieb 2
Kluckhohn, August 108, 133, 184
Könneker, Barbara 2, 16, 25, 27, 37, 44, 54, 78, 138, 150, 155, 184-85
Körner, Josef 2, 185
Kohlschmidt, Werner 2, 185
Kokott, Hartmut 74, 81, 185

Kolln, Caspar 156, 158
Koopmann, Helmut 15, 188
Krause, Joachim 18, 185
Kreutzer, Hans Joachim 9, 13, 14, 15, 16, 185
Kreuzer, Helmut 2, 15, 185
Krogmann, Willy 86, 185
Krohn, Paul Günter 155, 179
Kühnel, Jürgen 9, 180

Landgraf, Wolfgang 132-33, 185
Langosch, Karl 64, 78, 82, 86, 185, 188
Laube, Adolf 150, 191
Lehmann, Helmut T. 111, 114, 118, 186
Leitzmann, Albert 64, 188
Lenk, Werner 139, 153, 154, 182, 184, 186, 190
Lessing, Gotthold Ephraim 2, 181
Leuscher, Joachim 5, 7, 186
Liepe, Wolfgang 11, 12, 186
Lindow, Wolfgang 85, 87, 89, 185, 186
Lohse, Bernhard 112, 186
London 99, 102
Ludwig, Karl 18, 186
Lütge, Friedrich 20, 186
Luke, Book of 35, 116, 117
Luther, Martin 1, 5, 24, 61, 111-35, 137, 138, 140, 147, 149, 155, 172, 173, 177, 179, 180, 182, 185, 186, 187, 190, 192

Mackensen, Lutz 10, 11, 12, 186
Manger, Klaus 24, 27, 186
Mann, Thomas 98, 155
Mark, Book of 147
Marlowe, Christopher 155
Marx, Karl 6, 7, 187
Masser, Achim 14, 189
Matthew, Book of 113, 114, 115,

116, 120, 147, 153
Maximilian I (Holy Roman Empire) 24, 28
Melanchton 171
Merker, Paul 11
Militz, Helga 182
Mischler, Beat 25, 187
Mithal, Christine 3, 191
Moeller, Bernd 7, 55, 112, 187
Mölln 86, 93
Mörke, Olaf 108, 126, 187
Mohr, Wolfgang 24, 183
Mora, J.J. 66
Moses 49
Mottek, Hans 20, 187
Mück, Hans-Dieter 9, 180
Müller, Günther 12, 105, 106, 187
Müller, Jan-Dirk 15, 24, 187
Müller, Johannes 171
Müller, Ulrich 9, 180
Müntzer, Thomas 140, 149
Murner, Thomas 24, 27, 153-54, 184
Murray, James A.H. 17

Nadler, Josef 18, 187
Nantes 99
Nassau-Saarbrücken, Elisabeth von 10
Newald, Richard 76, 188
Nivardus 63
Novalis (Friedrich von Hardenberg) 2, 181
Nunnenbeck, Lienhardt 138
Nuremberg 20, 91, 138

Olpe, Bergmann von 26, 28
Opitz, Martin 10
Oppenheimer, Paul Eugene 85, 188
Otmar, Johann 98
Oxford English Dictionary 16, 17

Paris 100
Pascal, Roy 112, 187
Peasants' War 111, 150, 155, 191
Persia 100
Peter (the Apostle) 42, 153
Petrarch 139
Petsch, Robert 156, 190
Plato 139
Poland 91-92, 99
Pontus 12
"Poor Henry" uprising 121
Portugal 100, 130
Prang, Helmut 13, 14, 15, 188
Prien, Friedrich 64, 188

Raitz, Walter 98, 101, 108, 109, 182, 188
Reuter, Hans-Heinrich 2, 188
Reynke de Vos 2, 14, 19, 63-83, 85, 86, 87, 109, 138, 176-77, 183, 185, 188, 190, 192
Rhine River 26
Rieck, Werner 2, 188
Ritter, Gerhard 26, 188
Roda 163
Roloff, Hans-Gert 15, 16, 18, 98, 182, 188
Roman de Renart 63
Romans, Book of 127
Rome (ancient Rome) 6, 38, 39, 113
Rose, William 163, 165, 166, 184
Rupprich, Hans 16, 76, 188

Sachs, Hans 21, 24, 137-54, 155, 172, 173-74, 177, 179, 180, 185, 188, 189, 190, 191
Schellberg, Wilhelm 8, 182
Schenda, Rudolf 5, 189
Scheuer, Helmut 101, 108, 189
Schiewek, Ingrid 182
Schmidt, Peter 3, 189

Index

Schnabel, Hildegard 190
Schulze, Winfried 181
Schutte, Jürgen 150, 151, 189
Schwitalla, Johannes 189
Sedmann, Timothy 63, 64, 192
See, Klaus von 155, 185
Seitz, Dieter 182
Seneca 36
Shakespeare, William 2, 175
Sickingen, Franz von 154
Solomon 31, 32, 104, 105, 108
Soltau, Dietrich Wilhelm 66, 188
Spain 100
Spengler, Walter Eckehart 14, 15, 189
Spies, Johann 156, 158, 160, 161, 162, 164, 169, 172, 174
Sprandel, Rolf 20, 189
Spriewald, Ingeborg 97, 138, 140, 145, 147, 149, 150, 182, 188, 189
Stackmann, Karl 25, 184
Stadler, Ulrich 169, 190
Stammler, Wolfgang 11
Steiner, Gerhard 86, 97, 190
Steinmetz, Max 150, 191
Strasbourg 24, 27, 85
Strauß, Wolfgang 18, 191
Suchsland, Peter 162, 190
Szövérffy, Josef 12, 13, 190

Thirty Years' War 27
Tieck, Ludwig 4
Timothy, Book of 128
Trier 94
Trunz, Erich 2, 190
Turkey 165, 170

Ungern-Sternberg, Wolfgang von 3, 190
United States of America 175-76, 178

Unwin, George 145, 190

Van Cleve, John 64, 121, 190
Varty, Kenneth 64
Vatican 55, 65, 72, 73, 74, 75, 76, 80, 164-65, 166, 170
Vogler, Günter 150, 191

Wahle, Julius 2, 185
Waitz, Georg 108, 184
Walter, Monika 182
Walzel, Oskar 2, 185, 191
Weber, Ernst 3, 191
Weber, Gottfried 155
Wedler, Klaus 150, 191
Weimann, Robert 175, 176, 182, 191
Weimar 163
Welser family 21, 108
Wenzel, Horst 150, 189
Widmann, Hans 18, 191
Wiemann, Renate 108, 191
Winkler, Hannelore 139, 191
Wis, Marjatta 98, 191
Wiswe, Hans 97, 191
Wittenberg 138, 139, 141, 163, 165, 171
Witton, Niclas 63, 192
Wolf, Herbert 192
Worms 24, 137
Wunderlich, Werner 85, 86, 88, 90, 92, 183, 186, 191, 192
Wuthenow, Ralph-Rainer 3, 189
Wyclif, John 121, 181

Zarncke, Friedrich 25, 48, 180
Zeydel, Edwin H. 24, 25, 26, 27, 51, 162, 180, 192
Zimmer, Baron von 171
Zink, Burkhardt 98
Zorn, Wolfgang 20, 106, 158, 184, 189, 192